ENCHANTED LIFE:
THE MEMOIR OF A MAGICIAN

ENCHANTED LIFE

THE MEMOIR OF A MAGICIAN

HERBIE BRENNAN

ISBN: 978-1-7399949-7-6

Published by
SWEENEY & O'DONOVAN LTD.

www.sweeneyodonovan.ie

Printed in the EU.

CONTENTS

In the 1940s, my aunt lived in a cellar. If I had been older, I might have wondered why. She was, admittedly, widowed with two children to bring up, but she had a good job (as supervisor in the local telephone exchange) and no expensive habits. Perhaps housing was short during wartime and failed to improve with victory. In any case, when my mother—another widow—took me to visit, we entered premises identified as *Clarke's Opticians* but made a right in the hallway rather than pushing through the half-glass door that promised eye-tests.

The right turn took us down gloomy, dusty wooden steps to a cement floor and a dark cubby-hole packed with junk. To the left was a curtained entrance to the cellar that was Aunt Madeline's living quarters. The odd thing was she rented a drawing room with carpet and furnishings that smelled of polish (along with three perfectly respectable bedrooms) on the floor above the optician's, but the cellar was where she lived and entertained. There was an uneven, stone-flagged floor, a scattering of threadbare mats, a small dining table, a miserable stool, a broken-down armchair, a smallish sofa by the only window and, at one end of the sofa, a bookcase.

The bookcase was where it all started.

Family visits bored me. The sandwiches were nice, and despite rationing there was usually a piece of cake, but all my aunts ever seemed to talk about was illness, the temperature of their doctors' hands and whether he looked away while you undressed. I took as much of this as I could, then retreated inside my head. When I was a little older, I looked around for something to read.

I was a precocious and voracious reader, far ahead of my classmates at public elementary school. Everything was grist for my mill so long as it involved print on paper. The grist in my aunt's bookcase was mostly romantic fiction, but a striking exception was a six-volume matched hardback set of books on yoga.

It was a subject about which I naturally knew nothing. Strangely, neither did my aunt. In later years I quizzed her about that set, hoping she might offer to give it to me, or at worst leave it to me. (She did neither.) She proved utterly disinterested. She had never read the books, never so much as opened them. She could not remember where she got them. Her late husband—spoken about with caution, because she took his death badly—had no interest in the subject matter either. Neither had her son or her daughter, who were in any case only a year or two older than I was and consequently far too young for anything more meaty than *The Beano*.

The six books of the set were individually dedicated to the six main branches of Oriental yoga—*hatha, raja, karma, bhakti, jnana,* and tantra. On the fateful afternoon my hand reached out to grasp a volume, I elected to take down the work on raja yoga, the royal road to union with God which concerned itself largely with the practice of meditation. It fell open at a diagram of the chakras. I stared at it with the same tingling sensation I later came to associate with photographs of naked women.

As a child growing up in a mill village in Northern Ireland, I was what was known as 'odd.' I learned to read quickly, easily and early; and, having done so, supplemented the usual children's diet of fairy tales with how-to books on hypnosis. I no longer have the slightest idea how I got hold of these works, but get hold of them I did. I can still recall overhearing one of my teachers telling another that I was studying hypnosis more diligently than sums. "I wish he'd hypnotise my lot," her companion remarked sourly.

It was not long before I obliged. I achieved my first successful experiment in hypnosis with the aid of *Ripley's Believe it or Not,* a cartoon strip I followed with near-religious intensity. Since 1918, the American artist Robert LeRoy Ripley had produced a syndicated panel which dealt with events and items so bizarre that they beggared belief. One such item was the hypnotic blob, which, Mr Ripley assured me, was used by Oriental mystics to induce a state of trance. Helpfully, the piece included a drawing of the blob, an irregular black shape that might have been an inkblot. I tore it from the paper, folded it carefully and hid it in my schoolbag.

During break-time at school, I announced that I would hypnotise a willing volunteer and make him do tricks. Surprisingly, my best friend Reggie volunteered at once. I sat him down at a desk, surrounded by expectant classmates, and produced the hypnotic blob. "What am I supposed to do?" he asked as I smoothed the paper flat.

"Look at the blob," I said with the sort of confidence only Ripley could engender. Reggie looked at the blob.

I can only assume he was a naturally good subject, for his eyes began to flicker at once, then sank closed. His head bowed. I ordered him to stand up. When he did so, eyes closed, I decided he was faking it. I asked him to bark like a dog. *"Woof-woof,"* Reggie went, realistically. I still wasn't convinced and told him to sit down again. He did so, then slid slowly off his seat to fall heavily in a heap on the floor. At that point I panicked (there was no way Reggie would voluntarily have risked injury) and ordered him to wake up.

His eyes snapped open and he climbed to his feet. "What happened?" he asked.

I was nine at the time. I destroyed the mystic blob forthwith, and it was years before I attempted to hypnotise anyone again.

Despite this frightening brush with the arcane arts, I continued to read my aunt's yoga books each time we called on her. I was fascinated by chakras, by the idea of unseen energies. I was fascinated by the *asanas* of hatha yoga and tried to adopt some of the simpler ones from memory when I got home. I was fascinated by the art of meditation and even more so by the suggestion that it could, with practice, lead to the development of *siddhis*—strange powers like telepathy, precognition or even levitation. The trouble was, I never seemed to have time to meditate. Besides which, there were whole chapters devoted to the art and I could only read them piecemeal in bite-sized chunks whenever I visited my aunt's cellar.

Another cellar played a role in my early development. My father died when I was four years old, succumbing to pneumonia at a time when antibiotics were available only to wounded soldiers. For some reason my mother and her sisters decided to keep his death secret from me. I was bundled off somewhere to allow him a decent burial—because of a narrow staircase, the coffin had to be lowered from a first-floor window—and lived for several weeks under the illusion that he was still bedridden in the back room, too ill to receive visits from his only son. Eventually my mother admitted the truth and I entered the forbidden room to stare at an empty bed.

Thereafter my mother decreed that I sleep in the bed where my father died, which I did until the age of 21, when I finally left home. One night, Satan came to visit me. Appropriately, there had been a thunderstorm earlier, but I got to sleep eventually. I awoke at some unspecified hour with the realisation something was wrong. The only window in the room overlooked our kitchen roof. I climbed from the bed and drew the curtains to discover Satan—half of him at least—floating above the rain-slicked tiles. He had brown, leathery skin, a muscular torso and spreading batwings, but did not exist at all from the waist down. Years later, I mentioned the dream to my psychoanalyst who made much of the fact that Satan's nether regions were missing—something she suspected might relate to sex.

One result of the secrecy surrounding my father's death was that I developed an intense curiosity about him. I remembered him fragmentarily as a benign figure who doted on me sufficiently to try to give me a pony I didn't want. Somehow he managed to walk it into our kitchen, but at age three, the gigantic creature terrified me and I cried until it was taken away. Somewhat more successful was the miniature Lambeg drum he had made for me. I used to beat this small symbol of Protestant supremacy with great enthusiasm until my mother complained the noise gave her a headache—the first hint of the sickly psychosomatic lifestyle she was to adopt in later life.

My father used to read to me before I could do the job myself, seated comfortably on his knee with his warm hand on my thigh. But these few scraps of recollection were the only things that survived the shock of his death. Villagers later told me he was an immensely likeable man. My mother said he was 'too nice' and extended credit to the sort of low-life anyone might know would never pay him back. He made his living as a grocer, a difficult trade during wartime when food was scarce and rationing in full swing.

After his death, my mother reluctantly took over the shop, tightened up the lines of credit and began to exhibit signs of what I would now recognise as stress. She gave away some of my father's meagre personal possessions, notably clothing, but could not bring herself to give away others. The problem was she could not bear to live with them either, so she stored them in the cellar.

Our cellar was a vast, cold, rambling, gloomy, rat-infested labyrinth that underpinned the entire house. You reached it via narrow, dingy wooden steps that somehow resisted illumination by the single hanging electric bulb. Off the first landing was a coal-hole, which was as far as my mother ever went until I was big enough to bring up buckets of coal for the kitchen fire. I often went further. The cellar was a quest.

At the bottom of the wooden steps were three interlinked chambers and another, considerably more massive, coalhole. The whole place was gloomy and dirty: in my entire young life it was never cleaned. Part of the space was used as a bulk store for chests of tea (when tea became again available) and for meal, bought by local farmers as animal feed, which attracted water-rats from the mill race that ran behind the house. The creatures would scatter at my approach. I was so used to them I never gave them a second thought.

Alongside the tea-chests and the bags of meal were stacks of cardboard boxes chock-a-block with bric-a-brac. Much of it was household junk. My mother could never bring herself to throw anything away—a habit I have unfortunately inherited—and in wartime, of course, recycling was a necessity rather than a fashion. In the boxes I found traces of my father. Most of them were electronic.

During the 1940s, the leading edge of technology was radio. Until 1942, the only set in the village was in the home of our next-door neighbour, a blind man named Bob McIlroy who had somehow managed to build it from component parts. Helped by my father, he fastened a loudspeaker to his outside wall and villagers gathered to listen to the marvel. News broadcasts proved particularly popular and speeches by Churchill gathered exceptionally large crowds.

My father must have taken lessons from Bob, because in box after box I found traces of radios he had soldered together. There was even an early 'cat's whisker'—a simple, crystal-based wireless that worked, miraculously, without the input of electricity. I took it into my head that I might salvage enough spare parts from the various pieces of broken machinery to make a wireless of my own. But since my father worked without plans—or at least none I could find—construction was largely a matter of detective work, examining one piece after another to find out how bits were joined together. As a result, matters progressed very slowly indeed and I spent weeks, then months, squirrelling away in the cellar.

One day, in search of more spare parts, I opened a flat cardboard box and discovered a Masonic apron.

The headmaster of my primary school was a brutish, violent, bully of a man prone to flying into uncontrollable rages at the smallest provocation. I was so terrified of him that for my final few years at the school I threw up my breakfast each morning at the prospect of another day. My mother showed me little sympathy. She had problems of her own, not least of which was running the grocery business my father left behind, and a horror of my 'getting under her feet.' As a result, we drifted apart and I spoke to her very little about the things that concerned me. Nonetheless, I did ask about the curious garment I found in the cellar.

In Northern Ireland in the 1940s, Masonry was the tip of a Protestant iceberg. The Province was noted for several high-profile secret organisations, ranked by social standing. For a young boy like myself from a Protestant family, living in the shadow of the Presbyterian Church, my first step on the ladder, had I ever bothered to take it, was the Juveniles, a preparatory, all-male social club (with little sashes) designed to condition young Protestant minds for the important business of joining, at age 18, the Orange Order.

The Orange Order was a secret society formed in 1795 to maintain a Protestant ascendancy in Ireland in the face of rising demands for Catholic emancipation. Its lodges and Orange Halls were spread liberally throughout Northern Ireland and it held public parades in summer, notably on the Twelfth of July, which was not simply a date but a season of celebration. As a child, I had only the vaguest idea what was being celebrated, but I enjoyed the bands and the drums and, if the weather happened to be fine, the July 13 trip to nearby Scarva to watch the Sham Fight between green old King James and fine bright orange King Billy, who always won the day by shooting down his opponent's flag.

To become an Orangeman, as members of the Order were known, was to enter a social hierarchy as subtle as anything the British class system ever produced. For adult, Protestant males, membership was almost inevitable and virtually every man I knew throughout my childhood was an Orangeman. But if you were an Orangeman and nothing else, it marked you, more or less, as working class. The middle class were socially obliged to join the Royal Black Preceptory.

The Blacks, as they were widely known, came into being in 1797, a society formed from Orangemen for Orangemen. Although separate institutions, the RBP was seen as a progression of the Orange Order, and you could not become a member of the former without first joining the latter.

Most men stopped there, but a few with particular ambitions went further and joined the Masons. Masonry has, of course, no constitutional barriers to membership whatever your creed (beyond your acceptance of a supreme—and supremely vague—universal power) but in the Ulster of the 1940s you had no chance whatsoever of joining a Masonic Lodge, unless you first became a member of the Orange and the Black. My father, it transpired, had been a member of all three. So had one of my uncles, whose regalia I also discovered, along with an unloaded shotgun, while poking around his drawing room during a family visit.

My mother had nothing at all to say about the Orange Order or the Black Preceptory, but she did not like the Masons. It seemed she had expected a widow's pension from them when my father died but had not been awarded one. "What good are they?" she demanded sourly; adding, "Your father was faithful to them for *years.*"

As a child I couldn't answer her question. I knew the Orange Order (and presumably the Black Preceptory as well) was a bastion against the troops massed by the Pope in the southern half of our island, but I had no idea at all what the Masons were good for. All the same, their symbolism intrigued me. Spurred on by the apron, I stopped rooting for electrical components in the cellar and searched instead for any other sign of this mysterious organisation. Searched and found—there were several medallions inscribed with the same peculiar compasses I had seen on the apron. I squirrelled them carefully away and subsequently lost them. In the interim, I took to asking other adults about the Masons.

I received a variety of answers. One man told me thoughtfully they were a charitable organisation, good men who looked after the poor, especially deserving widows. Young though I was, I knew better than to pass this on to my mother. Another, somewhat unsophisticated, source suggested Masonry was a mutual-assistance club. "They look after their own," he said. "If you're caught and brought to court, all you have to do is give the secret sign and the judge will let you off. All the judges are Masons. You should join." My tender years would not have proved a barrier in his opinion. He knew my father had been a Mason.

At the time I had resisted a small degree of pressure—more expectation really—to join the Juveniles. I was a solitary boy with little interest in socialising, and despite my father's impeccable Protestant credentials, I managed to escape the brainwashing that turns children into fanatics. After my father's death, my mother made half-hearted attempts to send

me to Sunday School for about a year and dragged me to church service once a week for about two, but she was not a believer and the whole thing was just too much bother. In the twenty-four months following my father's demise, she worried about appearances, but as her solitary self-confidence solidified, she cared about them less and less. The whole Protestant-Orange thing somehow passed her by. She even stopped flying the Union Jack on July 12. "I have Catholic customers," she told me tersely. "I don't want to offend them." As a result, I was never driven towards the Orange or the Black, but I would have joined the Masons like a shot if I'd only known how. By the time I was old enough, my Masonic uncle was as dead as my father, and I could find no one else to ask. It was only very

School photograph taken at Gilford primary: I am at the extreme right on the back row. My best friend, Reggie McIlroy, the subject of my first foray into hypnotism, is the penultimate pupil seated cross-legged in the front row.

much later in life that I realised membership of the organisation was, in any case, by invitation.

As I investigated the nature of this mysterious group, I noticed something strange. The men I questioned about Masonry tended to admire it. The women, starting with my mother, tended to disapprove. "It's just a boy's club," one told me dismissively. An elderly crone went further. "They're trucking with Satan," she said bluntly and actually spat on the pavement as a prophylactic against the Evil Eye. But even the charge of Satanism—which one had to take very seriously at that time—was not enough to put me off. I had picked up bits and pieces of Masonic terminology and was fascinated by the fact that I was 'the Widow's Son.'

I was 16 when I discovered Madame Blavatsky.

My life had changed for the better by this time. The pattern of existence in the village where I was raised proved unrelentingly gloomy. The mill siren went off at ten minutes to eight each morning and within seconds the streets were packed with marching workers. At six each evening, the siren sounded again, and the pattern was repeated with the traffic flow reversed. During the war, the siren sounded at other times as well to celebrate the German bombers overhead, but no one paid much attention. The common consensus had it that they were on their way to Belfast and had no interest in such small fry as ourselves. My mother, a determined pessimist, told me gloomily they sometimes dropped bombs at random 'to lighten their load' but they never dropped one on Gilford. If they had, it might have livened things up a bit. Both before and after 1945, I found the place dull beyond belief. The lifestyle was succinctly described by my mother's accountant, an intelligent, cynical man: "They leave school at twelve and the next day you see them walking home from the mill and they're little old men in cloth caps."

I escaped from this cloth-capped fate by doing well enough in my Eleven-Plus to earn a place at Portadown College. Portadown was five miles and a world away from Gilford. I joined the college in a particularly good year, sharing my education with young versions of Ken Bell, the physicist, Gloria Hunniford, the TV personality, Mary Peters, the Olympic athlete, Dennis Hawthorne, the producer and Dennis Brennan (no relation), the actor. By the end of my first nervous week, I realised I had come home. I was no longer mocked for using words of more than one syllable or beaten up for being clever. I was surrounded by youngsters who were just as smart, just as ambitious, just as middle class as I was, and I loved it. I joined the Debating Society (where I soon discovered I could win debates by making people laugh), lost weight and indulged in small, popular acts of rebellion like wearing blue suede shoes with my school uniform.

But all this was surface. The internal process that started in my aunt's cellar was still working on me. I had taken to reading a great deal about Oriental mysticism, what Huxley was pleased to call the 'perennial philosophy' and was attracted to Buddhism as explained by Christmas Humphreys, the English barrister and author who, I assumed on the basis of his name, had abandoned the faith of his fathers as readily as I had. I later learned that Humphreys had first become a Theosophist while at Malvern College,

A first teacher: Madame Blavatsky

an English public school with the motto *Sapiens qui prospicit* ('Wise is he who looks ahead.') but later converted to Buddhism in his Cambridge days. My own path reversed this intellectual journey. As a teenager, Buddhism seemed a little dull to me.[1] But when I heard about Blavatsky, I could scarcely contain my excitement.

Helena Petrovna Blavatsky was born Helena Hahn at Ekaterinoslav in Russia in 1831. She was a peculiar child, prone to mesmerising pigeons and talking to invisible companions. Phantasmal forms glared at her with burning eyes, sending her screaming through the household until she met up with an imposing, ethereal protector who henceforth guarded her against ghostly attack.[2]

This wild, imaginative child, became a wild, imaginative adolescent. I suspect her family got fed up with her boyish behaviour and tried the

1   Or possibly just too much hard work.

2   And, apparently, physical injury. On one occasion when dragged by a horse after she got her foot caught in the stirrup, she claimed to have been buoyed up by an invisible power that prevented her getting killed.

corrective of marrying her off—aged 17—to the elderly General Blavatsky. The marriage lasted three months before Helena, who referred to her husband as a 'plumeless raven,' ran away, not simply from home, but from Russia itself.

For the next decade she travelled the world and returned to Russia with a fund of extraordinary tales and an accompaniment of weird phenomena. When Helena was about, raps, whispering and other unexplained noises could be heard all over the house. Mysterious winds blew out the candles and objects moved when she focused her attention on them. In one source I read that her clairvoyance was so well developed that she was successful in finding a murderer. The ungrateful authorities refused to believe in psychism and issued a warrant for her arrest as an accomplice.

Sometime in 1860, Helena became severely ill and fell into a lengthy, trance-like state. When she eventually recovered, the spontaneous phenomena all stopped. With her health restored she went travelling again and accumulated even wilder legends: she earned her living as a bareback rider in a circus, she disguised herself as a man and fought by the side of the Italian revolutionary Garibaldi, she had a miraculous escape at sea when her ship was blown up…

One thing she certainly did do was visit Egypt, where she founded a *Societé Spirite* in Cairo. It proved an ill-fated organisation despite—or possibly because of—its title and suffered a scandalous collapse.

Shortly before her birthday in 1873, Helena sailed into New York and set about making a name for herself within the Spiritualist movement that had been sweeping the States for the past quarter century. After a brief spell as a dressmaker, she turned to journalism and specialised in articles on Spiritualist topics. In one of them she claimed she had left the comfort of a wealthy home to become a 'wanderer upon the face of the earth' for the sake of Spiritualism. But while Spiritualism was fashionable, it was not her future. In 1875, she founded the Theosophical Society.

I learned most of this—in a slightly tighter and vastly more dramatic form—from a mailing I received offering me a paperback set of her master-work, *The Secret Doctrine*. The mailing must have been produced in America, for it contained the sort of selling copy only Americans seem able to write. Blavatsky, it claimed, had learned the mysteries of the universe at the feet of Indian gurus, Tibetan Lamas, Mongolian shamans. She had studied arcane knowledge, explored age-old doctrines, practised ancient magics. I don't know if any of this was true, but it certainly convinced *me*. I realised I wanted her *Secret Doctrine* more than I wanted anything in the world. Fortunately, I had a small stash of disposable cash saved from Christmas gifts. Besides, the books were offered 'on approval.' I filled in the order form at once.

Instead of receiving the books, I got back an apologetic note explaining that the paperback had, unfortunately, sold out. But the good news was they were able to supply me with a six-volume hardback edition of the work at a considerably higher price and without the on-approval offer. I smelt scam and fell into a paranoid fury which prompted me to send off a bitter, accusatory letter of recrimination. When this was ignored, I re-read the mailing several weeks later and ordered the hardbacks anyway. I have them still, on a high shelf of my library as I write.

I can remember the thrill of unpacking those books. My fingers traced the dramatic signature of HPB herself, embossed in gold on the cover. My eyes locked on the complex symbol above it—a composite of Egyptian ankh, Solomon's seal, and alchemical ouroboros surmounted by a tiny, surprising swastika and what I learned in later life to be the Tibetan rendering of the mystic syllable *Om*. My mind embraced the motto that circled the symbol: *There is no religion higher than truth.* After an upbringing in Northern Ireland where claims to know God's will were as commonplace as Gospel Halls, I could not have agreed more.

I opened Volume One, skipped the preliminaries and went straight to the Proem, which I judged would set me on the meat of this mystic tome. At first, I was in no way disappointed. Blavatsky began her book with the words:

> An archaic Manuscript—a collection of palm leaves made impermeable to water, fire and air by some specific and unknown process—is before the writer's eye. On the first page is an immaculate white disk within a dull black ground. On the following page the same disk, but with a central point.[3]

This was it, as I knew from the mailing. This was the first reference to the fabled *Stanzas of Dzyan,* a book so ancient some scholars dated it to lost Atlantis. I had started on my quest for arcane secrets. Unfortunately the quest did not last long. My eyes began to glaze as I read on:

> The first, the student knows, represents Kosmos in Eternity, before

3   H. P. Blavatsky, *The Secret Doctrine* vol 1 of the Olcott Lithographic Edition (Wheaton, Ill.: The Theosophical Press, 1952) p.69.

[13]

the re-awakening of still-slumbering Energy, the Emanation of the World in later systems. The point in the hitherto immaculate disk, Space and Eternity in Pralaya, denotes the dawn of differentiation.[4]

What was 'Kosmos in Eternity'? What, in the name of God, was 'Pralaya'? I began to skip down the page, which was densely packed with terms like 'Mundane Egg', 'Universal Soul' and 'Divine Thought.' There was a lengthy, obscure footnote that contained the mind-numbing passage, *'The "Unconscious," according to von Hartmann, arrived at the vast creative, or rather evolutionary plan "by a clairvoyant wisdom superior to all consciousness" which in Vedantic language would mean absolute wisdom...Mind as we know it is resolvable into states of consciousness of varying duration, intensity, complexity etc., all, in the ultimate, resting on sensation which is again Maya.'*
I had no idea what any of this meant, no knowledge of terms like 'Vedantic' and 'Maya.' Like the first, faint, opening bars of *Finlandia*, it began to dawn on me that, at 16, I was perhaps not quite intellectually prepared for Blavatsky. But I did not yet despair. What I was reading in the Proem was commentary, and commentary could be notoriously obscure. What I needed was the original source, the fundamental vision, the simple truth that shone a clear light on these obscurities. So I turned quickly to the *Stanzas of Dzyan* themselves; and discovered they were worse:

> The Eternal Mother (space) wrapped in her ever invisible robes (cosmic prenebular matter) had slumbered for seven Eternities. Time was not, for it lay asleep in the infinite bosom of Duration. Universal mind was not for there were no Dhyan Chohans to contain (hence to manifest) it. The seven Ways of Bliss (Moksha, or Nirvana)—were not. The great causes of Misery (Nidana and Maya) were not, for there was no one to produce and get ensnared by them. DARKNESS alone filled the boundless ALL...[5]

Darkness was filling me as well, driven by the nauseous suspicion that I had spent more than I could afford on a work as meaningless to me as if it had been written in Urdu. Madame Blavatsky might have been initiated into the mysteries of Maya, Moksha and Nidana, but I was not. Clearly one needed to do a great deal of study before one was equipped to tackle *The*

4   *Ibid.*
5   *Ibid,* p 102.

Secret Doctrine. In a half-hearted attempt at damage limitation, I turned back to Josephine Ransom's brief biographical sketch of Blavatsky's life in the introductory section of the book. Here, surely, was something I should be able to comprehend.

And it turned out I could. Ms Ransom was a vastly better writer than Blavatsky and while the piece had the whiff of hagiography about it, there were relatively few intrusive capitals and no obscure Sanskrit terms at all. What I did find, to my excitement and relief, was this:

> In 1873, H.P. Blavatsky went to the United States of America to do the work for which she had been trained…An unknown Russian woman, she plunged into the Spiritualistic movement… Scientific minds were anxious to discover the meaning of the strange phenomena…In two ways, HPB tried to indicate the explanation to them: (1) By the practical demonstration of her own powers; (2) By declaring that there was an age-old knowledge of the deeper laws of life, studied and guarded by those who could use it safely and beneficently; persons who in their higher ranks were called "Masters,' though other titles were used for Them—Adepts, Chohans, Elder Brethren , the Occult Hierarchy, and so on.

This was my first clear introduction to an idea tantalisingly hinted at in the mailing—the notion that there were, hidden in Himalayan fastnesses, occult supermen who looked after the spiritual welfare of our planet; and might, in certain circumstances, call on the services of Russians like Blavatsky or even (perhaps?) willing, bright young boys like me.

I made a few further half-hearted attempts to study *The Secret Doctrine*, enduring Blavatsky's interminable disagreements with Victorian scholars I had never heard of, before stashing the set on a bookshelf to await the day when I could better understand it. But from that point onwards, I made it my business to research everything I could about Blavatsky's Hidden Masters.

Eight years later, one of them turned up at my initiation.

Over the next year or so, I learned quite a lot about Theosophy, largely from the writings of Annie Besant and Bishop C. W. Leadbeater, and about the Masters, mainly from the *Mahatma Letters to A. P. Sinnett*. I could scarcely stop reading. Theosophical doctrines presented a picture of prehistory I found utterly fascinating.

Madame Blavatsky lived in an era of high controversy between the established doctrine of creationism and the newly launched theory of evolution.[6] Her own ideas, based on the mysterious *Stanzas of Dzyan*, allowed her to side with and irritate both camps. In a myth of sufficient potency to set against *Genesis*, the *Stanzas* began the story of humanity neither with ape nor angel, but with a conversation between the Earth and the Sun 2,000,000,000 years ago. At that time our planet was devoid of life and wanted the Sun to populate it. But the Sun refused, claiming the Earth was not yet ready, nor were the men who would eventually live on it. This exchange was packed with implications, chief among them the suggestion that souls were being prepared for incarnation long before their bodies had evolved. It was just the sort of unorthodox idea guaranteed to attract a teenager like a magnet. I particularly liked the timescale. Northern Ireland had its fair share of fundamentalists who claimed the world was created in 4004 BCE: I delighted in the thought that I knew better.

But greater delights were in store. Blavatsky embraced Darwin like a lover, then propounded a version of evolution he would have been hard put to recognise. To her, the *Origin of Species* was relevant only to the physical vehicles in which life manifested. The real story of humanity began with a race of spiritually advanced, immaterial beings called Dhyan Chohans who lived on the Moon (or possibly the Sun). At some point in an unimaginably distant past, seven of these creatures visited Earth, wiped out the soulless life-forms that had evolved there naturally, then created the first race of humanity from their own essence.

These early humans were mindless, sexless, almost formless and totally ethereal, but over aeons of time they evolved, state by stage into increasingly physical, intelligent and eventually even sexual beings. At one stage in their development, they roamed across the giant continent of Lemuria. At another, they established a high, technological sword and sorcery type

---

6   The Theosophical Society was founded only 16 years after first publication of *The Origin of Species*.

of civilisation on Atlantis.[7] Blavatsky even solved the dilemma presented by the similarities between humanity and the anthropoid apes. Far from humanity descending from apes, as many early evolutionists contended,[8] the apes descended from *us,* as the result of illicit sexual relations between early man and brute beasts.

In 1976, Futura brought out my *Occult History of the World* Volume One) (written as J. H. Brennan), which contrasted scientific and (largely) Theosophical ideas about prehistory. Volume Two was never published.

All this was a heady brew for a romantic teenager. But while there is no doubt at all that Blavatsky profoundly influenced my own ideas on prehistory—I have written several books suggesting the existence of an advanced prehistoric civilisation—I never joined the Theosophical Society, nor became in any real sense an intellectual Theosophist. The problem lay in Blavatsky herself. When, in 1860, her bout of illness put an end to the spontaneous poltergeist-style manifestations that had dogged her, she awoke to claim this was purely because she had brought them under conscious control. Later, as Ransom says, she sought to explain strange phenomena to the Spiritualists by practical demonstrations of her own powers. Later still, such demonstrations continued with manifestations of the Masters and claims of written communications teleported direct from the Himalayas.

I eventually read, with enormous interest, that two of Blavatsky's followers, a French couple named Coulomb, confessed to manufacturing many of the theosophical miracles in collaboration with Blavatsky. They talked about secret doors in the shrine where the astral letters were delivered and a dummy 'Mahatma' head that aided manifestations. They claimed Blavatsky was the real author of the Mahatma letters, disguising her handwriting to perpetrate the deception. Given the high profile of Theosophy at the time, it was no surprise to discover the Society for

7   Lest this appears a satirical interpretation of Theosophical doctrines, let me quote you a short abridged passage from one of Blavatsky's commentaries on the *Stanzas of Dzyan:* 'And the Great King of the Dazzling Face…sent his vimanas [flying machines]…saying "…The Lords of the Storm are approaching…The nether Lords of the Fires are preparing their magic fire weapon. But the Lords of the Evil Eye…are versed in the highest magical knowledge…"' and so on, in a style that would do justice to Edgar Rice Burroughs.

8   Nowadays, of course, most evolutionists would contend that both humanity and apes descended from a common ancestor who was, in fact, neither.

Psychical Research quickly mounted an investigation. After three months, Richard Hodgson concluded there had been widespread fraud.

I was not overly impressed either by the Coulombs' original claims—they struck me as a vindictive couple with axes to grind—or by Hodgson's conclusions. But there was no doubt that the scandal led Blavatsky, and indeed the entire Theosophical movement, to veer away from what was disparagingly called 'phenomena.' This was perfectly consistent with Oriental spiritual tradition, which warns practitioners against the development of *siddhis* (powers) that divert one's attention from God. But my problem was I *wanted* to be diverted from God by phenomena and it was my burning ambition to develop powers. If all Theosophy could offer was a new version of prehistory, then I needed to look elsewhere. Oddly enough, I found more satisfaction in the writings of another Russian.

P. D. Ouspensky sounded like hard work. The first book of his I came across—*Tertium Organum*—sounded harder still. So I started with *New Model of the Universe,* found it very much to my liking, and devoured *Tertium Organum* soon after. I can no longer remember much about either book, but one of them (or possibly some peripheral reading) brought up two matters of considerable interest: self-remembering and G. I. Gurdjieff.

Ouspensky introduced the problem of self-remembering, as I recall, by describing some thoughts he had about a walk home. Although he had taken the same route for years and knew every inch of the territory, he realised suddenly that details of a *specific* walk were a complete blank. So far as he was concerned, he set out to walk home, then arrived there with nothing in between. He might as well have teleported to his destination. Worse still, when he tried to recall details of the route he followed—like the number of panes in a window he passed each day—he could not.

Both these experiences are commonplace—they certainly rang a bell with me—but Ouspensky decided they shouldn't be. It seemed to him that if you walked the same route regularly, it should imprint on your mind like the two-times tables. How then was it possible to do so without any recall at all; and why should imprinted details, like the number of window panes, disappear completely?

A less creative mind might have viewed this as a problem of memory. Ouspensky decided it was actually a problem of perception. To him, any flaw in subsequent recall was related to the way he experienced the walk—and by extension the world—in the first place. He began to think carefully about how he normally perceived reality and found that he functioned much like a movie camera, an observer on an external world.

[18]

It then occurred to him that this was an incomplete perception, for just as the movie camera does not photograph itself, so his perception of the walk home lacked one vital element—his own participation.

Hard on the heels of this basic realisation came the recognition that virtually all of his life was like that: he went to parties, talked to people, ate meals, made love without ever experiencing the scenario inclusive of what should have been its central element. Effectively, he was forgetting to include himself in his own life. At once he determined to do something about it and embarked on a programme of self-remembering. On his homeward walks and as many other times as he could manage, he made a conscious effort to recall that he was part of the scene, an active participant in his own reality. This proved surprisingly difficult. He found he could self-remember for a minute or two, then old habits would reassert themselves and he would discover he had walked a considerable distance in a state of blankness. But he persevered and found that with practice not only did his memory improve (he could visualise the window and count the panes) but his awareness of the world became more vivid. Edges were sharper, colours brighter. When herculean efforts enabled him to extend his periods of self-remembering to hours rather than minutes, his perception of reality became almost mystical.

This sounded fun and I embarked on my own programme of self-remembering. My recall improved noticeably, but mystical perception eluded me, mainly because I did not have, at 16, anything remotely resembling Ouspensky's perseverance. I could self-remember for ten or fifteen seconds at a time, then my concentration would slip and I would sink back into my usual perceptual haze. Since childhood I had learned to live in my head, and even as a teenager I was vaguely aware my experience of objective reality was limited. I was also vaguely aware this was not necessarily a good thing; and besides, I was hugely interested in alternative states of consciousness, particularly the mystical. It seemed further investigation of Ouspensky's philosophy might be valuable. Further investigation led me straight to Gurdjieff.

George Ivanovitch Gurdjieff was an Armenian carpet-seller who life had some strong parallels with that of Blavatsky. Like her, he left home at an early age (20) and travelled through Tibet, India and Arabia in search of esoteric wisdom. Like her, he established a considerable intellectual following, first in Russia, then later in France, Britain and, by the mid-1920s, the United States. Like her, his followers credited him with mysterious powers, among them his ability to heal himself far more rapidly than medical science would expect—demonstrated after a particularly bad car crash—and his gift for bringing a woman to orgasm by looking at her.

At 16, there was little doubt which of these powers interested me most. I read with utter fascination the first-hand account of a woman who had been subjected to his orgasmic gaze. She was drinking coffee in a pavement café when she began to experience the uncomfortable feeling that someone was staring at her. She looked around and discovered it was a heavily moustached, middle-aged man at a nearby table. He had deep-set, piercing eyes and she found she could not look away. Then, without warning, she felt as though she had been 'pierced violently through her sexual centre,' an experience she found 'horrid.'

It seemed to me her reaction might have been triggered by hypnosis, although I could not quite think how.[9] But the account went some way towards reawakening my interest in the subject, which had lain more or less dormant since my successful, if scary, experience with Reggie as a boy. It was not until many years later that I discovered Gurdjieff had used a far more subtle occult technique than hypnosis for his venture into psychic rape. I was sorely tempted to try it for myself, but by then the moral implications must have been dawning on me, and I did not.

Stories like this encouraged me to read some of Gurdjieff's books. *Meetings with Remarkable Men* was interesting enough, but I found *Beelzebub's Tales to His Grandson* so bewildering I never attempted anything else. It was from the works of followers like Maurice Nicholl and Alfred Orage that I learned about Gurdjieff's fundamental teaching: his conviction that humanity lives in a state analogous to sleep and consequently no spiritual progress can be made until an individual manages to wake up.

In 1917, Gurdjieff established his Institute for the Harmonious Development of Man in Tbilisi, Georgia, to facilitate the wake-up process. Later the Institute was moved to Constantinople and later still to Fontainbleau in France, where it became firmly established and began to attract the attention of European intellectuals. Some went so far as to join the Institute for a rigorous training programme which involved considerable physical stresses and sometimes a degree of humiliation. Among them was the distinguished writer Katherine Mansfield who, according to the French author Louis Pauwels, was effectively killed by the rigours

9   Years later I met up with a retired Garda sergeant turned therapist who experimented on some of his female patients in a successful attempt to bring them to organism while they were in hypnotic trance, but even he never claimed to be able to do it at a distance without inducing the trance state first.

of Gurdjieff's techniques. But Pauwels' warning was still some years in the future—his biography of Gurdjieff was not published in English until 1964—and had Gurdjieff still been alive,[10] I would certainly have planned to enrol myself as his pupil. At age 16, I was absolutely convinced he was right about humanity (myself included) living in a state of sleep.

I still am.

10   He died in 1949.

Just before my seventeenth birthday I began to write my first novel, a self-conscious pastiche in the style of Eliot's *Wasteland*. From childhood I had wanted to be an author and now seemed a good time to start. I had read somewhere that authors should write what they knew, so *Song of Autumn* was chock-a-block with teenage angst, romantic longings, naive philosophical speculations and heavily repressed sexuality. It was about a boy suffering (profoundly) from unrequited love for a girl named Patsy. By the time it was finished, it ran to 55,000 words and ended with the words:

The song of Autumn.
Is.
Degeneration.

Since the autobiographical element was so strong, I was too embarrassed to show it to anybody and hid the bound copy away in a box. The work, produced in fits and starts, had taken more than a year and forced me to think seriously about my future. I was in my final year at Portadown College, sitting for my Senior Certificate examination. Most of my contemporaries were headed for university, if they got the grades. I was not so certain.

My mother had long expressed ambitions for me to take teacher training in Stranmillis College, a prospect that appalled me. I had vague ideas of trying something more creative—an English language degree, for example—but that prospect appalled *her*. "What *good* would it be?" she asked incessantly. "At least you'd have security as a teacher and there are nice long holidays."

In the event, I took neither the English degree nor the teacher training. My exam results were good enough for university entrance, but by the time they were announced, I had had enough of school. Classrooms had begun to feel like prison cells and I wanted freedom. Specifically, I wanted to get out into the big wide world and do some work. My mother, by contrast, wanted to stop work altogether. She had been forced into the life of a shopkeeper by my father's death and hated every minute of it. Her burning ambition was to retire, sell up and use the proceeds to buy a little house near her eldest sister in Bangor.[11] Funding my further education would have postponed the possibility for years. Each time the

11   The one in County Down, not the one in Wales.

subject came up, she complained about money. Eventually I took the hint and told her I planned to get a job.

A family friend alerted us to the fact that there would soon be an opening for a journalist in the *Portadown Times,* a local tabloid weekly. One of the reporters was planning to emigrate to Australia, leaving a vacancy to be filled. The job had not yet been advertised, but I wrote at once to the editor, David Capper. Within a week, he asked me to call for an interview.

Dave Capper was something of a controversial figure on the local newspaper scene. The *Portadown Times* had begun its life (sometime in the Middle Ages, it seemed to me then) as a single broadsheet page consisting largely of advertisements and obituaries. It existed in solitary competition with the *Portadown News* an altogether more forward-looking broadsheet which even managed to include the occasional photograph of local dignitaries. Both papers chugged along looking forward to the day when the *Times* would eventually die (probably when its owner, an elderly lay-preacher named W.H. Wolsey, decided to retire) and the *News* would sail on into a secure and prosperous monopoly. But this comfortable scenario reckoned without developments just a few miles away.

The local paper in Lurgan was the *Lurgan Mail,* a publication not unlike the *Portadown News*. The *Mail* was run by one of the old-school Masonic pillar-of-the-community churchgoing gentlemen named John Morton. Mr Morton—the formality was almost obligatory when referring to him—was satisfied with his newspaper, his printing works and the status quo. His son Jamés, who inherited the business on his death, was satisfied with none of them.

Jim Morton saw the future as one of expansion and modernisation. He upgraded his printing works from the old-style letterpress to the newly developed web-offset (which would allow him to print colour, if his staff ever got the hang of it). He dropped the *Mail's* page size from broadsheet to tabloid and set out to build himself an empire. One of his earliest moves was to buy the *Portadown Times*.

The development must have come as a chilling surprise for the aunt and nephew team who owned the *Portadown News*. Overnight, Jim Morton converted the creaking old broadsheet *Times* into a bright, modern tabloid, packed with pictures and features, all wonderfully displayed in up-to-date typestyles. To get the new show on the road, he searched around for a whiz-kid editor and found one in Dave Capper. Capper had many advantages. He was young, fearless, ambitious, hard-working and, frankly, a bit of a wild man. More to the point, he was not part of the Portadown

Establishment. This was particularly important to Jim Morton who had decided controversy sold newspapers. Establishment figures running newspapers avoided controversy like the plague: under John Morton, the old-style *Lurgan Mail* was discretion itself.

Capper took Jim Morton as his word and launched himself as editor with a front-page feature on slum housing under the banner headline, *THE LITTLE HELLS OF PORTADOWN*. It caused a sensation, not least in the Borough Council,[12] and boosted circulation of the revamped newspaper sky high.

All this had passed me by when I went for my interview—like most students, I had never read the local paper—but I was impressed by Dave Capper. He was rangy and relaxed, exactly the way I believed a newspaperman should be. I could have visualised him as a Humphrey Bogart figure in a grey fedora with a cigarette dangling casually from one side of his mouth. To my surprise, he seemed impressed by me as well. "How on earth did you know there was going to be an opening here?" he asked at once.

I had just enough sense to tell him I could not reveal my source—which impressed him even more—and he spent the rest of the interview filling me in on exactly what was going on. One of his junior reporters, Roger Donaghy, had scraped together the £10 it took to get to Australia in those days and would shortly be on the high seas to a better life. This left a vacancy on the editorial staff. Ideally, Capper wanted someone with reporting experience, but since I had demonstrated the most important journalistic characteristic of all—the ability to ferret out information—he was happy to offer me the job. Roger was not due to sail for a month, but if I started on Monday, he could show me the ropes before he left. I went home in a daze, and it was only when I was telling my mother the good news that I realised he had asked me nothing at all about my ability to write. But as it happened, that didn't matter. Having landed my first job, I was fired three days before it started.

What I took to be a letter of confirmation turned out to be a request from Dave Capper to meet him again on Friday. I had no intuition of anything amiss and presented myself at the appointed time. He told me apologetically that Roger Donaghy had changed his mind about emigrating and consequently the job I'd been offered no longer existed. When I looked suitably crestfallen, he told me confidentially that the senior reporter in the *Portadown News* had just been poached by the *Times*. Although

---

12   One member reached unusual depths of denial with the comment, "There are no slums in Portadown."

[24]

the *News* didn't know it yet, they were about to have a massive vacancy in their editorial team. "They'll be looking for an experienced man, of course," Capper told me soberly, "but it might be worth your applying: you never know. But leave it until the end of the month—Brian hasn't given in his notice yet."

Brian, the senior reporter, turned out to be Brian Courtney who, like Roger Donaghy, later turned into one of my closest friends. But at the time I didn't give a damn whether he'd given in notice or not. I reckoned somebody owed me something in the whole fiasco, so I walked round the corner to the *Portadown News,* asked to see the editor, and told him a) he was about to lose one of his best men and b) he should take me on as a replacement.

I was, of course, too inexperienced to become a replacement for Brian, but my cheek still got me a reporting job.

Journalism didn't turn out the way I thought it would. At the back of my mind was the idea that it was much the same as being an author—writing was writing, wasn't it?—while at the front my plan was to work for the paper during the day, then go home to write a great novel in the evenings. Neither of these ideas had much connection with reality.

First of all, being a journalist was a million miles away from being an author. Before I started work in the *Portadown News,* I went off for a seaside holiday with my mother. Originally it had been planned as a two-week August break, but I came home half way through because of my new job. The weather was oppressively hot and by the time I got off the train, there was thunder rumbling in the distance. The storm broke with a vengeance by the time I reached home and kept me awake throughout most of the night. (My mother had taught he to be very afraid of thunderstorms—she hid under things when there was lightning about.) As a result, I presented myself at the *News* office in a state of bleary-eyed exhaustion.

The editor, Dougie Sloan, had no idea what to do with me. Brian Courtney, the man I sought to replace, was still at work, with a week or two of his notice to run. Dickie Dale, the junior, was at his desk. Dougie was a reporting editor, who marked himself for the assignments—like meetings of the Borough Council—he liked best. The paper was fully staffed and running like a well-oiled machine. There was as yet no need for me at all. When I stood expectantly to attention beside Mr Sloan's desk, he looked at me blankly and asked, "What are you going to write?"

It was the last question I expected, and I answered with the first thing in my head: "What about a piece on the storm last night?"

"Good idea," Dougie grunted. "Ring the police and the Surveyor's Department for any reports of damage. Better check the Electricity Board as well."

And so my professional writing career began.

My plans to write the Great Irish Novel in the evenings never got off the ground. I quickly discovered a (junior) reporter's life is not a 9 to 5 affair. Most evenings I was marked to cover some function or other, usually in the highly unsuitable company of the *News* photographer, a hard-nosed, bullet-headed, middle-aged man named Jack Nicholson, who lost no time in introducing me to the pleasures of alcohol. Since Nickie did the driving and drink, at most functions, was free to the Press, I tended to stagger home in a daze. While there have been novelists who produced their best work under alcohol, I soon discovered I was not one of them. I would creep into the house to avoid waking my mother and fall into bed, frequently without bothering to undress. A youthful liver enabled me to meet the morning with an enthusiastic grin.

A novel of sorts actually *did* get started, but in office time, and in collaboration with Roger Donaghy. Although there was fierce rivalry between the two local papers, Portadown journalism was a single community with much fraternisation and a surprisingly high degree of information exchange. Roger approached me to apologise for not emigrating and I took to him at once. Later, when I was successfully head-hunted by the *Times,* I worked with him in the same organisation. In the meantime, we discovered we both had ambitions to become novelists and decided to cooperate on a joint venture.

The inspiration for our novel was a local politician named Dinah MacNabb who, we decided, was fair game for a lampoon. We worked out a hilarious plot and wrote an introductory paragraph along the lines of: *An anti-cyclone hung brooding over Ulster. The sun shone and there had been no rain for weeks. Parched crops were dying in the relentless heat. Children sought hosepipes in a vain attempt to cool down. But nowhere was more heated than Unionist Headquarters in Ballygomoron where local candidate Mrs Eusapia McConville was preparing to fight for her political life—* and so on. The first of Elmore Leonard's Ten Rules of Writing is *Never open a book with weather*: now you can see why. For several weeks we struggled on with this sort of rubbish, writing short alternate chapters, until sense belatedly prevailed and we salvaged the possibility of future reputations by abandoning it altogether.

I soon fell into a life routine. Mornings I arrived into the office and chatted for fifteen, twenty minutes to Mr Sloan, who would issue my instructions for the day. Then I'd head for my desk to write a little—usually work on some feature or other, since I was swiftly drifting towards a feature-writing specialty. At 11 a.m. I disappeared into Irwin's Café for breakfast and a journalistic conference with every other reporter in the district. By noon I was back at my desk or off on some job. Most evenings I headed for the pub. As often as I could afford it, I got very drunk on beer, as did all of my companions.

Although I was scarcely of age to drink alcohol legally, it played a surprisingly large part in my life then. No journalist I knew was capable of taking one or two drinks socially. We were all on a mission to get smashed. Our hero was a local office supplies executive named Joe Hynes, whose natural constitution allowed him to get legless on half a pint of Wee Willie Brown. He was the cheapest treat in town and we envied him enormously. One evening, after a particularly prolonged session with Joe and the journalism crowd, I was walking arm in arm with Roger Donaghy (both singing loudly) along a nice straight, quiet backroad we'd discovered when an RUC officer waved us to a stop with his torch.

"Where are you going, lads?" he asked.

"I'm taking my friend home," I told him.

"You might do better getting off the railway tracks," he said.

But all this was surface appearance. Beneath it, like some shameful, secret sexual practice, I followed my obsession with the occult.

These days, wherever you live, your local bookshop will have an extensive 'New Age' section packed with lurid paperbacks of varying worth, some of them even written by me. In 1958, it was virtually impossible to buy anything anywhere—and especially not in Northern Ireland—on esoteric subjects. But by some stroke of good fortune I no longer remember, I discovered George Sexton.

George Sexton was an antiquarian bookseller in the British seaside town of Brighton. He had two stores—in Ship Street and Dyke Road. I never visited either, but his partner, Mr Morley, used to post me out their monthly catalogue. I cannot begin to tell you how much I looked forward to those lists. Anthony Rota, an honorary president of the International League of Antiquarian Booksellers, described the Dyke Road shop as 'cavern-like premises that were for the book-hunter a veritable Aladdin's cave.' The catalogue reflected this reality. More to the point, it had a substantial occult section.

Many of the more intriguing titles were well beyond my means. I can still remember looking with longing at a copy of *The Book of the Sacred Magic of Abramelin the Mage* on offer at £78, an almost unimaginable sum at a time when my wage packet amounted to £1.10 a week.[13] I did, however, speculate precisely that (latter) amount on a copy of the 1922 Rider edition of *The History of Magic* by Eliphas Levi.

It turned out to be the best investment I ever made. Levi's work was everything a book on magic should be. I unwrapped a weighty hardback tome with a blue cover embossed in gold. The pages, every one, were rough cut and gold edged with just enough foxing to give them a heady scent of antiquity. There was a slim, aging, fabric bookmark. The frontispiece was

13 The same rare title is now available as a mass-market paperback.

a marvellous photograph of Levi himself, a stern, balding, heavily bearded man clutching a walking stick and wearing what I took to be magician's robes. There were other illustrations, far more strange, with exciting captions like *The Great Hermetic Arcanum* and *The Philosophical Cross, or Plan of the Third Temple.* I stared at them with a tingling fascination. But the illustrations were nothing by comparison with the text. In a single volume, Levi opened up an entire world for me. It began, curiously, with a reference to the *Book of Enoch* in his opening chapter.

As you probably gathered from newspaper reports during the Troubles, we make a great deal of fuss about religion in Northern Ireland. As the product of a Protestant family (nominal though it was, following my father's death) I was well versed in the Old Testament. I was never a fundamentalist, although I did believe in God and wondered, from an early age, why He behaved like such a bastard. By my teens, I had decided the early books of the Bible were a mixture of metaphor and ancient history. But there were aspects of some of them that raised interesting questions. The Ark of the Covenant, for example, seemed less of a religious artefact than a weapon of mass destruction. And I was even more intrigued by the *Genesis* reference to the 'Sons of God' breeding with the 'daughters of men' to produce giants. What was that about? I discussed it with a local theologian who told me the full story was in the apocryphal *Book of Enoch,* but added that I would lose my soul if I ever read it. The warning was seriously intended.

I didn't exactly believe the caveat, but I didn't disbelieve it either. (The hothouse atmosphere of a Northern Irish upbringing mitigates against the development of rational thought.) It seemed that if Levi was prepared to reveal the secret of the 'Sons of God' I might be safer reading him than searching for the dangerous original. So I turned at once to the relevant section and, only minutes later, was wondering what all the fuss was about. The story was that some 200 angels were so aroused by the beauty of human women that they 'consented to fall from heaven' (Levi's phrase) in order to have sex with them. They swore an oath to take mutual responsibility should God ever find out, flew down to Mount Armon and from there made contact with the human race. As well as taking human wives and breeding giants, they taught our distant ancestors magic, herbalism, astronomy and lunar lore. Predictably, the entire business ended in tears, not just for the angels, but for the human race as well.

Levi described the *Book of Enoch* as 'Kabalistic'—a very loose usage from a scholarly viewpoint—and interpreted the story as a symbolic presentation. It referred, he said, to the profanation of the Mysteries. The 'Sons of God' were initiates rather than angels.[14] It was they who taught magic to the rest of humanity and it was they who got distracted from their sacred duties by the lures of sex.

I could understand the latter point perfectly. As a teenager, I found it very easy to get distracted by the lures of sex. But I found Levi's interpretation curiously unconvincing. Not many years later, I met up with an alternative explanation presented in a blaze of publicity by the Swiss writer Erich Von Daniken and, far more soberly and thoughtfully, by the British archaeologist and academic Tom Lethbridge. Both men concluded the 'Sons of Gods' were visiting astronauts, whose high technology was mistaken for magic by primitive humanity. After a heady burst of initial interest, Von Daniken fell from grace amid accusations of skewing his evidence. Lethbridge's work,[15] in every way a far more interesting presentation, was overshadowed by the Von Daniken books and largely ignored both by the general public and his academic peers. All the same, to this day I still think there might be something to the 'ancient astronauts' idea.

The mysteries of Enoch were not the only thing I learned from Levi's marvellous book. He introduced me to the legend of Simon Magus, who was reputed to have taken on Saints Peter and Paul in a magical battle at the Roman Coliseum and lost his life while levitating after the Apostles prayed to God to make him fall. He introduced me to Apollonius of Tyana, a magician so powerful that, for a time, his following rivalled that of Christ. And he introduced me to the most appealing magician of them all, the thirteenth-century alchemist Raymund Lully.

There are major turning points in all our lives and Lully's came (according to the legend Levi lovingly recounted) on a 'certain Sunday' in the year 1250. A beautiful and accomplished young lady named Ambrosia di Castello was on her way to hear Mass at a church in Palma, Majorca, when she attracted the attention of a richly dressed cavalier. The man—Raymund Lully, Seneschal of the Isles and Mayor of the Palace—reined in his horse like one thunderstruck and then, as Ambrosia entered the church, spurred the animal and rode in after her to the astonishment of the assembled worshippers.

14   The British writer Andrew Collins echoes this idea in his intriguing work *From the Ashes of Angels* which postulates a lost prehistoric race of shamans who taught various arts to the rest of humanity. See Andrew Collins, *From the Ashes of Angels: The Forbidden Legacy of a Fallen Race* (London: Signet Books, 1997).

15   T. C. Lethbridge, *Legend of the Sons of God: a Fantasy?* (London: Sidgwick and Jackson, 1973).

My first book on magic was by the French nineteenth-century author Eliphas Levi.

Lully's action, prompted by a sudden passion, caused a huge scandal on the island. He was a married man with three children and should have known better. Worse still, Ambrosia was also married and enjoyed an impeccable reputation. Nonetheless, Lully wrote to her explaining that what had prompted his action was something 'strange, supernatural, irresistible' and he had been overwhelmed. He proposed expiation through 'great sacrifices, miracles of accomplishment, the penitence of a Stylite and the feats of a knight-errant.'

Such language would mark you as a stalker today, but it was common enough among the educated classes in the Middle Ages. Ambrosia sought the advice of her husband who, unusually for the standards of the time, counselled that she should let her would-be lover down gently, perhaps even humour him a little. Thus, Levi claimed, Ambrosia answered in the following terms:

'To respond adequately to a love which you term supernatural would require an immortal existence. If this love be sacrificed heroically to our respective duties during the lives of those who are dear to each of us, it will, beyond all doubt, create for itself an eternity at that moment when conscience and the world will permit us to love one another. It is said that there is an elixir of life; seek to discover it, and when you are certain that you have succeeded, come and see me. Till then, live for your wife and your children as I also will live for the husband whom I love; and if you meet me in the street, make no sign of recognition.'

The final sentence should have given him the clue. Instead, he took her missive seriously and embarked at once on an alchemical quest for the elixir of life. In a phrase that was to haunt me for years, Levi explained, 'Don Juan had become Faust.'

Little good it did him. Years went by. Lully's wife died, as did Ambrosia's husband, but the quest continued. Then one day Ambrosia had a caller, an emaciated old man holding a phial of red liquid. At first he did not recognise her, although she knew him at once as Raymund Lully and asked him what he wanted. Lully explained that the liquid in the phial was the fabled elixir of life, discovered as the results of his own painstaking efforts over thirty years. He had already drunk it and knew it worked, for he had become immortal, able to survive indefinitely without food or water. Now he wished Ambrosia to take the elixir and join with him in never-ending life.

But Ambrosia, ever the realist, pointed to her snow-white hair, then opened her gown to expose a breast eaten away by cancer. "Is it this you wish to immortalise?" she asked. Lully broke the vial and left to become a Franciscan monk. Months later he attended Ambrosia on her deathbed, then wandered the world, often injured but unable to die, until God intervened with a miracle to release him from his torment.

Having recounted the legend, Levi went on to outline a rather more believable version of Raymund Lully's life, but I remember nothing of it today. It was the legend that captivated me. I wanted my life to be a romantic adventure. I wanted to experiment with alchemy and delve into forbidden lore. Although I'd never been much of a Don Juan, I wanted to become Faust. Levi's book was something of a revelation. After years of interest in Oriental mysticism, yoga, hypnosis, alternative philosophies and Fortean anomalies, I had begun to feel an attraction to a whole other world of esoteric thought.

Although I wasn't sure where it might lead, I determined I would study magic.

Since Levi had served me so well in his *History of Magic,* it seemed rea-sonable to suppose he would be my ideal mentor in its technicalities. I cast around to find out what else he might have written—less easy than sounds in those pre-internet days—and discovered intriguing titles like *The Key to the Mysteries* and *The Magical Ritual of the Sanctum Regnum.* But the one that grabbed my attention was *Transcendental Magic: its Doctrine and Ritual,* which sounded exactly what I was looking for. The translation (from *Dogma et Rituel de la Haute Magie*) was by Arthur Edward Waite, the man who rendered *History of Magic* into English, so I felt comfortable there as well. The only trouble was I couldn't find a copy.

My prime source of esoteric literature was still George Sexton Books, backed up by a handful of lesser mail-order suppliers, including one in Paris who sent me catalogues in French that occasionally featured English-language titles. The problem was that all of them were second-hand booksellers, and while second-hand booklists are treasure troves for the browser, you take your chances when it comes to anything specific. I waited some months for a copy of *Transcendental Magic* to turn up some-where—anywhere—but in vain. Then I had a sudden inspiration and paid a call to Portadown Library.

Works of Eliphas Levi were not exactly conspicuous on the shelves—in fact there were none listed at all—but Dougie Sloan had recently handed me a library press release to rewrite and I recalled one vital piece of in-formation. If the book you wanted wasn't in stock in your local library, it was now possible to order it from any other library in Northern Ireland which *did* stock it; or, failing that, to bring it in from any associate library in Britain. That sounded the business. Surely even something as obscure as a book on ritual magic would be in some library somewhere.

As I approached the librarian to put in my request, I felt the sort of embarrassment usually associated with a taste for pornography. An interest in magic—real magic, practical magic, where you actually did something and hoped for strange results—seemed....I thought about it afterwards and decided it seemed somehow *sinful.* It was also hideously disreputa-ble. Those shadowy people apparently engaged in magical practice all seemed to end up in the *News of the World,* having desecrated a graveyard at midnight or kidnapped some poor child for unspeakable rites. I was still young enough to be fearful of authority and imagined the librarian would be profoundly shocked by what I wanted. But desire overcame fear, and I asked him rigidly if I could place an order for a book. He wrote down the details without a murmur and said apologetically, "This could take three weeks."

In the event, it took less than one. In response to a postcard, I went back to the library and collected my book. The first thing I did was check the stamps on the inside front. It had been loaned out only once before, to somebody in Belleek, a remote Northern Irish village renowned for the fact it was mostly in County Fermanagh but spilled over untidily into the Republic in County Donegal.

The book proved a disappointment. Its contents list looked hugely promising: *The Pillars of the Temple...The Triangle of Solomon...The Tetragram...The Pentagram...Magical Equilibrium...The Fiery Sword...*and so on. There were also some interesting illustrations, although one, entitled *Benediction,* looked oddly like someone making a shadow-play of a rabbit. But the text was a million miles away from the step-by-step magical operating manual I had been hoping for. If anything it was a book of occult philosophy with obscure, but thrilling, passages like: 'He who aspires to be a sage and to know the Great Enigma of Nature must be the heir and despoiler of the sphinx: his the human head, in order to possess speech; his the eagle's wings, in order to scale the heights; his the bull's flanks, in order to furrow the depths; his the lion's talons, to make a way on the right and the left, before and behind.'[16] There *was* some practical material on esoteric technicalities—notably Kabbalistic—but not enough to allow a beginner like me to put together any sort of magical experiment. My embarrassment with the librarian might have been entirely in vain were it not for two things.

The first was that the frontispiece of the book had been carefully torn out. I searched the list of illustrations and discovered that it had shown the constitution of a magic circle used to call up demons. It seemed that someone else in Northern Ireland—presumably the book's previous borrower in Belleek—shared my interest in magic, but with a darker complexion. Darker or not, I found that reassuring.

The second thing was a passage in the book itself:

> I was clothed in a white garment, very similar to the alb of our
> catholic priests, but longer and wider, and I wore upon my head
> a crown of vervain leaves, intertwined with a golden chain. I

16   Eliphas Levi, *Transcendental Magic: Its Doctrine and Ritual,* A.E. Waite trans. (Chicago: The Occult Publishing House, 1910.)

held a new sword in one hand, and in the other the "Ritual".
I kindled two fires with the requisite prepared substances, and
began reading the evocations of the "Ritual" in a voice at first
low, but rising by degrees. The smoke spread, the flame caused the
objects upon which it fell to waver, then it went out, the smoke
still floating white and slow about the marble altar; I seemed to
feel a quaking of the earth, my ears tingled, my heart beat quickly.
I heaped more twigs and perfumes on the chafing-dishes, and
as the flame again burst up, I beheld distinctly, before the altar,
the figure of a man of more than normal size, which dissolved
and vanished away. I recommenced the evocations and placed
myself within a circle which I had drawn previously between the
tripod and the altar. Thereupon the mirror which was behind the
altar seemed to brighten in its depth, a wan form was outlined
therein, which increased and seemed to approach by degrees.
Three times, and with closed eyes, I invoked Apollonius. When
I again looked forth there was a man in front of me, wrapped
from head to foot in a species of shroud...[17]

Levi put the story in context and, some years later, I managed to do
the same for Levi. Despite his fearsome reputation and a lifetime spent
studying the esoteric arts, he remained at heart a theoretical magician.
Where others ventured to experiment, he preferred to speculate. Until,
that is, the spring of 1854.

Levi was then visiting London at the invitation of Edward Bulwer-
Lytton, a well-known writer and Rosicrucian, when an incident occurred
that might have come directly from the pages of a Bulwer-Lytton novel.
Levi returned one evening to his hotel to find a note waiting for him. It
was unsigned and said cryptically, *'Tomorrow, at three o'clock, in front of
Westminster Abbey, the second half of this card will be given you.'* Enclosed
with the note was half of a calling card, cut transversely, on which was
printed the Seal of Solomon, the hexagram of interlaced triangles now
often called the Star of David, but used for centuries as an occult symbol
by Western magicians.

When a curious Levi kept the assignation, a carriage drew up and a foot-
man invited him to join its passenger, a heavily veiled woman, dressed in
black, who promptly presented him with the second half of the card. She
was, it transpired, a titled lady and a friend of Bulwer-Lytton. She believed

17   Ibid.

Levi to be an adept, offered to show him a 'complete magical cabinet' of ritual equipment and eventually convinced him that a theoretical magician was no magician at all—hence the evocation of Apollonius described.

This elderly, anonymous woman (Levi never revealed her name) managed to convince me as well. I was fascinated by her collection of magical vestments and weapons. I was spellbound by Levi's description of her turret room with its four enormous concave mirrors and marble-topped altar encircled by a chain of magnetised iron. I knew then it would never be enough just to study magic. I had to put it into practice.

My external circumstances were changing. Jim Morton discovered that while controversy might sell papers, it had a negative effect on advertising. Dave Capper left the editorial chair of the *Portadown Times* to be replaced, incredibly, by its former owner and lay preacher, W.H. Wolsey. Roger Donaghy changed his mind again and decided to emigrate to Australia after all. By now we were the closest of friends, so I was privy to his thinking before the announcement was made. (It was either Australia or the French Foreign Legion—he was bored out of his mind with Portadown.) The night he made his decision he told me firmly, "You should apply for my job. The *Times* pays better than the *News.*" We compared notes and I discovered it was brutally true. Roger handed in his notice (again) at nine o'clock on Monday morning. By nine thirty, I was knocking at the door.

I got the job, of course. Experienced reporters were few and far between; and by this time I qualified as experienced. There was an overlap of several weeks between my joining the *Times* and Roger's actual departure, so we continued to spend time together even though Jim Morton decreed that he should work out part of his notice on the *Lurgan Mail,* which was short-handed at the time. One afternoon he returned to the *Times* office with an odd, lustful expression on his face. "There's a new bird in the Lurgan office," he told me at once. "She'd do you nicely—wears blue stockings."

To this day, I have no idea why Roger imagined blue stockings would light my fire, but he was right. The Lurgan office, which housed the *Lurgan Mail,* was also the administrative headquarters and printing works of the entire Morton Newspapers Group. The day each weekly paper went to bed, its editorial staff descended *en masse* to oversee layouts, write last minute copy and be pushed around by the printers. I arrived as part of the Portadown contingent and went straight to see Louis Malcolm. Louis was a handsome, blond young man with a wicked wit and a taste for beer that exceeded even my own. (He used to say the fastest way out of Lurgan was through the Brownlow Arms.) At the time he was senior reporter on the *Mail* but was destined to become its editor when the incumbent, John Murray, eventually left. "Where's the new bird with the stockings?" I asked.

The new bird with the stockings turned out to be Helen McMaster, a tall, slim, attractive, blonde girl just out of art school. She had been hired to illustrate and design advertising. The blue stockings were the least of her fashion eccentricities. We hit it off at once. I even discovered that she was sympathetic to esoteric interests. More than sympathetic, in fact. Her Belfast landlady, Eileen Boyd, was a Spiritualist medium. Helen herself was a member of what I took to be, not altogether accurately, a Spiritualist organisation, the White Eagle Lodge.

This was almost too good to be true. I had read enough about Spiritualism to know it was a movement that concentrated on practical experience. Spiritualists did not, by and large, sit around discussing how many angels could dance on a pinhead. They held séances at which a medium would bring through messages from the dead, often accompanied by spectacular phenomena like levitations, spirit voices and *apports*[18]—magic by another name as far as I was concerned. I could not wait to get in on the act and demanded an introduction to the landlady.

Eileen Boyd was a pale, slender, neurasthenic woman of a certain age who lived with her elderly father in a large, gloomy Victorian house filled with large, gloomy Victorian furniture, in one of the more respectable quarters of Belfast. The senior Boyd, who had been a master cabinet-maker before his retirement, looked on his daughter's interests with benign tolerance. "Can't say I hold much with talking to spirits," he told me quietly, "but I don't see it does much harm either." Eileen herself was considerably more down to earth than I'd imagined. She parried my suggestion that we hold an immediate séance by explaining that she was purely a 'developing medium' of small ability. If I wanted to investigate Spiritualism (she had somehow formed the impression that my interest was journalistic rather than personal) then I should attend a meeting run by an experienced professional. She had, of course, someone in mind.

The conversation led to one of the more interesting periods of my life. The man Eileen wanted me to see in action I shall call 'Mr Sludge', partly because I can no longer remember his real name, partly because I want to pass on the scurrilous and unsubstantiated rumour that he had been dismissed from the SNU (Spiritualists' National Union) for faking a trumpet séance.

A trumpet séance, as I was later to discover, is designed to bring through direct voice communications from the dead, who use the trumpet like a megaphone. Unlike most séances, it is held in total darkness with the position of the trumpet marked by luminous rings around the mouthpiece and rim. On the rumoured occasion, sitters were thrilled when the trumpet began to tremble, shift and finally levitate some feet off the ground. A cynical participant saw fit to switch on the light; and there was Mr Sludge,

18   The mysterious appearance of small objects.

on his hands and knees, waving the trumpet above his head. "But he does have genuine powers," Eileen assured me. "You'll see that for yourself."

Despite his shattered reputation, participation in one of Mr Sludge's séances was by invitation only. Fortunately, Eileen proved to be something of a celebrity in Belfast's Spiritualist circles and managed easily to wangle three. Eileen, Helen and I attended the following Saturday night.

I'm not sure what I expected, but it was certainly nothing like what I experienced. Eileen led us from her Victorian respectability to one of the more run-down areas of the city where the (unmarked) entrance to the séance rooms was sandwiched between a greengrocer's and a bicycle shop. We climbed flight after flight of dusty wooden stairs urged on by the Doppler approach of a sound so strange I could not begin to identify it. I was of an age when one fears to show ignorance, so I refrained from asking Eileen. "Through here," she said as we reached the top floor and the sound reached a crescendo. She pushed open a door.

Northern Ireland, in the Fifties, was peppered with Meeting Halls—small, simplistic buildings erected by small, simplistic Protestant sects dedicated to freedom of worship so long as it involved no Roman ritual. The interiors of these Meeting Halls were all the same: plain rooms with a lectern at one end, faced by excruciating rows of upright wooden chairs. As Eileen pushed the door, I realised I was in just such a Meeting Hall: Ulster's cultural imperative had swallowed the weirder trappings of Spiritualism whole. But Spiritualism was fighting back. Protruding from one wall was a red darkroom light on an erectile fitting, and around this and the remaining walls were scores, perhaps even hundreds, of songbirds in cages, the source of the peculiar sound I'd heard on our approach.

We took seats near the front. A glance around confirmed the first impression of a Meeting Hall. I'd been to enough of them in the course of my journalistic career to recognise a typical congregation: predominantly female, working class and middle-aged. A great many of them made it their business to greet Eileen and shake her hand. Then Mr Sludge came in.

Mr Sludge was a small wiry man with the dirtiest fingernails I've ever seen. He wore a crumpled black Sunday-go-to-meeting suit and didn't seem to know how to smile. The room fell silent, except for the cage-birds, as he walked to the lectern, opened the Bible apparently at random and read a passage, eerily appropriate to the occasion, about speaking in tongues. Then everybody sang a cheerful hymn.

Just when I thought the similarities with a Gospel meeting were moving close to absolute, Mr Sludge made a signal and the atmosphere changed.

[39]

Someone near the back scurried to switch off the lights. At once we were plunged not into darkness, but into a ruddy gloom. The cage-birds stopped singing. Mr Sludge, now seated on an upright chair next to the lectern, closed his eyes and began to breathe heavily. "He's going into trance," Eileen whispered in my ear.

I had never seen a mediumistic trance before and in the event, it proved disappointing. There are mediums and mediums. Some are taken over by spirits, who use their vocal cords to deliver messages. Some conjure voices from thin air. Some produce ectoplasm that takes on ghostly shapes. Mr Sludge was what was called an 'impressionistic medium.' He saw visiting spirits mentally and formed an idea of what message they wanted to pass on through some foggy process analogous to telepathy. "I have the impression of a grey-haired old man standing behind your left shoulder," he told one woman with fruit in her hat.

"That's my grandfather," she said promptly.

"I think he may be your grandfather," Mr Sludge echoed soberly. "He sends you love and tells you not to worry."

My own impression, after fifteen minutes or so of this drivel, was that, as a medium, Mr Sludge left a lot to be desired. He also ran out of steam very quickly, for less than half way through what was supposed to be a one-hour séance, he emerged abruptly from trance to ask his congregation, "Anyone else getting any impressions?" The congregation needed little urging. For the remaining forty minutes, women were up and down like yo-yos, giving each other messages from dead, banal relatives and, occasionally, claiming they could smell the scent of ethereal flowers. I had the strong impression they all knew one another because names were thrown around with reckless abandon: "There's a woman I think might be your Martha. She says you're fretting about Timmy."

In retrospect, I should have seen it coming. I was the only new face in the room. (Even Helen had been before.) The woman with fruit in her hat stood up to fix me with a gimlet eye. "Has your father passed on?" she asked without preliminary.

I blinked. "Yes. Yes, as a matter of fact he has."

"I see him in uniform. He was a soldier, wasn't he? No don't tell me anything, you're someone who needs proof. He died in the First World War, didn't he? Flanders Fields—he's showing me a poppy. He says you're not to worry about the exam. Everything is going to be all right."

"I'm not sitting an exam," I said.

"This is an exam that's gone by. You mustn't be embarrassed, dear, about not doing well. We all have difficulties with exams. He says, your father says, it doesn't matter. He sends you love and flowers."

As we were walking Eileen home, I encountered for the first time the deep-seated human instinct to bend facts to fit theory. "What was that business about the exam?" Helen asked.

"I've got a beard," I said. "I think she must have thought I was a student." What I really thought was that the woman in the fruity hat had been on a fishing trip for all her urging not to tell her anything. But I wasn't sure how deeply committed Helen was to this sort of thing and didn't want to endanger our budding relationship with an open expression of cynicism.

"Have you failed an exam recently?"

"I haven't sat many, but I've actually never failed an exam in my life."

"Maybe it's something to come," Helen said.

"She said it was an exam that had gone by."

"It can be difficult to sort out past from future," Helen said.

"But your father is dead?" Eileen put in.

"Yes, she got that right."

"And he died at Flanders?"

I lost patience. "No," I said firmly. "He was never a soldier, never wore uniform, didn't die in World War One. He died in bed, of pneumonia."

"Did you have any relative in the Army?" Eileen persisted.

"I had an uncle killed in the First World War, long before I was born. I never knew him."

"That would be it, probably," Eileen said. But her beliefs must have been slightly shaken, for she added, "It wasn't very good tonight. I think Mr Sludge is getting past it."

"Why don't you let him come to one of your private séances, Eileen?" Helen said brightly. "You're a much better medium than Mr Sludge."

And Eileen, having earlier refused the same request from me, said, "Yes, all right."

It took more than three weeks to organise the private séance with Eileen Boyd. In the meantime I continued to step out with Helen and, in the process, learned more about the White Eagle Lodge.

I might perhaps have been forgiven for imagining it was a Spiritualist organisation, for that was certainly how it started out. During the 1920s, a London medium called Grace Cooke worked diligently with the Stead Borderland Library to provide grieving relatives with post-mortem messages from their loved ones. She might have continued to do so until her own death, but in 1930 there arose one of those situations that are accepted without question by Spiritualists but seem bizarre in the extreme to the rest of us. The year marked the death of Sir Arthur Conan Doyle, creator of Sherlock Holmes and tireless campaigner for the Spiritualist cause. It also marked the first contact between Grace Cooke and the Fraternité des Polaires, a mysterious Parisian group founded on the instructions of an 'oracle of astral force' discovered by an Italian hermit in 1908.

The Polaires told Grace the late Sir Arthur wished to appoint her as his personal medium so he could continue to communicate from the other side. To help with the work, she was given a symbol—a six-pointed star— and a helper, in the imposing shape of a native North American named White Eagle. Although Helen seemed to think White Eagle was a spirit guide of the type common to Spiritualist mediums—Eileen Boyd had one called White Feather and my friend Ian Graham has one called White Bull—this was not actually the case. Grace Cooke's husband subsequently revealed that, like Blavatsky's Masters, White Eagle lived on a mountain in the East and controlled his medium from there until sometime around 1956 when he seems to have passed permanently into the spirit realm.

After the initial communications with Conan Doyle, Grace Cooke more or less ceased to function as a medium in the traditional Spiritualist sense. She became what would now be called a 'channel'[19]—a psychic in touch with some highly evolved, discarnate entity who her uses to teach humanity spiritual truths. Grace Cooke's highly evolved entity was, of course White Eagle, and the White Eagle Lodge, founded in 1934, was based on her mentor's teachings. What were these teachings? Helen, who was keen to have me join the Lodge, loaned me one of her White Eagle books. Although I sympathised with much of the information in it—doctrines like karma and reincarnation, for example—the writing style was so saccharine

19 While working in France, Ian Graham became known as the English Channel.

I found it impossible to stomach. I returned the book to Helen, politely declined her invitation to become a Lodge member and silently vowed I would never, ever have anything to do with such a crackpot organisation. White Eagle must have been listening, for he continued to turn up in my life until I finally discovered that his Lodge, in its inner workings, was a far more magical establishment than its public face suggests.

But that was in the future. In the meantime, there was a formless aspiration to practice magic and an immediate excitement about the prospect of another séance. My intuition told me, correctly as it transpired, that Eileen Boyd was not a female Mr Sludge. Although a Spiritualist through and through, there was a severely practical air about her—as there often is about women who look after an aged parent—and I could not believe she would waste her time on the sort of woolly communications Sludge and his followers had produced. Then and now, I could not understand why she had recommended him.

I arrived at Eileen's home on the appointed afternoon to find Helen already there, as was another of Eileen's tenants, an agricultural student named George. George, I quickly discovered, had no belief whatsoever in Spiritualism, magic, mediums or psychical phenomena; and precious little interest in them either. He was there purely on the promise of a free meal. Eileen explained that she'd invited him in order to balance the sexes in the coming sitting, this apparently being an important element in a successful outcome.

The séance itself was scheduled to take place after supper and after dark. We whiled away the afternoon in one of those etheric conversations guaranteed (in retrospect) to send someone like George into paroxysms of disbelief. He was polite enough about it, but Eileen eventually grew tired of his scepticism and suggested a ouija experiment.

"Do you have a ouija board?" I asked delightedly. I had been trying to find one for ages, but without success.

"No, but I have a wine glass."

The wine glass turned out to be a tumbler and was accompanied by a pack of *Lexicon* cards. With the sort of expertise that suggested she'd done this before, Eileen dealt the letters of the alphabet in a large circle on her polished dining table and upended the tumbler in the centre. "Rest one fingertip lightly on the rim of the glass," she ordered.

You are doubtless familiar with this parlour game: the glass moves to spell out answers to questions in the same manner as the pointer of a ouija board. Whether the movement is the work of spirits, as Eileen believed, or involuntary, unconscious muscle movements, as George insisted, is a matter of debate and was indeed debated hotly on that occasion. For me the session remains memorable on two counts. The first was my observation that, during a particularly vigorous movement, the glass lost two of its fingers—the participants simply couldn't keep up—then elected to move *towards* the remaining two. It is difficult to see how this could have been caused by involuntary muscle movements. The second was the fact that the glass told Helen she had a Guide, a long-deceased Spanish nun named Carmen. Helen looked quite pleased with the news, and I remember wondering what she was going to do with it.

After supper, Eileen's father was dispatched to the cinema like the younger brother of a woman on a date and the rest of us set about preparing for the séance. The heavy Victorian setting could not have been more appropriate. Modern Spiritualism began in the Victorian era with the Rochester Rappings of 1848. Two young American sisters, Kate and Margaret Fox, claimed they were communicating with spirits and by 1850, everyone was doing it. The movement, now institutionalised as a church and hence claiming some sort of respectability, swept across the Atlantic to take Europe by storm. The Continent's crowned heads, with little else to do, took to it in a big way, as did Queen Victoria, who was moved to award one medium a medal for 'meritorious clairvoyance.'

We set comfortable chairs in a semi-circle around the open fire. "I may or may not fall into trance," Eileen said. "If I do, don't be concerned and above all don't touch me—a medium should never be woken unexpectedly. I don't know what will happen, if anything, but I would ask every one of you to keep watch carefully."

"What's *likely* to happen?" I asked her.

"I don't know that either. But whatever does will happen to me, so no one else has to worry." In the event, she proved wrong about that.

I wondered if she would produce some sort of darkroom light like Mr Sludge, but the séance was held by firelight, which cast just enough of a ruddy glow for the sitters to see one another while leaving the proceedings in a comfortable, relaxing gloom. Not that I was *actually* relaxed. My feeling was that this was the real thing. I more than half expected 'phenomena'—raps or strange lights or the touch of ghostly hands—even though Eileen had insisted in the course of the afternoon that she was not that sort of medium. For the first few minutes, my heart was pounding wildly, but boredom soon settled it down. Sixty seconds is a long, long time when you're sitting in the gloom, waiting desperately for something to happen and nothing does. Or almost nothing. Eileen's eyes slid closed behind the firelight reflected in her spectacles. Her breathing deepened. The performance was very similar to that of Sludge and I presumed she was falling into trance; but if so, there it stopped. She voiced no 'impressions,' manifested no phenomena, did nothing more. She might as well have been asleep and, as the minutes ticked by, I suspected she was.

I looked at the others. For the life of me I can no longer recall what Helen was wearing, but George had on an outrageously bright yellow sweater. They were both wide awake and seemed, from their expressions, amused by whatever it was that Eileen was doing. I half suspected a conspiracy, some elaborate conjuring trick agreed between the three of them designed to pull my leg, produce a convert or generate a favourable newspaper report. It occurred to me I knew nothing about George: his scepticism could easily have been play-acting. And despite our occasional cuddles in the cinema, I knew precious little, in any real sense, about Helen either, beyond the fact she'd pledged allegiance to an Amerindian spook. A woman who could do that might seem capable of anything.

So I stared into the fire, watched my fellow sitters, listened to the steady ticking of the grandfather clock and then, after a period of time I can no longer determine, something quite extraordinary happened: a window opened up across reality and I was no longer in the séance room but staring out across a well-kept summer parkland. White-robed figures, in groups of two and three, strolled across manicured lawns or paused to chat beneath the trees. No one paid me any attention.

I suppose this is as good a place as any to tackle a problem I have encountered over the years when discussing experiences of this sort. One's listeners, sympathetic or critical, tend to nod, purse their lips, then ask kindly, "Are you sure you weren't dreaming?" There was a time when the question made me feel defensive. Today, I consider it little more than a mindless reflex. If you were tempted towards it yourself as you read the preceding paragraph, let me ask you a question in return: *Can you tell the difference between your sleeping dreams and your waking experience?* If the answer is *yes*—and I strongly suspect it may be—then why on earth should you imagine that I cannot? While caught up in a sleeping dream, one can and does often mistake it for life, but once you awake there is no doubt whatsoever. Dreams, even vivid dreams, have an unmistakable quality, usually manifesting in irrational elements that were readily accepted while dreaming, but easily recognisable for what they are in the waking state. Besides, however vivid (and apparently rational) a particular dream might be, it does not integrate readily with waking experience. In retrospect, you see it plainly as an aspect of sleep. So I can tell you categorically that, in my vision of the parkland, I was not asleep and dreaming.

But such a denial tends to raise another problem. Most of us have an either/or mentality. We see experiences like this in terms of sleeping or waking, dream or reality. This is unfortunate, for I do not believe for a moment that the séance room somehow metamorphosed into a physical parkland, nor, indeed, that I was physically transported into a different area of reality, although I suspect that 'transported' in its religious sense may bring us closer to the truth of the matter. It seems to me that there is a third state of perception, neither dreaming nor normal waking consciousness, which allows us glimpses of (objective) realities that are generally unavailable.

I watched the parkland, fascinated, for a few moments before it faded, and I found myself staring into the anxious faces of my fellow sitters. "Are you all right?" Eileen asked.

"Yes." I wondered vaguely what the fuss was all about.

"Your eyes were open, but we couldn't get you to react," Eileen said.

Helen put in, "You were covered by a sort of cloud. At one point you disappeared completely."

"We thought it might be a trick of the light," Eileen said, "but when George put his arm into it, his arm vanished." I looked at George's yellow sweater. It was the one thing in the room that stood out brightly in the firelight.

They stared at me a moment longer, then gave a collective sigh. "I think I'll make us all a cup of tea," said Eileen.

Roger disappeared into Australia, hated the job that was waiting for him and settled in Tasmania instead, working for a daily newspaper. Thrilled by his example, I decided to do the same. For a Protestant journalist in Northern Ireland, the traditional route to advancement was to spend a year or two in a provincial weekly, then head for Belfast and join either the morning *Belfast Newsletter* or the evening *Belfast Telegraph*. (Catholic journalists had it a little rougher: their only Belfast option was the *Irish News*.) The *Telegraph* was my preferred choice. It had always seemed to me to be the better paper of the two and recently it had passed out of Baird family ownership—it was founded in 1870 by William and George Baird and run by their descendants ever since—to become part of the growing empire of Roy Thompson, a Canadian newspaper magnate. The injection of fresh blood—and, I suspect, money—had created a lively publication and word in the business was that Thompson paid his reporters well. I only had one problem: I didn't really want to work in Belfast. But Providence was looking after me. The *Telegraph* suddenly advertised for a Mid Ulster correspondent. Portadown was as Mid Ulster as you could get. I applied at once.

At the interview, the paper's managing editor had a sudden wobble over my name and asked if I was a member of the Orange Order. Names were a subtlety of Northern Irish life that few outsiders ever came to understand. From the cradle, both sides of the religious divide were taught how to recognise their own on the basis of a name. Someone called, for example, 'Billy Wilson,' could, with ninety per cent accuracy, be placed in the Protestant camp, while 'Finbarr O'Rourke' was assuredly a Roman Catholic. Unfortunately, I was one of the ten per cent minority where the name-religion linkage didn't work. 'Brennan' was a Catholic name, yet my upbringing was Protestant. But I was keen to get the job and quite prepared to be anything the *Telegraph* wanted: the unofficial apartheid that would later lead to decades of slaughter was then accepted as a way of life. "I'm not," I told him truthfully, "but my father was. And a Black. And a Mason."

"So you're a Protestant?" he asked.

"Oh yes," I lied. My current religious beliefs were more or less summed up by the expression 'A plague on both your houses.' He bought it, smiled with relief, and offered me the job. So I joined the *Belfast Telegraph* and God decided to punish me for the lie through His instrument, Freddie Gamble.

At first everything went well. The *Telegraph's* management had decided that Mid Ulster—the area around Portadown and Lurgan—was of growing importance and required an editorial presence. Since it wasn't *quite* important enough to warrant opening a proper administrative centre, the idea was to hire a feature-writer cum reporter, have him rent a phone and cheap office accommodation, then supply the paper with a flood of exclusive local information. This suited me down to the ground. It meant I would be my own boss, keeping my own time and picking jobs that suited me. It also gave me lots of local clout—there wasn't a tinpot politician in the country who didn't quail at the mention of the *Telegraph.* "We'll want you to spend a trial period in Belfast, of course," said the managing editor happily. "Just to make sure you're not *absolutely* useless."

"Perhaps I should set up my new office first," I suggested. He bought that too and I left feeling as happy as he looked. I *really* didn't want to work in Belfast—the city was too big, too bustling and, frankly, too scary—but I thought that if I set up in Mid Ulster, did my job efficiently and fed them lots of copy, they would soon forget the idea of a trial period.

I resigned from the *Times* and walked around the corner to Hynes Office Supplies, a business run by two brothers, Joe and Cecil Hynes. If you've been paying attention, the name Joe Hynes will already be familiar to you as the man who could get legless on a half of Wee Willie Brown: in other words, one of my old drinking cronies. I was aware that Joe's business, still very much in its establishment stage, was run on a shoestring and reckoned—accurately as it turned out—that he would welcome a contribution to his rent. I suggested that he set me up one of his many desks at the back of his showroom, organise a second phone and cut me off from public view by means of a free-standing screen. I would get a set of keys cut so I could come and go without involving him. If anybody phoned me while I was out, I would expect young Cecil to take a message. In return, the *Belfast Telegraph* would pick up the entire company phone bill, pay half the light and heat, and contribute a rent equivalent to two thirds of what Joe was paying for the whole building. I also promised to buy him a pint once a week, whether it was my round or not. He jumped at it.

The arrangement worked brilliantly. I liked Joe and Cecil enormously and they liked me. When things were slack, as they frequently were, we entertained each other with the latest jokes. When things were busy, we managed not to get in each other's way. I established a fortnightly comment column, alternating with a feature round-up of local gossip and kept up my old contacts so I stayed on top of any hard news the *Telegraph* needed to know. Both the comment column and the feature round-up were by-lined, so I reckoned I was establishing a solid name for myself. As the weeks slipped by, it was obvious my plan had worked: nobody was talking about a trial period anymore.

Then one day the phone rang. "Where the hell are you?" asked an angry voice, which I recognised at once as belonging to the *Telegraph's* news editor, Freddie Gamble. Freddie was a swarthy man of middle height with a permanent. I'd met him briefly during the interview process and he terrified me.

"What do you mean, *where the hell am I?*" I asked aggressively. I subscribed then to the old-fashioned notion that it was best to stand up to bullies.

"I mean why aren't you here? You're supposed to be doing a month's trial."

"I was setting up the office."

"How long does that take?"

"It's done. I've been sending you copy."

"Have you? I hadn't noticed."

"You should have—you've been running it in your paper."

He changed tack. "Why didn't you come up here after you'd set up your bloody office?"

"I was waiting for somebody to tell me when you wanted me."

"I want you here tomorrow—I'm short-staffed."

I panicked. After weeks as my own boss, the thought of working under this scary man in a strange environment was a nightmare. "I can't come tomorrow," I said quickly. "I have things arranged."

"Report to me on Monday then," he said and hung up.

Freddie—or Mr Gamble as I liked to call him to his face—was an exception, possibly the sole exception, to the rule that only Protestants should work for the *Belfast Telegraph*. He was Jewish, but in the mindset of the time, anything was better than a Catholic. (*Pro Tanto Quid,* the Queen's University rag-day magazine, once ran a telling cartoon showing an Orangeman holding a broken bottle to the face of a loin-clothed Indian. 'Aye, but are you a Protestant Hindu or a Catholic Hindu?' the Orangeman was saying.) He was also the hardest man I'd ever met. I never, ever, saw him smile. He was always busy, always in a hurry, scathing at the slightest sign of ignorance or weakness. I tried to hide my weakness, but there was no hiding my ignorance.

"I'm marking you for City Hall."

"How do I get to City Hall, Mr Gamble?"

"Oh, for Christ's sake—ask somebody!"

My trial period, working essentially as a junior reporter in Belfast, was scheduled to last a calendar month, but in less than half that time I awoke one morning to discover I was now so terrified of Freddie Gamble that I could not leave my bedroom. I remained there for several weeks, fed on a tray by my patient mother, before I tackled the root of the problem by sending a letter of resignation to the *Belfast Telegraph,* explaining that I was unable to work a period of notice for medical reasons and suggesting they adjust my severance pay accordingly. (They paid me in full anyway.) Then I called the *Portadown Times* and asked for my old job back. It turned out to be gone, but Jim Morton, who never seemed to nurse a grievance if his staff left to better themselves—and returned when they didn't—found me a job in the *Lurgan Mail.*

The *Telegraph* survived without me, although the Mid Ulster office did not: to Joe Hynes' chagrin, it was closed as a failed experiment. Not all that long after, Freddie Gamble complained to a friend that his shirt collars had somehow grown tight. Medical investigation revealed a virulent throat cancer. When I heard the news of his death from a colleague in Belfast, I mentioned that my fear of Freddie had driven me into a nervous breakdown.

My colleague nodded soberly. "Most of us were afraid of him," he said, "but if it's any consolation he thought you were a good journalist."

Back on familiar territory, my fears disappeared like morning mist and I settled into a comfortable routine at the *Lurgan Mail*. John Murray was editor when I joined and within months became editor-in-chief of the entire Morton Group. He was, if anything, a harder man than Freddie Gamble, but for some reason I was never afraid of him. (Except possibly during the lunch-time poker games when he regularly took me to the cleaners.) My senior on the editorial staff was Louis Malcolm whom I liked enormously and since the print works was in the same building, I soon made friends with several of the men who worked there. The friendships were cemented over poker and pints and even the occasional fist fight as tempers frayed under the strain of deadlines.

Apart from poker, the favourite form of gambling in the print works was horse racing. One of the apprentices, a nervous boy named Fred, collected bets for placement each lunchtime and was dispatched again late each afternoon to bring back any winnings. I had no interest at all in horses until the day I managed to acquire a curious little book called *Thought Dial* by Sidney Omarr, an American astrologer with the *Chicago Sun-Times.* Sidney had invented a circular cardboard device (which he generously included in a slip-pocket on the inside cover) that allowed you to dial up three numbers, reduce them by addition, then look up the result in a chart. By doing so, you were able to find lost objects, answer yes/no questions and work out lucky numbers. You were also able to predict the winners of horse races.

The device appealed to me enormously. Since there were no particular questions I needed answering and I had lost no objects, I decided to test it on the horses. I found runners and riders in the morning newspaper, worked out who was going to win the 3.30 and then, to make it interesting, decided on a small bet. Since I had never been inside a bookmaker's door in my life, I had no idea how to go about it, so I asked Fred to do it for me. My stake was half a crown—about 10p in today's money: I didn't have *that* much faith in the Thought Dial—and I emphasised I wanted it placed on the nose.

What happened next was a comedy of errors. My disinterest in racing was well known. A puzzled Fred began to wonder why I suddenly wanted to place a bet and discussed it with several of his colleagues. A consensus gradually emerged that, as an investigative journalist, I must have had information that the race was fixed. There was a stampede to get money on my horse and several hundred pounds were lost—as well as my meagre half-crown—when it failed to show.

The incident, farcical though it was, illustrates that my esoteric interests had survived the recent upheavals in my life. I still wanted to practice magic and I still had no idea how. What I desperately needed was someone to show me. I was aware of the occult cliché *When the pupil is ready, the teacher will appear,* but either I was unready or my teacher was late. Even my relationship with George Sexton was going through a hiatus. His esoteric listings had shrunk over the years, probably as a reflection of diminishing customer interest. Even I wasn't buying very much. My problem was I really didn't know what books I needed. I was desperate for occult guidance, and occult guidance, as the Sixties dawned on Northern Ireland, was hard to come by.

I did, however, have better luck with another of my passions. I had been devoted to science fiction since childhood when a new comic called *The Eagle* introduced me to the exploits of the space pilot Dan Dare and his implacable Venusian foe, the Mekon. When I outgrew the comic, I read my way through every work by H. G. Wells, including the bewildering *In the Days of the Comet,* which dealt with 'free love', a term I was too young to understand. Wells was available in libraries because his books were considered classics, but any other science fiction was almost impossible to find. Most of the genre was produced in America and very little of it ever got as far as Ulster. I remember my astonishment, years later, when I discovered Belfast had its very own science fiction author, James White; and very highly thought of he was too.

One Saturday I was rummaging through a bookstall in Portadown Market and attracted the proprietor's attention by picking up a book of glamour photographs called *Diana Dors in 3D.*[20]

"I'm afraid it will actually cost you Three and Six D," he remarked and we got talking. I asked him, without much hope, if he ever carried any science fiction. He shook his head, but recommended Smithfield Market. Smithfield Market was in Belfast, a long way to go on the off chance of buying a book, but I was desperate and had time on my hands so I drove up that afternoon.

It was like finding a goldmine. One whole corner of Smithfield Market was occupied by a massive bookstall jam-packed with science fiction pa-

---

20   Much later in life, when I was in my Seventies, I became friendly with Mim Scala, one-time Rolling Stones road manager, who knew Diana Dors personally. I felt a pang of jealousy when he told me.

W.E. Butler: the aim of the true magician
is to realise his true self.

perbacks imported from America. There was Asimov, there was Kornbluth, there was Pohl and Anderson and Bradbury and Heinlein and dozens more winking at me from behind their lurid covers. There were copies of *Astounding, Galaxy, Analog* and *The Magazine of Fantasy and Science Fiction.* I was like a child in a sweetshop. Thereafter, Smithfield Market became a weekly destination.

One Saturday afternoon I found among the science fiction a slim, small paperback entitled *Magic: Its Ritual Power and Purpose* by someone called W. E. Butler. I bought it without hesitation and read it at a sitting that evening.

For such a small book, it had a lot to say. Butler began, rather obscurely, by discussing the Biblical 'Kings of Edom', then launched into a survey of the history of magic from pre-Christian times to the discoveries of Jungian psychology. He claimed that the aim of the genuine magician was to realise his true self—the normal personality being little more than a mask. Most importantly, he claimed there was a living (if hidden) Western Esoteric Tradition that embodied doctrines and practices handed down from antiquity, the central philosophy of which was contained in a corpus of Hebrew mystical wisdom known as the Qabalah. Magic itself, he insisted, was not an irrational superstition, but a body of techniques based on profound psychological laws. I was fascinated.

The following week, I was back at the stall, science fiction forgotten, searching for anything else W.E. Butler might have written. Sure enough, there was a single copy of a hardback—and a full-sized book this time—entitled *The Magician: His Training and Work*. I didn't know it, but I picked up a whole new way of life when I reached for that book.

Although not particularly well known then (or now, come to that) Ernie Butler was one of those interesting individuals whose influence far outreached their fame. He was born in Yorkshire in 1898 into a large, poor family. Very little is known about his early life except that it seems to have been fairly grim. His parents were rumoured to have ended their lives in a workhouse and Ernest himself was brought up by a relative. Like many another poor boy, he joined the army and was shipped off to India in what must have been another of those life-changing moments. India, of course, has never been short of spiritual teachers, and Ernie studied under several of them. He was interested in Theosophy, but here my sources part company. One claims he became a Theosophist, asked Annie Besant if he could study with her and was politely refused. The other maintains he was refused membership of the Theosophical Society but *did* study under Besant. The dichotomy is unimportant. Theosophy was not his path in any case.

When he returned to Britain he continued his spiritual training under Robert King, a bishop in the Liberal Catholic Church. Although founded by a Theosophist, the orientation of the Liberal Catholic Church was distinctly Western. In 1925, Butler joined the Fraternity of the Inner Light, an organisation with an intriguing provenance.

Spiritualism wasn't the only Victorian craze. Towards the end of the nineteenth century, there was a growing interest in the occult, particularly among Freemasons. Some of the Scottish Lodges were already working Rosicrucian degrees and in 1867 a handful of master masons formed the Societas Rosicruciana in Anglia, which leaned more towards magic than traditional masonry. Its members began to work rituals and hold lectures on esoteric subjects, including Kabbala, (as it was commonly spelled at that time), symbolism and the ubiquitous spiritualism.

In 1888, three members of the SRIA, Wynn Westcott, MacGregor Mathers and W. R. Woodman, formed the Hermetic Order of the Golden Dawn, an organisation that was magical through and through. There's been a lot of nonsense written about the origins of the Golden Dawn, much of it based on romantic statements issued by its founders. Westcott was particularly culpable, claiming to have received rituals and a charter from a mysterious German adept, Fraulein Anna Sprengel, whom I suspect was a fictitious as my own creation, Eddie the Duck. MacGregor Mathers, on the other hand, was a capable scholar of occult lore and created many of the Order's rituals based on his knowledge of spiritual Hermeticism, Kabbala and, to a lesser extent, the evocatory 'Solomonic' magic of the Middle Ages.

But wherever its doctrines came from, the Golden Dawn had one distinct advantage—its system worked. Somehow these scholarly masons had managed to put together a sort of yoga for the West, based on sound psychological principles, that offered its members genuine opportunities for spiritual awakening through meditation training, esoteric practice and a graded structure of complex initiatory rituals. It should have been a school for supermen, but human nature intervened.

Into the Golden Dawn in 1898 came a wild man named Aleister Crowley. He'd had a hard time with his mother, a rigidly religious woman who responded to his childhood peccadilloes by calling him the Great Beast (from *Revelation,* the final book of the biblical *New Testament).* He spent much of his later life trying to live up to the name. It took him just two years to sow the seeds of the Order's downfall. Crowley was an extraordinarily competent magician, who did the work diligently and swarmed up the initial degrees of the Golden Dawn like a monkey. The trouble was, he wasn't very likeable. In the repressed Victorian atmosphere of his day, his priapic behaviour was appalling—and might well raise a few eyebrows even today. He was bombastic, argumentative and far too sure of himself. He was flamboyant and theatrical. He liked to shock. He exploited others—particularly women—and treated them badly. Perhaps worst of all, he had a schoolboy sense of humour.

Crowley swiftly got on the wrong side of his magical superiors, notably William Butler Yeats, the Irish poet who was head of the Order at the time. They tried to slow his progress, Crowley fought back and the resultant quarrel—which eventually ended up in Court—split the Golden Dawn so effectively that it never really recovered. It did, however, stagger on, fragmented and fragmenting, a shadow of its former glory, for a good few years thereafter. In 1919, it admitted a new member called Dion Fortune.

Dion Fortune is a pen-name derived from a magical motto: *Deo Non Fortuna* (From God, not Chance). Its owner was Violet Firth, a Welsh girl born into a Christian Science family in 1890. Violet showed signs of psychism from childhood—she was having visions of Atlantis at the age of four—and studied psychology and mysticism as an adult. By 1918 she was working as a therapist in a London clinic and listening to lectures on esoteric subjects. A year later, a childhood friend introduced her to the Golden Dawn, where she learned trance mediumship and various other magical techniques. She was, however, careful to point out that she did not disturb the dead, but rather channelled an intelligence from a higher plane of existence.

Unfortunately Dion Fortune was a writer as well as a psychic and magician. In 1922, she published what today might seem to some, and certainly does seem to me, to be a rather silly book called *The Esoteric Philosophy of Love and Marriage.* But at the time it caused something of a sensation and greatly irritated the head of her Lodge, Moina Mathers (wife of MacGregor) who accused her of disclosing Golden Dawn secrets. When Dion responded by publishing an article that mused on why occultism attracted so many charlatans, Moina first suspended her membership, then threw her out altogether. Dion continued to publish books and articles packed with technical details of magical techniques and in 1924 established her own Order, the Fraternity of the Inner Light, which trained its students in Kabbalistic spirituality and offered an initiatory structure comparable to the original Golden Dawn. The public face of the Order came to be known as the Society (rather than Fraternity) of the Inner Light. This was the organisation Ernie Butler joined a year after it was formed. This was where he learned Western Esoteric Tradition magic.

The Magician: His Training and Work proved one of the most interesting books I had ever read. Butler's style was a lot less portentous than Levi's (at least in the Waite translation) and he had a very pleasing habit of explaining exactly how a magician trained without recourse to jargon or obfuscation. My excitement grew with every page. He even gave some exercises in relaxation and breathing and one basic ritual for readers to try out. But the most useful segment of all was a four-page bibliography of recommended reading. High on the list were the works of Dion Fortune, of whom, at this point, I had never heard. One that sounded particularly interesting was her *Psychic Self-Defense.* I bought a copy mail order direct from the publisher. On the penultimate page was the address of the Society of the Inner Light: 38, Steele's Road, London, NW3. I wrote to them at once.

While I was waiting for a reply, I decided to experiment with magical ritual.

Until this point, despite a burning ambition, I had never found the necessary information that would allow me to try out a magical ritual with any degree of confidence. Now, with books under my belt by Dion Fortune, Israel Regardie and, especially, W. E. Butler, I decided I could give it a go. The decision was not without its problems. First among them was the fact that I was still living with my mother.

Our relationship was far from easy. As she grew older and more unhappy, my mother retreated down two escape routes from the twin worries of her grocery business and an only son who must, at times, have seemed as alien as Dan Dare's Mekon. One was the cinema. There was a single Picture House in Gilford which changed its movies three times a week. My mother went to every fresh showing without fail or discrimination. On the days when no new film was being screened, she selected her alternative escape and presented herself at the doctor's surgery.

The local G.P. was Dr Sproule, a man I remember for his aroma of disinfectant and his look of perpetual exhaustion. He had saved my life as a child by lancing an abscess in my ear that had generated a high fever and coma. What he made of my mother I cannot imagine. For years he would find her lurking in his waiting room every other day, week in, week out, without respite, complaining about her eyes, her headaches, her cramps, her leg pains, her shortness of breath, her tendency to blood clots (due to standing behind the counter of her shop) which threatened to kill her if they ever reached her heart or lung. She had blanks in her vision, tingling in her fingers, numbness in her feet and before she told Dr Sproule about them, she told me. After a few years I lost my capacity to care, but he did not. He was generous with his time, listened to her sympathetically, examined her thoroughly, reassured her emphatically and sent her home with a new collection of tablets that, he must have known, would last her only until the Picture House next changed its show. She liked the little pink pills best—they 'did well' for her—but something in me suspected she liked the attention more: she always looked bright-eyed after a full examination. With the march of time, the perpetual worries about business, finance and her health, she looked forward to nothing so much as retirement. I looked forward to the day when I might leave home but could not see it coming. When my father died, each of my aunts, in turn, admonished that I was the man now and must look after my mother. I took their words as seriously as only a four-year-old can and they still haunted me as I became an adult. How could I leave home when my mother needed me? How could I leave home when my *poor sick* mother needed me? She told me at least once a week I was everything she had.

My home in Gilford was not extensive. Apart from the rat-infested cellar, there was a tiny vestibule before you entered the shop from the street. Beyond the shop was a hallway with doors into our living room (called the kitchen), a lavatory, the cellar and stairs up. There was no bathroom—we washed in a tin contraption in front of the fire, filled with saucepans of water boiled on an electric cooker. The only other downstairs room was a tiny pantry off the kitchen where my mother did the cooking. Upstairs was no more impressive. There was a front room overlooking the street, once kept as a parlour but now my mother's bedroom, the cramped back room where I slept on my father's deathbed and, up another flight, a low-ceilinged attic full of junk. None of it lent itself to works of ceremonial magic.

Fortunately there was the Press Club.

The Press Club was the brainchild of a dapper, journalistic womaniser named Fred Miller, who worked on a paper in Armagh, but lived in Portadown. He needed somewhere to take girls who succumbed to his charms and reasoned, not without justification, that there were others in the same boat. Thus he called a meeting of local reporters and proposed the formation of a Press Club. The name sounded reassuringly professional, but all Fred's idea amounted to was that we should club together to rent a convenient room and furnish it with a couch. Each member of the Club would have a set of keys. We might hold an occasional meeting there for the sake of appearances, but the Club would really come into its own on those nights when we got lucky. If we knew in advance, we might book the room for the evening—or at least an hour or so—by phoning fellow members and negotiating. If we didn't, we could take pot-luck. Should there be someone already in residence, the door would be locked from the inside: a sign to creep discretely away. Although some of us were nudging twenty, we were still essentially a group of horny teenagers and the idea sounded wonderful. The rental cost of a single room was small and we were all in gainful employment. The proposal to form the Portadown Press Club was passed by acclamation and another pint.

Helen never saw the inside of the Press Club, although I did take an earlier girlfriend up there, usually accompanied by a bottle of cheap wine. But in the event, it was hardly used, except, I suspect, by Miller. We were a sad bunch on the whole who talked about sex more often than we got it, but since nobody wanted to admit that, the rent continued to be paid, the Club continued to exist. It was private, it was curtained and, apart from the miserable second-hand couch that could be pushed easily to one side, it was empty. In short it was the perfect place to practice magic. I lifted the phone and negotiated myself a free night.

It probably goes without saying that I did not know what I was doing, even with written help from experts like Dion Fortune and Ernie Butler. I wanted to try something that promised tangible results, while unsure exactly what. I was attracted to the idea of evocation—calling up a spirit form to visible appearance—but the Spiritualist literature I had read warned against it, speaking darkly of the dangers of possession, and I was frankly frightened. So I decided on something safer, something more familiar, something (and I blush to write it) closer to prayer. My idea was to request an unusual item, like a rare book which, if it turned up, would constitute proof that results were not due to chance.

My feeling was I should turn the Press Club into a magical temple, but since I still had no idea how to do that, I compromised by pushing the couch to one side and setting up a tiny table in the middle of the room to serve as an altar. Then, in a state of nerves that bordered on hysteria, I worked the Lesser Banishing Ritual of the Pentagram.

I have learned that ritual by heart now. Then I used a script laboriously retyped from Appendix B of *The Magician: His Training and Work*. Ernie Butler had explained this was perhaps the most fundamental rite of Western magic, used to prepare and protect a place of working before any other form of magic is attempted—the equivalent, one might say, of disinfecting the operating theatre before taking out an appendix. He also explained that all magical ritual had an inner and outer aspect. The outer aspect was everything you could see, hear, touch, smell and, if you were especially intimate with the magician, taste. The inner aspect was what went on in the magician's head while he was working it.

What went on in the magician's head during the Lesser Banishing Ritual of the Pentagram was a complex series of visualisations. These began with a short sub-ritual called the Qabalistic Cross. (I had by now learned that the acceptable modern spelling of Kabbala was Qabalah, with its various derivatives following suit.) To work the Qabalistic Cross effectively, you imagined cruciform shafts of white light penetrating your body to energise energy centres in your aura. The remainder of the ritual involved the (imaginal) establishment of a fiery circle around the room with fiery pentagrams drawn at the cardinal points. Beyond them were established four vast archangelic guardians—Raphael in the East, Michael in the South, Gabriel in the West and Uriel in the North. This cleaned the working space of undesirable elements and prevented psychic intrusions while you were otherwise engaged.

Although nobody had said so, I had the idea that everything was likely to work better in gloom, so I placed a nightlight in the centre of the little table and flicked the electric light switch at the door. The familiar Press Club took on an eerie appearance. After a moment, I found my courage and walked to the East.

I never did get to ask for my rare book. I must have had a talent for ritual since the Banishing Pentagram went all too well. As I intoned the words, made the gestures and engaged with the inner working, I found myself slipping into a state of consciousness not entirely unlike the one I experienced in the séance when I saw the parkland. The first thing that happened was that I stopped worrying about being interrupted. There was something about the work that forced you to focus only on the task at hand. Very quickly, the mundane world beyond the room ceased to exist.

Although still untrained, I was naturally good at visualisation and had no trouble at all with the inner working. Even the complex visions of the archangels, with their specific colours, clothing and adornments sprang up easily before my inner eye. But as the rite was completed, a very odd thing happened. I was struck by the acute sensation that the world ended immediately behind me, so that I was standing with my back to a precipice and the slightest motion would send me toppling over the edge. The feeling was intense, physical and very, very scary. I glanced cautiously over one shoulder. The room was at it had always been. I began cautiously to turn on my own axis. There was no visible precipice, but the sensation that one existed by my heels moved with me as I turned. It was an extraordinarily unpleasant sensation and one that made me feel nauseous. Clearly, there was no way I could continue any magical experiment while feeling like this. I crept towards the door and flicked the light switch again. The precipice sensation vanished at once.

I blew out the nightlight, moved the couch into its former position, picked up my tiny table and went home. Ernie Butler maintained that, once established, the Banishing Ritual of the Pentagram remains in place and functioning until the next change of the solar tides—that is, until the next sunrise or sunset. I often wondered afterwards whether any of my colleagues brought their girlfriends to the Club that night and did the deed observed by four imaginary archangels.

In the fullness of time I received an information packet from the Society of the Inner Light. What they had to offer—provided you were at least 18 years of age—was a four-year study course, under personal supervision, based on the Hebrew Qabalah. The course was broken down into monthly lessons and students were required to submit coursework on the same cycle. There was a substantial reading list of esoteric works with which the student was expected to familiarise himself. It was a daunting prospect, an equivalent workload to a university degree. It also sounded, as I read through the literature, as if it might be hideously expensive.

There were no examinations, but students who completed their coursework to an acceptable standard became eligible for admission, by initiation, to the Society itself, although not without certain conditions. One was that you had to be at least 24 years of age: the Society had no interest in accepting starry-eyed youngsters attracted by the glamour of magic. Another was that you submitted yourself for interview by officials of the Society whose decision on your admission must be accepted, without question, as final. Another was that you swore off recreational drugs. But that was probably no hardship since you had to swear off recreational drugs, (and all other esoteric practice, come to that) for the duration of your training. Even medical treatment had to be reported to your supervisor. It was not that the Society disapproved of drugs *per se;* or rival esoteric systems. It was simply that some things interacted with magical training to produce unforeseen results. After initiation, you were required to attend monthly meetings at the Society's London headquarters in Steele's Road, although overseas students might, by arrangement, reduce this to attending quarterly to celebrate the solstices and equinoxes.

As I waded through a plethora of literature, I suddenly discovered, to my astonishment and delight, that the fee for the four-year supervised course was astonishingly low…and even then, it was payable per lesson, in instalments. SIL clearly was not a money-grubbing organisation. In fact, I was hard put to understand how they covered their costs.

The discovery removed the last potential barrier to my magical training. I was over 18, I was engaged with no other esoteric practice, and had no problem at all with recreational drugs which, in the Fifties, were part of such a rare and exotic sub-culture that nobody I knew had the least idea where to find them. I searched out an envelope, reached for my chequebook and enrolled as an esoteric student.

It was around this time that things started to get serious between Helen and myself. While I was still working for the *Belfast Telegraph*, another member of staff took a fancy to me. She was the ideal date, attractive, sexy and in personal charge of vetting my expenses, but I gently parried her advances since I was dating Helen at the time and held to the Fifties ideal of one-at-a-time. Within the mores of the day (at least in Northern Ireland) only cads and bounders played the field. Nice young men like me had to dump Girl A before moving on to Girl B, however casual the relationship with either might prove. Alluring though my finance department executive undoubtedly was, I did not want to dump Helen. In fact when I got over my nervous breakdown, I proposed to her as part of the general reorganisation of my life. She responded by taking me home to meet her parents.

Helen's mother was a short, mildly overweight, religious woman, who made tea a lot and plumped up the cushions behind me after I sat down. She brought in the local vicar—presumably for a second opinion—and emptied my ashtray, then polished it, each time I finished a cigarette. She asked me my religion and was delighted when I told her I had been brought up in the Church of Ireland, which was true, but not very. She insisted both the vicar and myself should eat many home-made buns. She never sat still and when she was not listening intently, she talked. Helen's father, by contrast, scarcely said a word. He was a slim, slight man who worked for Harland and Wolff, the Belfast company that built the *Titanic*. His favourite chair was set right up against the Aga in the kitchen.

I must have passed muster for, after a respectable interval for thought, Helen agreed that we should get engaged. We drove to Belfast to buy the ring together. I had small savings due to prolonged outgoings on cigarettes and beer, but Helen had made some arrangement with Uncle George (the title was honorary), a jeweller she knew in King Street. "My life, but what a handsome man," he said effusively when we were introduced. "But you should be so lucky to find yourself a girl like this!" It was like stepping into a Dickensian novel. Uncle George congratulated us on our engagement, flattered us both outrageously for fifteen minutes, then announced he had exactly the ring we needed at a price so special to us, and us alone, that he was cutting his own throat. He laid out an antique ruby engagement ring on a little velvet cushion and I bought it. "You tell him he doesn't treat you right, he has to answer to your Uncle George," he called after Helen as we left.

We discussed wedding plans. Helen wanted a church ceremony, mainly to please her parents, and a small, intimate reception. That suited me fine, but I was hesitant about marriage in the Church of Ireland. I was no longer a believer, and some mindless prompting of principle made me feel awkward about using their facilities. But, surprisingly, I did have one friend in Holy Orders. The Reverend Tom McIlroy was church correspondent of the *Lurgan Mail* and I liked him. "How would you feel about officiating at the marriage an atheist?" I asked him without preamble, overstating my position so that he would realise the seriousness of the situation.

"Are we talking about you?"

"Yes."

"I'll do it. You know you have to stand there afterwards while I lecture you about the way you have to live your life?"

I expected protests from Helen's parents—Tom was Presbyterian—but they obviously decided another Protestant denomination was not the worst thing that could have happened and gave their blessing. We formalised arrangements and set a date. Then I took a deep breath and went off to tell my mother.

One of the few lessons I have learned from life is that my motivations are not always what I believe them to be. Had you asked me at the time why I was in such a hurry to marry Helen, I would have told you that I loved her. Which was true, but surely not the whole truth, since it explains only why I wanted to marry her, not why I wanted to marry her so quickly. I was scarcely out of my teens and a nervous breakdown. She was not pregnant, nor likely to become so. (We were both virgins.) Neither of us was particularly well-off. It would have made sense to wait. But I could not wait and did not wait. The reason, I believe, was that I had become desperate to get away from my mother.

The *geis* laid on me by each aunt in turn after my father's death—*You are the man now, you must look after your mother*—was silly, thoughtless and destructive as a curse. At the age of four, I was manifestly not a man, nor was I in a position to look after anyone. But I believed I should and since I could not, I worried incessantly. If my mother went out, I worried that she might not come back. If she did not return at the promised time, my mouth would turn dry, my stomach tighten and I became almost incapable of speech. Worse still, she took great pains, both by instruction and example, to teach me her philosophy of life, which was that the world was an extraordinarily dangerous place. Cars waited to run over you. Lightning crouched in the summer sky to strike you. Criminals lurked in the shadows to rob you, mug you, then cut your throat. If, miraculously, you managed to escape, there was always disease. I might be too old for infantile paralysis, but the country was filled with diphtheria, tuberculosis and the pneumonia that had carried off my father.

Curiously, for someone convinced the outside world was so lethal, she had no compunctions about throwing me into it. "I don't want you under my feet—I have a shop to run." To this day I enjoy rainy weather. It was the only time I was allowed to stay safely at home.

As a lifestyle, it was utterly exhausting. During my early years I lived in a state of perpetual terror, crouching behind our closed front door listening for the silence that meant the street was empty before I could venture out. Later, the terror was replaced, more or less, by stress and frustration. Despite the fact I was now earning a wage, most of which was contributed to the family budget, I continued to be treated as a child and no decision was made with my participation. Over time, I became heartily sick of worrying about my mother, heartily sick of having her control my life, heartily sick of being a dutiful son. I wanted independence, to strike out on my own. What stopped me, in a word, was guilt.

The *geis* was still there and it produced guilt as effectively as a churn produces butter. How could I lead a life of my own when my mother needed me in hers? (*You must look after your mother.*) How could I follow my own star when my mother's desires were paramount? (*You must look after your mother.*) How dare I feel angry, miserable, frustrated when I was only doing what had to be done? (*You must look after your mother.*) Above all, how could I possibly leave home when my mother was perpetually ill? I strongly suspected the headaches and the tingles and the chest pains were psychosomatic in origin, a call for help and attention of a sort I was in no position to give. But that made no difference whatsoever: I still felt guilty and the guilt forged unbreakable chains.

Or *almost* unbreakable. Although it pains me to admit it, there seems to have been another factor in the situation. I was concerned about what people might think of me. One of the most common comments made about my father was that he was a decent man, and something in me tried hard to live up to this ideal. Despite the guilt, I might have found the strength to break away, but I simply could not face the additional burden of public disapproval. Yet this very fact provided its own loophole. While it was unthinkable that a boy should leave his poor, sick, aging mother to lead his own life (no doubt of selfish pleasure and debauch) it was absolutely reasonable that he might leave to get married. The certainties of Ulster culture held that a man's first duty was to his wife, not his mother.

[64]

A wife was an escape route.

When I told my mother I meant to acquire one, she realised the implications at once, burst into tears and pleaded with me to postpone the wedding. "Just for a year," she said. "Just so I can save up and get you on your feet."

On March 28, a date suggested by my tax advisor, I married Helen in Portadown's First Presbyterian Church.

I was 21 years old.

The Society of the Inner Light had a sneaky marking system. The first lesson of their instruction course required me to keep a meditation diary record, read a portion of a textbook, write comments and post all coursework to the Society at the end of the month. I was then instructed to get on with the next lesson, which was more of the same. In the fullness of time, I was promised, my work would be returned with comments and a mark by my appointed supervisor.

My appointed supervisor turned out to be somebody called Margaret Lumley Brown. The name meant nothing to me, which was just as well because I would have been terrified had I known who she was. She had round, legible handwriting and used it to scrawl encouraging comments on my diary record. She wrote a little letter of welcome, hoping I would enjoy my studies. She marked my entire effort as 'adequate.'

I'd put a lot of effort into my first month's work and thought 'adequate' pompous and a little mean, not at all like the warm persona Margaret had projected through the rest of her comments. Then I found the enclosed slip that explained, for the first time, the Society's marking system. *All* first lesson submissions were marked 'adequate' whatever their standard. From that point on, there were four possible gradings—'adequate', 'adequate plus', 'adequate minus' and 'inadequate.' 'Adequate' meant you had reached the standard of your enthusiastic first lesson. 'Adequate plus' meant you'd actually done better. 'Adequate minus' signified that you'd fallen below the measure of your first lesson. 'Inadequate' meant that you'd fallen so far below that you had to do the whole thing again. The effect was that each student unwittingly set his own standard with his first submission. I read the slip with a surge of admiration. It struck me our entire education system might have been improved by adopting the system.

The practical aspect of the Inner Light course was concerned with exercises in meditation, concentration and visualisation. The study aspect revolved around Qabalah and since it became such a central part of my life, the time has come to explain what the term denotes.

According to Hebrew myth, the Holy Qabalah was taught to Adam in the Garden of Eden by the Angel Rezial. The historical reality is only marginally less romantic. The story began with a priest named Ezekiel, exiled to Babylonia in 597 BCE and living in a Jewish settlement on Tel Abubu, the Hill of the Storm God. During the fifth year of his exile, he was working with some fellow captives by the Chebar River when, in his own words, the heavens opened and he saw visions of God.

You can read a full description of his visions in the Old Testament (Ezekiel 1:4 ff). They were so complex and obscure that for a time in the 1960s and '70s, it became quite fashionable to speculate that he might actually have seen some flying saucers. Ezekiel himself was under no such illusion. He believed he had been granted sight of the very throne of the Almighty. The experience made a prophet out of him, and he formulated a set of doctrines—including the revolutionary notion of personal responsibility—that he eventually persuaded his followers to take seriously.

But by the first century AD, Jewish mystics in Palestine were becoming less concerned with his ethical teachings than with duplicating his original experiences. They too wanted ecstatic visions of celestial hierarchies and the throne of God. So they developed techniques to obtain them, involving fasting and magical formulae known as seals. Thus prepared and armed, they embarked on perilous soul-journeys through seven spheres ('heavenly dwellings') guarded by hostile angels who had to be placated by the seals. It was, apparently, vital to match the correct seal with the right angel because any mistake could prove fatal. The Talmud warns that of four men who engaged in the practice, one died, one apostatized, one went mad and only one, Rabbi Akiba ben Joseph, managed to achieve the visionary goal. Nonetheless, these hardy mystics, the *yorde merkava* ('explorers of the supernatural world') were the direct ancestral source of Qabalah.

The earliest known Qabalistic text, the *Sepher Yetzirah* ('Book of Creation') turned up sometime between the third and sixth centuries AD, reflecting an older oral tradition. It was a book of magic and cosmology, a mixture that has characterised Qabalism ever since. According to the *Yetzirah*, God did not create the universe all of a piece, as explained in *Genesis*. Rather, creation was a process of emanations—ten in all—out of the Almighty's unknowable essence, each one progressively different until, at length, the world as we know it (*Malkuth)* was produced.

The study text for the Inner Light's course was not the *Sepher Yetzirah*. The Society showed little interest in the history of Qabalah which had, in any case, evolved considerably since the days of Rabbi Akiba. For one thing, it was no longer exclusively Jewish. Elements of astrology, alchemy, tarot, neoplatonism, Gnosticism, hermeticism, Rosicrucianism, Freemasonry, Oriental yoga and Christian mysticism had all been grafted onto the Hebrew root. The result was a new Hermetic Qabalah with emphasis on a broadly-based magico-spiritual practice that had largely ceased to concern itself with the throne of God. At its heart was a peculiar diagram called, for reasons I have never really been able to fathom, the Tree of Life.

As you can see on the following page, the Tree of Life looks nothing like a tree...it is rather a diagram of interlocking paths and spheres. If you count the spheres, you will find there are ten in all. (The black sphere just visible on the central pathway, one down from the top, doesn't count because it's not really there—a Qabalistic mystery I may or may not chose to tackle as this memoir continues.) Each has a name, and each represents one of those emanations of God I mentioned earlier.

I have studied Hermetic Qabalah for more than forty years now and am sorely tempted to give you a complete philosophical exposition of the Tree. But I suspect it might bore you rigid, and besides it would not be at all relevant to the stage of my life under discussion. Although magic, if pursued long enough, often glides seamlessly into mysticism, that journey for me had scarcely started. What I learned in those early days was how to draw a perfect diagram of the Tree using ruler and compasses—a skill of which I am still childishly proud—the names of the individual Sephiroth (the spheres) and a whole host of correspondences linked to both Sephiroth and paths. And even that wasn't the important part. The important part was the exercises in mind training, the meditations and visualizations that gradually increased my ability to concentrate and enabled me to experience various deep contents of my psyche that might otherwise never have emerged into the light of waking consciousness.

I had no idea how dangerous all this might be.

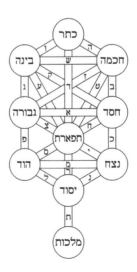

In the early days of our marriage, Helen and I lived in a flat on Belfast's University Road. The set-up suited Helen, who had now left the employ of Morton Newspapers to work as an occupational therapist in Purdysburn Mental Hospital: she only had to get as far as the Saintfield Road. I commuted to Lurgan by train and rather enjoyed it. The train times were convenient, the journey relatively short, but long enough to let me read the *Daily Mirror* every morning, and there was a sort of commuter camaraderie that produced interesting conversations with interesting people should I feel like talking. If there was any downside at all, it was the cost. Like most newly weds, we were counting pennies.

Our plans for the future were conventional. After a respectable interval, Helen would leave her job and get pregnant, not necessarily in that order. We would have two children, spaced about a year apart, so one would be company for the other. Neither of us, as I recall, expressed any preference for a boy or a girl, but for all my protestations, I knew I wanted girls. There was something in me that was frightened by the prospect of rearing a son.

We shared the Belfast flat with Ned, a large, neutered tiger of a cat who would take your arm off for a piece of melon. I make mention of Ned because he proved to be one of those turning points in my life that are invisible at the point when they actually turn, but glaringly obvious in retrospect. Until I met Ned, I had been a dog man. I was brought up with a blind terrier named Slippers (who still managed to kill rats in the cellar), and the only cats I remember from childhood was an independent black-and-white queen capable of disappearing for eighteen months at a time, and a cute little kitten who broke my heart by running under the wheels of a moving car only hours after we acquired her. I vowed then I would never give my heart to a cat again. But Ned turned me. Something in his personality led to a fixation that has endured ever since. Helen was already ahead in the cat-worship stakes and encouraged the development vigorously. It was an aspect of our life together that was soon to get completely out of hand.

One evening, with the casual indifference to fate that is only possible in one's early twenties, we moved from the passive idea of starting a family sometime to the equally passive notion of starting one *now*. Helen became pregnant instantly.

The Sixties, in Northern Ireland, had not yet become the Swinging Sixties. In my quiet little world at least, Fifties attitudes were still very much with us. There was no question of a wife and mother going out to work. A woman's place was with her children. Thus we decided that Helen should continue with her job until the bump (which had not yet begun to show) became onerous, then stop. Henceforth, I would be the sole breadwinner. In order to prepare for this inevitability, we decided to make a home in Lurgan, where I worked, thus saving on travel costs. Since I was on the spot, I was entrusted with finding one.

I hit pay-dirt almost at once. The Mayor of Lurgan at the time was Alex Greer, the only man I have ever known who could speak Mandarin Chinese. Since local journalists and local politicians tend to live hand-in-glove, I was among the very first to learn he was converting some outbuildings into flats. I asked him if I could have one and he said yes. He even offered a small reduction in the rent in return for my writing an admiring article about the development. I returned home that night with one of Alex's brochures and told Helen we were about to move into a country estate. "That means we can have another cat," she said. In fact, within four months, we had another sixteen.

While we were living in Woodbrook—the Greer estate—I passed another invisible turning-point, this one self-generated. During the time I worked on the *Lurgan Mail* I began, increasingly, to specialise in feature-writing and did less and less reporting. I had also begun to sell fiction. The way this came about was the first indication that I have, in many ways, led an utterly charmed life. In this convoluted story of love, marriage, nervous breakdown, journalism and magic, you may have lost sight of my ambition to become an author, but I had not. In a burst of misplaced self-confidence, I pulled the manuscript of *Song of Autumn* from its drawer, bought a copy of the *Writer's and Artist's Yearbook* and sent it off to the first entry that happened to catch my eye in its literary agent listings—Curtis Brown Ltd of London. I was unaware then, and for a long time afterwards, that it was at the time the largest, most successful literary agency in the world.

Curtis Brown held the manuscript for about three months then demonstrated their professional expertise by declining it. But they declined it with an encouraging letter. The work, they said, 'showed promise.' And they wanted to see anything else I might have. What I did have was a short piece of romantic fiction called *Theresa's Well*.

The title was a pun. Theresa was an English girl who fell ill after her fiancé ditched her at the altar and came to the south of Ireland to recuperate. While there, she found a holy well, dedicated to her namesake, Saint Theresa, where a strange little man, who might or might not have been a leprechaun—I was much more subtle in my writing then—gave her a prayer that went:

Holy Saint Anthony,
Holy Saint Ann,
Bring me a man,
As fast as you can.

Theresa eventually used the prayer and was rewarded by the appearance in her life of a very nice young man who made her feel much better, thus completing the arc of the story and the pun of the title. It was pure candyfloss, and not very well spun. I'd written it under the encouragement, by letter from Tasmania, of Roger Donaghy who told me that while short stories in the women's magazines were total crap, they paid an *absolute fortune.* (The italics were his.) With a family now in the offing, I badly wanted to be paid an absolute fortune for total crap and after a few false starts, Theresa was born. Curtis Brown liked her. More to the point, Curtis Brown managed to sell her—to *Woman's Realm* as I recall—for £50; an absolute fortune, as Roger had predicted.

So I signed up as a client of Curtis Brown who clearly hoped I'd write another, better, novel. Instead, I began to churn out short stories as if there was no tomorrow. I developed two appealing characters named Stanley and Olive, newly weds based loosely on Helen and myself, who did silly and amusing things as they faced into the mild, middle-class problems of modern life. They obviously had some bizarre zeitgeist appeal because Curtis Brown kept selling their adventures—to *Woman, Woman's Own, Woman's Realm* and the rest—until, at the peak of my output, I was apparently the most widely read short-story writer in the British Isles. But that was sometime in the future and not, as you may have imagined, the turning-point I mentioned.

One early outcome of my short-story success was to focus my attention on the world of magazines. I had no particular interest in women's magazines beyond their ability to send me money, but I paid lively attention to magazines aimed primarily at men. *Playboy,* founded by Hugh Hefner less than a decade earlier, had made the transatlantic trip to the shelves of UK newsagents, joining *Esquire* which was already there. I loved *Playboy* which, like most men, I bought for its literary excellence rather than its pictures and wanted to see more of the same. But Guccione's *Penthouse* was still a few years away, the old *Lilliput* had gone by the board, swallowed by

[71]

Men Only which was not yet the raunchy title it became, and *Town*, with little enough circulation outside of London, was only irregularly available. There was a handful of other men's titles—*Razzle, Spick and Span* and the extraordinary volleyball-obsessed *Health and Efficiency* are the only ones that come to mind—but these were little more than glossy vehicles for photographs of naked women which, while welcome, quickly palled. It seemed to me there was a gap in the market for a home-grown man's magazine with literary pretensions, lively local features and a few well-chosen nudes that would compete successfully with *Playboy* in Northern Ireland in the same way that local weekly newspapers competed successfully with the city dailies. I woke up of a morning and wrote a letter to Jim Morton suggesting he launch one.

I posted the letter on Thursday night and was summoned by its recipient on Monday morning. He had a windowless, businesslike office behind the printing works so that I walked a gauntlet of suggestions that I might be getting sacked. I grinned at the printers who made them, wondering if there was the slightest possibility my own suggestion might be taken seriously. On the whole I thought it unlikely: I was, after all, still a junior reporter despite my feature-writing and short stories.

Jim Morton wore suits created by his tailor using the code RRS or Raised Right Shoulder. He was diminutive in stature, (but, as his works foreman once remarked enviously, 'a big man when he's standing on his wallet') with a ruthless reputation that made most of us afraid of him. I was quite relieved to discover he was smiling. He waved my letter. "I read it in bed on Saturday morning. Didn't get out of my pyjamas until nearly noon. Were you thinking of including nudes?"

"Yes."

"Controversial. This is Ulster."

"Yes."

"I suppose you want to edit it?"

I grinned at him as well. "It did cross my mind."

"I talked to Courtney about it on Sunday." Courtney was Courtney Hutchinson, his brother-in-law and fellow director, an ex-RAF pilot of exceptional looks and social skills who was the public face of Morton Newspapers. Jim didn't like meeting people and was vaguely aware that it showed.

"Yes?"

"There's a lot of work needed before you launch a new title. Market research, costings…" He shrugged helplessly when he couldn't think of any more. "We'll keep it in mind."

And that was that. After my brief moment in the spotlight, I returned to the routine of the *Lurgan Mail.* Jim Morton never launched a man's magazine, never spoke to me of the idea again. But my decision to write the letter was a turning-point just the same. It was, I suspect, the reason he made me editor of the *Ulster Star.* It was certainly the reason he gave me *Scene.*

On October 22, 1962, Helen and I were visiting her parents when my attention focused on the background radio broadcast playing in the kitchen. A presenter interrupted the music with a news flash: President Kennedy had scheduled a broadcast to the nation to make an announcement about what was believed to be a deepening crisis involving Cuba. I had an instant premonition of doom. There had been a series of increasingly worrying news items over the past few days: Kennedy had cut short his holidays to return to Washington...Kennedy had held urgent meetings with his special advisors...Nobody was saying publicly what was going on, but there was speculation that, whatever it was, it involved Cuba, an island that had last been in the news more than a year before when American-backed troops attempted an abortive invasion at its Bay of Pigs.

Later that evening, I listened to the actual presidential broadcast. It began with the chilling words, *"This Government, as promised, has maintained the closest surveillance of the Soviet military build-up on the island of Cuba. Within the past week, unmistakable evidence has established the fact that a series of offensive missile sites is now in preparation on that imprisoned island. The purpose of these bases can be none other than to provide a nuclear strike capability against the Western Hemisphere."*

One drawback of reading science-fiction throughout the 1950s was that I knew exactly what this meant. I had followed endless fictional versions of the same scenario: a political misstep...the clash of two great super-powers...the slide into World War Three...the deployment of nuclear weapons...millions dead on the first strike, millions more dying from the effects of residual radiation...retaliation, total war and the grimmest of all prospects, nuclear winter. The final scene was always the same: a barren, lifeless planet in lonely orbit round its sun. As I listened to Kennedy, I felt suddenly very much afraid.

The rest of his speech did nothing to reassure me. He announced a seven-point plan to counter the threat, only one point of which impinged on me: he had instigated a quarantine zone around Cuba. All island-bound ships would be stopped and searched. Any found carrying cargoes of offensive weapons would be turned back. He almost managed to make the response sound mild, but I recognised the implications here as well. What happened if a Soviet ship declined to be searched? What happened if it refused to turn back? The world was clearly on a collision course.

"Sounds serious," remarked Helen's taciturn father.

Over the following week it got worse. For six days, news broadcasts and newspapers were concerned with little other than the Cuban Crisis. Hours of airtime and acres of newsprint were devoted to reports and analysis of what was going on. But what it all came down to was that several Soviet ships were steaming towards the American blockade with their captains insisting they had no intention of stopping. It was like a global version of *High Noon*. Every morning the newscasters announced how much closer the ships were getting, then went on to waffle about how neither the Americans nor Soviets seemed to have the least idea how to defuse the crisis.

I cannot remember when I'd felt more frightened about anything; and I was not the only one. At the time I was having problems with my car and cadged a lift to work each morning from the print foreman's brother who was driving in several of his colleagues. Cuba was the only topic of conversation. The car radio stayed on and there was sudden silence at each news flash. "Has your crap turned yellow?" one of the printers asked me conversationally. It transpired everyone's had. We were all terrified.

Four or five days into the crisis I awoke to a morning newspaper that announced a mid-day deadline. The two sides were on target to clash on the high seas at exactly noon. I should have smelt journalistic flim-flam, but fear had squeezed all analytic ability out of me. For days I had known we were all going to die. Now I knew when. I tuned into the midday news broadcast, confidently expecting to hear the nuclear bombs go off, but the Soviet vessels were still steaming quietly towards the quarantine zone. The morning paper had got its timing wrong. But later that day, a miracle occurred. The closest of the Russian ships turned back. True to the old maxim that good news is no news, the newsreader took pains to emphasise that the crisis was far from over. But I knew differently. Somebody had blinked.

On October 28, the Soviet Premier, Nikita Khrushchev publicly agreed to remove the missiles from Cuba. The world gave a collective sigh. The crisis was officially over. Several of my work colleagues were in the cellar bar of the Brownlow Arms that evening for a celebratory drink. Their relief was palpable.

But my fear wouldn't go away.

According to a friend of mine who runs an esoteric school, more than a third of those who enrol for magical training drop out after the first lesson. Another third don't make it through the first six months. Very few indeed actually complete the course. Part of the problem is simple disillusionment. Becoming a magician sounds terribly glamorous before you start, but while the theoretical study can be interesting, the mental training is repetitive and dull. Furthermore—and this is another part of the problem—training the mind is like herding a cat: you meet with huge natural resistance. Nonetheless, I managed to hang in there until the day came when I received back my last diary record, appropriately marked as 'Adequate plus.' My studies were over. I now knew quite a lot about Hermetic Qabalah, particularly the correspondences associated with the Tree of Life. I was instructed in the subtleties of God's manifestation which, I must say, were not a million miles away from the discoveries of quantum physics. I had even tackled, with a conspicuous lack of understanding, Dion Fortune's channelled revelation, *The Cosmic Doctrine*, which described the universe in terms of mystifying rings. But far more importantly, at least in my view, was the fact that my concentration had improved to an almost trance-like degree and I had developed a facility for extraordinarily vivid and detailed visualisation, both of which were proving extremely useful to me as a writer. Thus equipped, I could not wait to become an Initiate, work magic with my well-trained peers and learn the *real* secrets of the Society. But to do so, I had to pass my interview.

My circumstances had changed again. After propelling me into a part-time career as a short-story writer, Curtis Brown eventually woke up to the fact that I was a wholly uneconomical client. Within a couple of years it became clear to them I would never write another novel. Meanwhile, postage costs were rising, as was the value of executive time. Neither was covered by their percentage take on my meagre earnings, so they wrote me a Dear John and dumped me. It was something of a blow, because while my earnings were meagre from the viewpoint of the world's largest literary agency, to me they amounted to a lucrative little sideline. There was, of course, nothing to stop me submitting future stories direct to the British women's magazines—my name was known by now and I was already in correspondence with all the fiction editors who counted—but Curtis Brown routinely sold overseas rights in my stories, which was something I was not at all equipped to do. So I faced a sharp decline in income.

But when the Lord taketh with one hand, He sometimes giveth with the other. By the time I lost my literary representation, I was no longer a junior reporter in the *Lurgan Mail* but had become, at an unusually early age, editor of the *Ulster Star,* another Morton weekly based in the County Antrim town[21] of Lisburn. (Years afterwards I asked Jim Morton if he felt he'd taken a risk appointing such a young man editor. "You weren't half young enough," he replied bewilderingly.)

There was a sensation of *déjà vu* about the *Star.* Like the old days in Portadown, it was a bright, modern tabloid opened in competition to an existing pictureless, ads-on-the-front-page broadsheet established sometime in the nineteenth century. The day I took up my new post, Courtney Hutchinson (who lived in Lisburn and considered the *Star* his baby) took me to one side and warned me soberly, "You have complete editorial freedom, but you must not, under any circumstances, upset our advertising manager." I had no trouble complying. The advertising manager was a small, dapper man named Charlie Hunniford who had a neatly trimmed moustache and a remarkable facility for sleight of hand. He was the father of Gloria, my schooldays' classmate, now well on her way to fame and fortune as a television presenter. I knew Charlie of old and we got on like a house on fire. The management, Jim and Courtney, considered him the most valuable asset of the entire Morton Group—his ability to sell advertising was almost as astonishing as his magic tricks.

Since the Cuban Missile Crisis, I had been plagued by inexplicable panic attacks. I was prone to waking up terrified, but without knowing of what. Sometimes I found a peg to hang the fear on—a rumbling crisis in the Middle East, perhaps, or, closer to home, the familiar worries of a young man with a wife and family—but mostly it just squatted unattached, like a cloud that gradually dispersed over the day until, by evening, I felt fine. At this point of my life, it didn't happen every day, but when it did, the same sequence could run for weeks at a time before stopping as mysteriously as it started. Oddly enough, the massive responsibility of an editorial chair relieved the anxiety rather than increased it. For the first year or so, the new job—and the move to a new town—was such a challenge I had no time to feel afraid. I organised the newspaper to run the way I wanted it, put my systems in place and had lunch with Charlie every day in a local café where he entertained me by pulling coins out of the owner's ear. In the evenings I went home to Helen, my daughter Aynia and a benign new baby named Sian. We lived harmoniously in the three-bedroomed

21   Now city.

semi-detached house I had purchased for the risible sum of £900. Helen and I shared one bedroom with the baby, Aynia occupied another with two invisible companions called Ali Garten and Ali Macgorran, while the third was turned into a cattery. The seventeen cats of Woodbrook had been reduced to nine by a virulent outbreak of feline enteritis, but Helen would not let them leave the house for fear they might be slaughtered on the busy road.

I liked being an editor. It gave me a freedom of action unavailable to a mere reporter. So when the Society of the Inner Light summoned me for interview, I had no need to ask anyone for time off. I just took it and slipped away to London.

It was my first plane flight, and I felt a little nervous. But as I climbed aboard the aircraft at Nutt's Corner—Belfast's major airport at the time—I spotted a familiar face. One of my fellow passengers was the husband of a woman I knew well from an amateur dramatic group I'd helped to set up. I was aware that his job, something to do with computers, involved incessant travel, so I hailed him like a long-lost brother, took a seat beside him and settled myself to enjoy the reassuring presence of a seasoned flyer.

"This is your Captain speaking," said the intercom through an unpleasant burst of static. "I'm afraid there will be a short delay before take-off. Please remain seated and thank you for your patience."

"Listen to that," hissed my companion. "They can't even get the bloody intercom to work properly. Why do you think there's a delay? You don't suppose it's engine trouble, do you? Christ, the more I fly in these things, the more I realise how much can go wrong. God, I hope we don't hit turbulence—I was reading just the other day about a plane that hit turbulence and both the wings broke off."

Against all odds and turbulence, the flight made it safely to Heathrow and I was met at the airport by a grinning Roger Donaghy, long back from Tasmania, married to a delightful girl named Ray, and now living in London where he worked for the BBC. "I'll show you the city," he said. "Where would you like to go?"

There was only one place in London I wanted to see, the quarter regularly featured in the *News of the World* as a den of unspeakable vice and corruption. "Soho," I told him promptly.

Soho turned out to be more of a den of delicatessens, although we did pass a handful of sleazy strip joints and spent some time in a gloomy store that sold the sort of glamour magazines I could buy at home, but more of them. While we wandered through the disappointing streets, I discovered that London made me feel uncomfortable. I could not shake off the feeling that I was standing on a sheet of concrete that stretched to infinity in every direction. Soho itself reminded me of the instructions given by the novelist Gerald Kersch on how to reach his miserable fictional district, Fowler's End: *You start anywhere in London and keep moving in the seediest direction.*

The following afternoon, I took a taxi to Steele's Road. "Most be toffs live here," remarked the driver as we turned into the tree-lined avenue. Inner Light headquarters, unmarked by any plaque or sign, was a large, imposing building that might indeed have housed a toff. I was interviewed in a comfortable living room by two serious men. The elder of the two was the Society's Warden, Charles Ulric Arthur Chichester.

At the time I met him, Chichester must have been teetering on 60—he was born in 1904—but from my early twenties perspective he looked older, and wiser, than God. I assumed from his accent he was English, but his family was actually as Irish as my own. After a Roman Catholic education at Stonyhurst public school he first emigrated to Canada then took up an executive post with a petrol company in Tokyo. While in Japan he seems to have developed an interest in esoteric subjects generally and Dion Fortune in particular. During the Second World War, he served as an intelligence officer with the Air Ministry in London and used the freedom granted by his position to track her down. At first he was less than impressed, but she took to him and insisted he investigated the occult more deeply. The upshot of their meeting was that he joined her Fraternity of the Inner Light, and by 1943 he was functioning as Magus. When Dion died three years later, he succeeded her as Warden.

The younger of the two men, whose name I am mortified to admit I can no longer remember, was the current Secretary of the Society. He looked scarcely a decade older than I was despite his prematurely balding hair and actually impressed me more than Chichester, probably because of the fierce intensity of his gaze.

The interview was brief and surprisingly informal. Both men held papers which I suspected were copies of my diary records: Chichester's opening remark was, "Well, you managed to get through the course." They asked me a bit about my background, but frankly didn't seem all that interested in the answers. I had the feeling of people going through the motions and wondered half seriously whether their decision would be based on some sort of psychic evaluation. At one point, the Secretary asked me why I wanted to join the Society. It was the first question I should have expected and the last I actually did. I waffled at him for a while, trying to collect my thoughts. "I'll put that down as 'spiritual itch' then," he said, making a note.

Eventually it ground to an uncomfortable halt. Chichester ostentatiously consulted the mantel clock. "If you *are* admitted," he said ponderously, "how do you think you will feel about joining an occult society?"

I smiled at him endearingly. "A bit like my first plane flight—a little nervous."

It struck me that the question was a good sign: surely he would not have asked it if he planned to reject my application? But all he did was gather up his papers and say, "We'll let you know."

Back in Lisburn, life became a bit of an anticlimax for a week or two. To take my mind off my esoteric future, I flung myself into my favourite hobby, the creation, at home, of fine wines and beers. Helen much preferred the former, and not simply for reasons of taste. I was a purist when it came to beer and eschewed the all-in-one easy-brew kits that were just coming on the market in favour of a start-from-scratch approach which involved boiling up vast quantities of hops and grains. Helen said it stank out the entire house.

Oddly enough, I was not nearly so fussy when it came to wine. I has a series of one-gallon demi-johns in various warm cupboards fermenting delicacies like rhubarb Chardonnay and elderflower champagne, but all I really knew about wine-making was that a gallon wasn't enough. Before you start, a demi-john (approximately six standard-sized bottles) looks as if it might last you for months, but once you have the finished product, produced for pennies a bottle, you knock it back like tea. What I needed, what I *knew* I needed, was a substantially larger fermentation vessel.

When I first took to the hobby, I had to travel to Belfast for my supplies, but recently there had been a pleasing development closer to home—a man named Arthur Gibson had opened a home-brewing shop in Lisburn. Arthur was born and bred in Northern Ireland, but with his brown skin and brown eyes, he looked like an Indian. He was a remarkably successful business executive, a professional managing director who'd already proved himself capable of running companies in various different sectors. His career spanned several continents—including India, oddly enough—and for years his earning power had been enviable. But one day he realised he was tired of the rat-race, resigned from whatever highly paid post he was holding, and opened up the little Lisburn home-brew business. I was his first customer, demanding entry before the shop actually opened because I was the pushy editor of his local paper and could offer him much-needed publicity. I liked Arthur at once and the feeling proved mutual. From then on, I stopped driving to Belfast for supplies and gave Arthur all my business.

He looked pained when I explained my problem, but this was an habitual response and meant very little.

"I think…" he said slowly, "…they've just developed five-gallon fermentation vessels. They're heavy-duty plastic in a fold-up cardboard casing. They come with a tap so when the wine ferments out, you can draw it off above the sediment. Is that something like what you're looking for?"

"Get me three," I told him.

The interesting thing is that making wine in large quantities is actually easier than making wine in the traditional one-gallon batches. The yeast works much more quickly, there are far fewer problems with stuck ferments and, for some reason, you usually end up with a better quality of wine. Not that the latter benefit influenced me unduly: what I was after was strength, and bulk fermentation facilitated that as well. Soon I had fifteen gallons of dried elderberry red plopping quietly in three gigantic cardboard cubes set side by side on a living room table. This was not elegant living, but space was at a premium and I reckoned the end result would be worth it. When I finally tasted the finished wine—before breakfast one morning—I knew I had been right. I went into the office and boasted about both the quality and volume.

That night, about 1 a.m., I was awakened by a thunderous knocking on the door. I answered it in pyjamas and dressing gown to find a police car in my driveway and two uniformed members of the Royal Ulster Constabulary on the doorstep. "We have information," one told me soberly, "that you are storing commercial quantities of alcohol on these premises without a publican's licence."

"You'd better come in," I said.

We continued to sample the alcohol stored on the premises until 5 a.m. when my friends—I knew them both well, of course, as I knew most of the Lisburn constabulary—called for someone else to drive the police car and staggered off home. It was too late to go back to bed, so I had an early breakfast and walked to a bleary-eyed morning at the office. When I came home that evening, battling an anvil chorus of a headache, there was a letter waiting for me from Arthur Chichester, the Warden of the Society of the Inner Light. I had been accepted for membership with my formal initiation set for a date to be agreed. In the interim, I was required to choose my mystery name.

The mystery name was an interesting tradition dating back to the original Golden Dawn. To mark what was supposed to be a spiritual transition, initiates were never known by their real names while engaged in hermetic activities, but by a special 'mystery name' instead—or rather, by its initials, since the name itself was never supposed to be revealed to anyone. Thus Yeats was known as Frater D.E.D.I., (Demon Est Deus Inversus), Crowley became Frater P (Perdurabo) and so on. Choice of name was not arbitrary, Mr Chichester explained: I was required to meditate in an attempt to discover my innermost essence, belief or aspiration, then express it in the form of a motto. The nature of the name was why it was kept secret. To reveal your innermost essence to others was to put yourself in their power: the only reason we know about Yeats, Crowley and the rest is that they are dead.

It was one of those deceptively simple spiritual exercises that have far-reaching consequences. To discover your mystery name requires genuine self-knowledge and, even more difficult, self-acceptance. I worried over the problem for weeks and finally decided on an aspirational motto, the initials of which were V.V. I wrote back to Chichester, rather proud of my decision, and told him I was now prepared.

I also suggested a date for my initiation.

On the evening of July 5, 1964, I was back in London, facing a 7.30 pm deadline and utterly unable to find a taxi. Even when I stumbled across a whole rank of them, the first two declined to take me anywhere, possibly mistaking my panicked expression for lunacy. The third looked blank when I asked for Steele's Road. "Chalk Farm," I told him tersely in my best *I'm a bloody Londoner and I know my way around* voice. He sucked his teeth. "That's a long way out, gov." I'd had enough of taxi drivers by this time. My experience was that an out-of-town accent encouraged them to find the longest way around while reciting their life stories. At home, as a sensitive and caring individual, I would have taken the hint that this one really did not want to drive to the distant jungles of Chalk Farm and found myself another cab. As it was, I settled myself firmly in the back seat and said, "Can you make it by 7.30?"

In fact he made it by 7.25 and I rang the bell of No. 38 with minutes to spare. A stern, unsmiling man opened the door. He seemed to know who I was because he gestured me to come in without asking my name, then led me to a small room somewhere in the bowels of the house. "You've brought your robe?" The robe was something else I'd acquired with my mystery name, purchased mail order from an ecclesiastical supplies store in London. In the catalogue it was identified as a single-breasted cassock, half lined, a neck-to-feet black garment that buttoned all the way down the front. I was disappointed to find it did not have a hood. I patted my briefcase. "In here."

"Please robe," said the unsmiling man. "Then I would suggest you meditate until someone comes to collect you." He closed the door silently behind him.

I put on the cassock—the buttons were fiddly and took forever—with the black socks and soft black slippers specified in the Society's instructions. Then I sat down on the straight-backed wooden chair, the only piece of furniture in the room, closed my eyes and worried. The reality of my situation fell on me like an avalanche. I was alone in a strange city, in a strange house, filled with strange people who engaged in weird rites and believed in magic. I realised suddenly how little I actually knew about the Society of the Inner Light. Every Sunday newspaper headline I had ever read began to jostle for my attention until one came out on top: SATANISTS SACRIFICE SECOND VICTIM. Why second? I had no idea. Who was the first? I didn't care. Roger didn't know where I'd gone.

Helen didn't expect me home for a couple of days. I could be murdered and dismembered with the pieces scattered throughout London's dustbins before anybody bothered to report me missing. I tried to console myself with the thought that occult sacrifices were usually virgin which, thankfully, I was no longer, but this weak attempt at internal humour made not the slightest difference. My nerves were stretched to breaking point by the time the door opened again.

A tiny woman in her seventies came in wearing a black robe and an Egyptian nemyss with a stylish golden cobra rising from the forehead. She had the sort of lines on her face that come from laughter. She had dark, twinkling eyes. "Hello," she said. "I'm Margaret Lumley Brown."

Apart from listings of the few books and articles she wrote and some surviving correspondence with Arthur Conan Doyle, the little that's known about Margaret Lumley Brown's early life tends to be anecdotal. But what anecdotes. Her eccentric father taught her to read using only books published in the eighteenth century and introduced her to Ovid—at the age of 8—by way of a Latin grammar and a dictionary dated 1715. In the 1920s, she worked with Marie Stopes, campaigning for sex education and birth control. Then, out of nowhere, she began to develop fearsome and peculiar psychical abilities.

It started with a weird mental version of the moving glass I'd witnessed with Eileen Boyd and Helen. A letter of the alphabet would slide into her consciousness, and then, when it had clearly impinged, fade away to be replaced by another. In this way words, then whole sentences would be spelled out. The messages themselves were of no great importance, almost as if someone was chatting to her. Margaret mentally answered back, but after three nights she was losing sleep, increasingly confused and occasionally subject to threatening hallucinations. She was living on London's Edgware Road at the time and discovered there was a black cloud enveloping her house.

Her situation grew steadily worse. At one point it seemed as if a multitude of voices entered her head, all seeking her attention, all speaking at once. When she looked out of a window, misshapen figures crawled among the debris of former houses. There is sometimes a very narrow dividing line between psychism and madness and Margaret seemed close to crossing it. She found herself taken over, in the way that Spiritualist mediums are possessed by spirits of the dead. But the entity, a male, proved calming and protective. Poltergeist manifestations broke out. Flying discs of light appeared in her room, candle-like flames flickered at

[85]

random, then went out. Black shapes manifested, like Medieval woodcuts of demons with their faces grotesquely sunk into their bloated bodies. She was terrified and paralyzed.

At this point a new voice spoke to her, telling her not to be frightened because fear 'only makes them worse.' The creatures were, he said, devils and the haunting was associated with the room she was in. Margaret had a brief out-of-body experience in which she found herself floating near the ceiling, then returned to normal consciousness and fled.

Unfortunately she was in no position to leave the house altogether, so she endured days of illness while the phenomena continued. These included foul smells, apparitions, voices, glowing letters traced on a window blind and the spontaneous movement of objects like a rug and a dressing gown. Eventually the family called in an occultist and clairvoyant, who told them their home stood on the site of a much older building that had once housed an opium den, and this was where the current manifestations were coming from. What had caused the trouble, he said, was the interaction between the conditions existing in the house and Margaret's rare psychic qualities. Powerful and unusual spirits had been trying to communicate with her. He advised her to leave the building as soon as possible, otherwise the experiences might kill her. The occultist in question was Bishop Robert King of the Liberal Catholic Church, the man who trained Ernie Butler in Western magic.

I don't know if Margaret did leave the house at this point, but she clearly survived the trauma. More to the point, she got her psychism under control. And extraordinary psychism it was. Like William Blake, she had constant visions of nature spirits, elementals and even, to judge from her sketch pad, towering angelic figures. She developed a particular affinity for the fairy kingdom. A friend of mine once described how she would gently brush the little creatures off cushions so visitors could sit down. She made contact with what she believed to be the spirit of Oscar Wilde, who acted as her guide and mentor for a time. In the mid-1940s, she joined the Fraternity of the Inner Light. For a few years she maintained a low profile, but following Dion Fortune's death in 1946 she moved abruptly into a central position within the organisation, taking over from the founder to channel those inner plane communications on which the spiritual life of the Society depended. Although virtually unknown outside the fraternity, she was recognised within it as the finest medium and psychic of the century. She eventually became known as a 'cosmic mediator', a term that described someone capable of contacting the very highest of spiritual entities. Although I had no idea of her background or position at the time, this was the woman who had been patiently training me in magical techniques for the past four years.

"You're not wearing a watch, are you?" she asked me, then took my wrist and looked for herself. "You'll have to take that off—it'll be quite safe here. No other jewellery? They don't like jewellery on the Inner Planes. You can keep your wedding ring, but that's all. They'll spot watches and pendants like a shot. They're very eagle-eyed on the Inner Planes."

"Just the watch," I said and took it off.

Margaret looked me up and down like a sergeant-major inspecting troops, then did a strange thing. "It's your birthday, isn't it?" she said. I nodded. I was 24 that day, the youngest age at which the Society would accept an initiate. Margaret leaned forward and kissed me. She was so tiny she had to stand on tip-toe to do it. "Happy birthday," she said, smiling.

She produced a length of black cloth. "Are you ready to go? You're not nervous, are you? There's no need to be nervous—I know you're going to be fine. I have to blindfold you now, so you'll have to scrunch down: you're far too tall for me to reach." I scrunched down like a lamb, wondering how Helen would take it when I told her I'd fallen in love with a little old lady.

Had I been seeking admission to the original Golden Dawn, I would have been required to swear a ritual oath of secrecy under penalty of expulsion and voluntary submission to 'a deadly and hostile current of will set in motion by the chiefs of the Order by which I should fall slain and paralyzed without visible weapon as if slain by the lightning flash.' The Inner Light was less dramatic. Although members valued their privacy— and still do—you were required only to exercise discrimination in deciding with whom you would share details of the Society's activities, although any papers you might receive containing Inner Plane communications were to be kept under lock and key and returned to the Society if you ever resigned. I'm not sure whether discrimination would reasonably stretch to sharing my initiatory experiences in a published book, but that is, in any case, an academic question since now, more than forty years later, my memory contains only impressionistic glimpses of what happened.

Margaret led me from the waiting room to the door of the Lodge room. I recall the feel of her hand, small as that of a child, in mine. She knocked and answered a muffled response. I heard the sound of the door opening and felt the most extraordinary sensation as Margaret gently nudged me over the threshold. It was similar in many ways to that feeling you get when you walk from a cold street into a heated building, as if you have met with an invisible wall. There was an invisible wall across the threshold of the Lodge room, but not a wall of heat. It was comprised in equal parts of incense scent and something I can only reasonably call energy. I have experienced the same phenomenon again since then, but never to quite the degree I experienced it then, perhaps because being blindfold sharpens the senses.

Being blindfold also forces you to visualise when you are involved in an initiatory ceremony. Dramatic pictures certainly swam into my mind as I was ritually challenged by the guardian of the threshold and gave the ritual response prompted by whispers from Margaret. It was all very Masonic, similar in some respects to what my father must have gone through when he joined his Craft. The guardian (presumably) stood aside, and Margaret assisted me into the room. Underfoot felt like carpet, but my mental impression was of a vast outdoors.

After that, the experience becomes even more impressionistic. I felt Margaret let go of my elbow so that I stood vulnerable and alone. There might have been more ritual questions and responses, but I can scarcely remember. There was certainly a homily from the magus, who had, I noted with relief, a reassuringly Northern Irish accent. Then the blindfold came off and I was in a room that was both surprisingly small and surprisingly large—small by comparison with the vast open spaces of my visualisation, large by any other measure, since it readily contained more than twenty people, an altar, twin pillars and a magus throne. Margaret reappeared to lead me around the assembled company in a ritual possession of formal introduction. I was grinning smugly by this stage. I was one of them now.

Everyone who attended the rite, myself included, was required to submit a report of what they saw, heard and experienced. (I wrote mine before I left London.) All but one were simply held in Society archives. The exception, a description by the Society's Cosmic Mediator of Inner Plane activity during the ceremony, was circulated. When I received my copy, I discovered Margaret had been psychically aware of an unusual intruder. One of Blavatsky's spirit guides, the Master M, had turned up to witness my initiation.

My return from London marked my fourth plane flight and as I left the airport I knew I had a problem. All four journeys had been without the slightest incident—I don't recall even a hint of turbulence—but as I stepped off the aircraft that fourth time, what had begun as minor nervousness brought on by unfamiliarity had transformed itself into something close to panic terror. I had spent the entire flight in a cold sweat, hunched over in my seat, aware there was no more than a thin skin of metal between me and the hard ground 30,000 feet below. I knew, beyond all possibility of doubt, that the engine was about to stop, the wings fall off and the remaining fuselage carry us all downwards screaming to our deaths. I knew that since the pilot had not managed to crash on take-off, he would certainly crash on landing. Paradoxically, I also felt trapped and wanted to wrench open the door and hurl myself out. I listened to every change in engine note. I watched the faces of the air hostesses for the slightest indication of impending doom. I had developed a phobia: the fear of flying.

I was too ashamed to discuss it with Helen: our conversation revolved around the sights of London since she was far too polite, or possibly just disinterested, to ask me about the details of my initiation. I lay in bed that night, staring at the ceiling. I knew I would never step on board a plane again.

But while I recognised I had a problem, it was far from critical. I was not exactly an international jet-setter and Helen's modest background left her with few expectations of Continental holidays. My work took me no further than the bounds of County Antrim, the rough circulation district of the *Ulster Star,* nor was it likely to. What was really on my mind was the Inner Light requirement for its members to attend London meetings. I had already arranged with Chichester that I would be excused the monthly rituals—he recognised at once that ongoing travel and accommodation costs would be prohibitive—but there was no leeway at all when it came to attendance at the solar festivals. The summer solstice had already passed. My next London trip was not scheduled until the autumnal equinox on September 22. I decided to worry about it nearer the time.

Unfortunately the fear associated with flying started to crawl sideways and infect the rest of my life. The bouts of floating anxiety that had started with the Cuban Missile Crisis intensified, then gradually expanded until panic terror was my normal condition, at least first thing in the morning. I would lie there, eyes open in the dark, listening to the pounding of my heart, feeling the cold sweat on my brow, wondering how I could possibly get through the day. Then I would force myself to get up, shower and dress. Breakfast was always a problem since the lump in my throat made swallowing difficult, but as I had no appetite anyway, I ate minimally. I drove to the office to begin a morning of pretence. I would pretend to be normal. I would hold conversations, brief my reporters, hold meetings with Charlie, phone contacts, plan articles as if I were a fully functioning professional. When people asked me how I was, I'd say *Fine.* I could even smile and laugh at jokes. I must have been very good at it, because nobody suspected my secret: day after day I was strung out to the point of collapse. Or at least morning after morning. By lunch time, typically, I would have started to feel a little better. By mid-afternoon, the stomach knot had transformed into gently fluttering butterflies. By early evening I felt human again. I could eat a decent meal, watch a little television, play with the kids without fear. The only cloud on the horizon was that I knew it would all start up again next morning.

In this state, time passes abnormally quickly. I had scarcely returned from my July initiation before I found the autumnal equinox was looming. There was no question of my attending the Inner Light ceremonial. The very thought of stepping on another plane turned my insides to water. At the same time the shame was overwhelming. I saw my condition as weakness, even cowardice, something to be kept secret at all costs. Thus I honed my techniques of the brave face, lived a lie and managed skilfully to navigate my days. I wrote to Chichester explaining that financial problems would preclude my attending the equinox meeting. He wrote back including a cheque to cover my air fare and accommodation.

I stared at his letter in utter disbelief. No organisation I'd ever come across would have dreamed of subsidising a wholly unimportant junior member within weeks of his joining. I read it again. It was not even the offer of a loan, simply the solution to my problem as I had expressed it. Chichester said the Society would continue to underwrite my expenses at the four festivals 'until I got on my feet again.'

After a while, I wrote him another letter, returning the cheque. This time I told him the truth. Shortly afterwards, since there seemed no other way out, I resigned from the Society in good standing and returned my papers. My future as a magician had ended before it even began.

There was no concealing this development from Helen who, in any case, had already begun to suspect the emptiness behind my smiling façade. Bit by bit she winkled it out of me: the flying phobia, the morning terrors, the constant fear. "This isn't normal," she said when I had finished.

"I don't suppose it is," I agreed.

"I'll talk to Uncle Ozzie," Helen said.

Like Uncle George the jeweller, the designation was purely honorary. 'Uncle' Ozzie was Dr Oswald Proctor, a psychiatrist Helen had got to know during her Purdysburn days. I'd met him once and remembered him as a teddy-bear of a man whose wife held high office in the Women's Institute movement. I didn't want to see a psychiatrist—I thought such an action would irreversibly stamp me as mentally ill and open me up to treatments like lobotomy—but if I had to see one, Uncle Ozzie seemed less threatening than most.

As it happened, Uncle Ozzie would not see me. He was not, he told Helen, the man for the job, but he could recommend someone who was. In less than a week, I was driving to Belfast for an evening consultation in his Balmoral home with Dr Whitely. Dr Whitely—I never did learn his first name—was a slim, aesthetic-looking individual who wore rimless glasses and a well-cut suit. He sat behind a desk and listened carefully while I listed my symptoms. "Your wife is right," he said when I had finished. "What you are feeling is not normal stress: you are ill and need treatment."

With my new fears of lobotomy, a barbaric psychiatric procedure still in common use at the time, his words should have sounded like a death knell, but actually came as a relief. I no longer had to pretend, no longer had to keep up a front. By the act of admitting my symptoms, I had made them somebody else's problem. "Can you help me?" I asked, knowing he would say yes.

"Yes, I can," said Dr Whitely confidently.

After a moment I said, "So what happens now?" I was wondering if he would suggest admitting me to hospital. I knew nothing at all about the man or how he worked.

"You have two choices," Dr Whitely told me briskly. "I can see you as a private patient for—" He named an hourly figure that made my hair curl. "This is the comfortable option. Your appointments will be here, in this room. You can come in the evenings which will be convenient for someone like yourself who has to work, and I will see you on time so you will not have to wait. There is the added benefit that I would be able to see you right away—before the end of the week. Alternatively, you can book in under the National Health at my Belfast clinic. It's not so comfortable, of course, you will have to take time off work since I can only see you during the day and I do not have an appointment there for another three weeks. But as against that, you do not have to cover the costs."

Three weeks sounded like an eternity, but his private fees were well outside my budget. "I'll take the National Health," I said. To be fair, he didn't seem in the slightest disappointed.

The three weeks passed in a haze of fear, leavened by the expectation that if I could just get through them, something would be done to make me feel better. On the appointed afternoon I drove to his Belfast clinic, read women's magazines in the waiting room for ten minutes, then was shown into his office by a nurse. It was a fairly stark affair with a coat-rack beside the door and framed certificates on the walls. Dr Whitely sat gravely behind a large wooden desk. The only other items of furniture were an armchair and a black leather couch. The couch seemed a bit of a caricature and I managed a grin. "Am I supposed to lie down?" I asked.

"If you want to," he told me soberly.

I was a bit nonplussed, but thought I'd better play the game and stretched out on the couch amid embarrassing sounds of creaking, farting leather. I waited. So did Dr Whitely. The silence grew uncomfortable, then more uncomfortable still. After an eternity I said, "I expect you'd like me to talk about my mother."

"If you want to," he said.

Dr Whitely proved to be what's called a non-directive psychiatrist, or, less kindly, a 'grunt shrink'. He positively refused to offer a diagnosis or advise me in any way. My most startling revelations were met with a grunt. Any questions I ventured were reflected or deflected. The techniques were fascinating in themselves.

Reflection:

"I think perhaps I may have been angry with my mother."

"You think anger was an aspect of your relationship with your mother?"

Deflection:

"Is it possible, Doctor, that I unconsciously resented the way my father's death was hidden from me?"

"What do *you* think about that?"

But there was little enough of even this limited dialogue. Most of the time Dr Whitely sat impassive as a lizard behind his pristine desk and encouraged my monologue with the occasional grunt. I talked about my early childhood and its Oedipal longings not because I wanted to, or even because I thought the process might somehow calm my panics, but because, having read a good many books about psychiatry, I thought that was what I was supposed to do. The good doctor patiently permitted me to do it, without comment or challenge, week in and week out until many months down a tortuously long line, I decided this was getting nowhere. For a few weeks longer, I wrestled with the idea of confronting Dr Whitely with the failure of his treatment. My symptoms had not abated and while talking relieved them, the effect lasted no more than an hour or two. But like many a patient before me, I was in awe of my psychiatrist and tended to assume if things were going badly this must somehow be my fault. I dreaded the thought that he might break his stony silence to explain to me in detail what a miserable failure of a human being I actually was. Nonetheless, in the fullness of time, I did lay off slandering my mother long enough to point out timidly that my life was still as full of terror as an Inquisition victim and wonder aloud if he had any ideas about an alternative approach.

"What alternative approach would you suggest?" he asked me.

I had a momentary flash of anger. He was supposed to be the bloody doctor. I was just the patient. How was I to know what we should do? All the same, I heard my mouth answer without a second's hesitation, "Drugs."

What I had in mind was LSD. There was a bit of a fashion for therapeutic psychedelics at the time—among more experimental psychiatrists at least—and while I couldn't really see how tripping would ease my panics, I thought it might be nice to have a mystical experience. Dr Whitely would have none of it, but he did catch fire on the broader principle of drug-based therapy. "I'm afraid something like LSD would not be suitable for a case like yours," he told me in the longest speech he had made since my initial consultation. "But there is a process known as abreaction which can be induced by certain drugs. Broadly speaking, it allows you to discharge suppressed emotions associated with childhood traumas. Sometimes it can have a dramatically beneficial effect." He looked at me through his rimless glasses. "Do you think this is something we should try?"

It occurred to me all of a rush that he was trying to avoid his Hippocratic responsibilities. From the word go he had ensured I was the one who made decisions about every step of my therapy. Which meant if anything went wrong—the drugs killed me, for example, or abreaction drove me completely insane—he could always claim I asked for it. "Yes," I said, still without a second's hesitation.

The following Thursday, Helen took me to the clinic since Dr Whitely had warned I would be unfit to drive after the treatment. Instead of the consulting-room couch, I was herded into a tiny box-like ward by a nurse who instructed me to take off my shoes and lie down on the narrow bed.

She covered me up with a blanket (which was rather nice: like a mother tucking in a baby) and assured me Dr Whitely would be with me in a moment; and so he was, equipped with a syringe and a selection of glass vials. He gently slid a colourless liquid into a vein in my arm.

"What's going to happen?" I asked breathlessly. My panic was particularly bad that day and I was anxious for anything that might afford relief.

"You could experience a change in perception," he told me, possibly recalling my interest in psychedelics.

What I did experience was a wave of muscular relaxation that disappeared in seconds. After a minute or so, I said, "Nothing's happening."

Dr Whitely began to pack up his gear. "We have to experiment to get the dosage right. That was obviously too little."

"Can't you give me some more?" I asked desperately. I had a huge emotional investment in the new treatment—abreaction sounded just the thing to drain away my fear—and I could not bear the thought that I would leave the clinic just as panic-stricken as I entered. There was not even the temporary relief of talking for an hour.

"I'm afraid not," he said without further explanation. "We'll see you same time next week." With which he took his leave.

The following week proved much more satisfactory. Dr Whitely's new improved injection triggered my first Out-of-Body Experience.

The ward was slightly bigger this time, with a chair beside the bed. I was rolling up my sleeve when Dr Whitely came in. "We'll use the right arm today," he said. "I find it best to alternate, otherwise there can be bruising." I stopped rolling up my left sleeve and started rolling up my right. My fear was under control—I was determined not to repeat the shattering disappointment of the previous week—spun into a ball and locked away somewhere deep in my long-suffering stomach. Over the past year or so, as the panics increased, I had learned how to function while in their grip. The trick was largely one of dissociation. I would separate myself from my fear and act as if everything was normal. This enabled me to carry out my responsibilities as an editor, enabled me really to get through anything that life delivered me, but at a terrible cost to my digestion.

I lay down, offered my arm and received the needle. The effect was almost instantaneous and quite wonderful. The tiny wave of muscular relaxation I had experienced the week before rolled over me again, but this time it was tidal. Every hint of fear was washed away. The release was glorious. My limbs felt like lead, far too heavy to move. A sense of marvellous well-being washed over me. I lay there feeling happier than I had been in years. Then, just when it seemed life could get no better, I floated out of my body.

This is not a metaphorical description. I felt myself rise upwards like a stage levitation until I was floating supine some three or four feet in the air. At the same time, I was aware that my physical body had remained on the bed. In other circumstances, the sheer oddness of the situation might have worried me—I was well accustomed to worrying about *everything*—but the drug in my system left me incapable of feeling the slightest concern. In its place was an elated fascination. *I was floating in the air!*

Dr Whitely was now sitting on the chair beside the bed. "Any changes in perception?" he asked quietly.

His voice entered my physical ear, then travelled upwards to arrive after an acceptable microsecond delay inside the mind that belonged to the second me floating above. I considered the question, wondering (without worry) whether I would be able to answer it while my vocal cords were *down there* and my consciousness *up here*. But when I made the attempt, I discovered I was still in control of my (physical) body, albeit in a very strange way. I could twitch a finger, even move an arm or leg, but the process felt exactly like controlling a puppet on strings. When I went to speak, my physical throat and tongue worked in much the same way. "Yes," I whispered.

I was aware Dr Whitely was smiling when he asked, "Nice?"

"Yes," I croaked again.

"I think this time I'll just leave you to enjoy it. Next week we'll chat a little."

The following Thursday, we did it all again and the 'little chat' turned into a monologue of marathon proportions. Despite the puppet difficulties, I could not stop talking. I no longer droned on about my mother but spoke animatedly about anything and everything—my job at the *Star,* the latest political scandals, books I'd read, ideas I had…all was grist for a mill that never stopped grinding until my psychiatrist declared the session over. Clearly he had added another ingredient to my injection.

So it was from then on: I floated and talked and talked and floated. And it worked, at least up to a point. At the end of each session I felt purged. My panics were gone, as was the free-floating anxiety. I felt optimistic for the first time in years. The effect lasted over Friday and all through the weekend. On Monday, the fear, worry and anxiety began to creep back, but that didn't matter. I had my magic injection to look forward to on Thursday. It was possible to survive until then. Hell, after what I'd been through, making it to Thursday seemed downright easy.

Dr Whitely eventually grew bored with my prattle and turned over the listening to a staff nurse named Sister Eileen, a slim, attractive and ultimately comforting presence who neglected to take notes. As a result I found myself telling her things I shouldn't, about my occult interest and my sex life, on the drug-induced premise that without notes she would forget them five minutes after I left. One week Sister Eileen was a little late and Dr Whitely had administered the injection before she arrived. Lying on the bed while simultaneously floating above it, I manipulated my head to watch her walk across the room. Somehow she managed to do this outside of time, manifesting in various parts of the room like a stop-motion movie. I bent her ear about it for most of the session.

"What's in that injection?" I asked Dr Whitely next time came he came to administer it.

The sun was shining through the window, and he was obviously in cracking form. "A pinch of this…a soupçon of that," he cried gaily. "I sniff the wind and consult the stars!"

"No, seriously…" I said; and the potion turned out to be a mix of a powerful muscle relaxant and methedrine, an amphetamine known on the street as 'speed' and widely used by students—who could buy it as a slimming pill—wishing to stay awake and party all night. It was the methedrine that persuaded me to talk incessantly, but, under Dr Whitely's expert administration, failed to keep me awake at night. In fact the only downside of the drugs was that they made me feel incredibly randy while simultaneously taking away the means to do anything about it. (I got an erection easily enough but could not climax.) By the time the effect wore off, the randiness had gone as well. I found it a small price to pay.

My life turned into a routine that focused entirely on my Thursday sessions. Although I was still completely spaced out after each of them, I refined my coping mechanisms to the point where Helen would collect me and drive me directly to the office where I came down slowly over the course of the afternoon, chatting animatedly to anyone unfortunate enough to come within range. I was convinced my work colleagues must have known what was going on—my coordination was affected and my pupils were dilated to the size of saucers—but when, years later, I discussed my illness with Derek Adams, the *Star's* staff photographer, he told me no one had suspected a thing. As weeks drifted into months, a part of me was aware I had received a new management system rather than a cure, but I did not really care. My quality of life was so much improved on what had gone before that I was willing to accept a compromise. I was happy to keep attending Dr Whitely weekly until the two of us grew old and died. Just so the methedrine kept coming.

Despite my disaster with the Inner Light, my esoteric interests continued. I still hunted for magical books, and while my supply from Smithfield Market had dwindled I eventually found a substitute for the now defunct George Sexton in a new mail order list that was entirely devoted to occult works. It was called the Helios Book Service and it functioned out of a Gloucestershire hamlet named Teddington. When I received the mimeographed catalogue, I failed, once again, to sense a life-changing moment.

Helios Book Service was run by John and Mary Hall, a couple who were, I believe, both initiates of the Society of the Inner Light. By the mid Sixties, at around the time I joined and left so hurriedly, the Society was undergoing a sea change. The scope of magical workings was severely reduced. The structure of the administration altered. Margaret Lumley Brown's key position was eroded as the belief grew that her type of mediumship had become outmoded. There was an increasing emphasis on personal development at the expense of traditional magical practice. New editions of Dion Fortune's books were issued with a disclaimer suggesting that her ideas about psychical contacts were now outdated. Not everyone welcomed these developments and several members voted with their feet and left. Among them were John and Mary Hall, Ernie Butler and Basil Wilby, an initiate now better known by his pen-name, Gareth Knight. All four shared the worry that with SIL's changed direction, there was now no reliable source of traditional magical training. John and Mary decided to do something about it and approached Gareth Knight to write a new training course. Gareth started the work and produced several lessons, but found circumstances precluded him from completing it. The Halls asked Ernie Butler to finish the job. The result was the *Helios Course in Practical Qabalah*, a five-year supervised training in traditional magical methods. They advertised it in every book catalogue they distributed.

I read their advert and enrolled at once.

On Press Day, the editorial staff of the *Ulster Star* got up early and travelled to the printing works in Lurgan to put the paper to bed. My job was to oversee the layout, decide where stories went, write headlines and cut copy that proved too long to fit. At least in theory. In practice, most of the decisions were made by the comps, who called me only when there was a problem. Some other editors in the group resented this system, which they felt devalued their status. I welcomed it. Press Day for the *Star* was a Wednesday, so my weekly injection had well and truly worn off. It was as much as I could do to face the few decisions I was called on to make, so I got through the day with as little involvement as possible, consoling myself with the thought that Jim Morton could expect no more for £26.10 a week, less tax, superannuation and insurance. One benefit of my dissociation was that I was popular with the printers. I let them get on with it so the paper went to bed quickly and they got out before the pubs closed.

One Press Day, the works foreman, Jim Ferguson, handed me a magazine with the smiling face of Milo O'Shea on the cover. It was mast-headed as *Scene*, 'Ireland's new international magazine' and promised features on Irish millionaires, Mrs Haughey at home and a new short story by J. P. 'Ginger Man' Donleavy. "What's this?" I asked.

"Something Morton's printing for some fat git of an Englishman," Jim shrugged.

The fat git of an Englishman turned out to be a company executive named Norman Ames who had arrived in the Irish Republic a year or so earlier to take up a junior management post with Dublin's Dartry Laundry. He was a lifelong magazine fanatic and couldn't believe how poor a choice there was on offer in local newsagents. What surprised him even more was the paucity of home-grown offerings. There was a popular woman's magazine called *Woman's Way*, an arty, literary, politico comment semi-broadsheet called *Hibernia* and a weekly tabloid glossy with the self-explanatory title of *Business and Finance*. Apart from that, nothing...or at least nothing worth writing home about. Ames found the situation incredible and decided to launch his own. What he had in mind was a quality monthly that focused on modern Ireland but set such high standards of lay-out, illustration, text and print that it would have international appeal. The only trouble was he had no funds for such an ambitious project and soon discovered Irish banks were hesitant to back a risky venture mounted without collateral, track-record or experience.

Nothing daunted, Ames decided to go it alone. His plan was to commission a few original articles from Irish writers and buy cheap second serial rights to obscure pieces already published by big-name authors, both to be paid out of funds generated when the magazine actually went on sale. The rest of the content would be features supplied by syndicates who could be held at bay financially for months. Photographs would come from Walter Pfeiffer, a talented young German photographer lately arrived in Dublin, on the promise of company shares and a permanent job on the magazine staff. Ames, already publisher and editor, reckoned he could be his own art director as well by copying layouts from existing magazines. On this basis, he put together a pilot issue—called *Scene 67*—and went searching for a printer who would allow him three months' grace before asking for payment.

It was here he hit his first major setback. Ireland at the time had a reputation for ordering material like leaflets, brochures, wedding invitations and the rest, then stiffing the printer on payment once delivery was made. As a result, Irish printers had become extraordinarily cautious about extending credit. Ames hawked his pilot from one to the other, increasingly frustrated by refusal after refusal. Eventually he decided to try north of the border where, he hoped, he might find less suspicious printers. As a result he ended up in Jim Morton's office. Morton was impressed. Ames was confident, well-dressed, well-spoken and persuasive. More to the point, Morton smelt a business opportunity. A regular print order for a monthly magazine would fill the spare capacity in his print works without interfering with the weekly schedules of his newspapers and could become a very welcome profit centre. Never one to baulk at risk, he offered to print the pilot issue of *Scene* on extended credit in return for an ongoing print contract if the magazine succeeded. Ames agreed.

The final stage of the launch plan was a stroke of genius. Ames planned to sell magazines door-to-door, like encyclopaedias or brushes, dispensing with the middleman and maximising profits on the cover price, which in turn meant the publication would not be reliant on advertising. Since he had neither the money nor the patience to set up a proper sales force, he decided to test his distribution scheme by teaming up with a major charity. His offer was to publish and supply the magazine which the charity would then offer door to door in return for any profits generated. A major charity accepted.

The test-marketing exercise went like a dream. Morton printed the pilot issue with a lot of complaints from his works staff but no real problems. The charity sent out its teams of volunteers with colourful copies under their arms. Householders starved of interesting reading reached for their purses and *Scene 67* (which actually came out in '66) roared in with a circulation of 35,000 copies, an astounding figure for the first sale of a brand-new Irish magazine. Ames resigned from his laundry job and started in at once to turn *Scene* into an ongoing commercial proposition.

I was scarcely aware of *Scene 67* beyond a degree of bitching in the print works and knew nothing of the foregoing history when Jim handed me the first commercial issue. But I was very, very impressed. It was an eclectic mix of content. The opening article, by *Irish Times* motoring correspondent Wesley Boyd asked if the Irish car assembly industry was doomed; he answered yes. This was followed by a gossipy local news and entertainment round-up, *Scene on the Town,* and an in-depth interview with that pillar of the Irish Establishment, Lt-Gen. M.J. Costello. The whole package was what it promised on the cover: a witty, well-written, in-depth slice of Irish life of interest to an intelligent international audience. The only jarring note was a four-page illustrated feature starting on page 26 startlingly entitled *The Ten Thousand Silken Poems of Ch'i Pai-Shih,* a Chinese writer who seemed to have no Irish connections whatsoever. I felt vaguely envious. It wasn't exactly the man's magazine I'd once suggested, but it was a classy substitute and arguably a far more workable idea.

The next couple of issues were just as good and I began to view *Scene* as an opportunity. Here was a sophisticated international magazine published on my doorstep and printed by the man who paid my wages. Surely such proximity could be turned into a source of income? I imagined a glossy monthly must pay more—and probably a lot more—than the women's weeklies for whom I was writing fiction. I had visions of regular features, maybe even a comment column, and extra earnings of several hundred pounds a month. To set the ball rolling, I put together a satirical 3,000-word account of my Spiritualist experience in Belfast and sent it off. I discovered it had been accepted when Ames ran it in his next issue. There was no money forthcoming, but when I pressed him, he sent me a cheque for a tenner. It was my first indication that *Scene* might not be everything it seemed.

But by this stage, I later discovered, the magazine was no longer the sole property of Norman Ames; in fact it was hardly Norman Ames's property at all. What happened was a matter of speculation, but the cynical consensus of the printing works was that Jim Morton had royally screwed him, withdrawing his line of credit, then demanding his company as payment for the outstanding print bill. My own feeling was that Ames had probably run through his lines of credit without encouragement from Morton or anybody else and been forced to sell out voluntarily. The fact was, Morton *hadn't* ended up with *Scene* in full and final settlement of any debts, although he did have effective control. Company shares were now split three ways: a third to Morton, a third to Courtney Hutchinson and a third to Ames, who was also named as publisher and the only one to draw a salary. It didn't look so much like an outright corporate grab as a routine business arrangement to keep the magazine afloat. The new structure had obvious benefits. The Morton-Hutchinson partnership provided much needed capital and print services at cost, while the majority shareholding gave the brothers-in-law overall management control. Ames, as publisher, retained editorial control, earned a regular salary and would be rewarded by the income from his remaining shares if he made his brainchild a success. I wished him good luck. The tenner cheque had seriously drained my interest.

But it soon revived. On another Press Day, Jim Morton materialised unexpectedly and asked if he could see me in his office right away. I was in my usual Wednesday horrors and followed him through the print works convinced I was about to be sacked. Instead, he picked up the latest copy of *Scene,* threw it on his desk and said, "*Scene*. Would you like to edit it?"

"Yes," I said. "I would."

I agreed to edit *Scene* without hesitation, but also entirely without thought. It was, as Morton reminded me quickly, something that should be discussed for hours, even days 'but there are never hours and days to discuss anything in this place.' He was delighted with my response but touchingly concerned about my welfare. "You know this means you'll have to move to Dublin?"

I supposed it would. It also meant I would have to sell the house, arrange somewhere to live in the Irish Republic, organise a school for the girls, find out about health insurance, adjust to a new country, find my feet in an unfamiliar organisation, work out how to edit a different type of publication, and I didn't give a toss about any of it. I wanted *Scene* the way men want a glamorous woman, and for much the same reason. The magazine was so beautiful on the outside I didn't care to think about what problems might be underneath. "When will I be going?" I asked him.

To my surprise, Morton said, "I was hoping you'd say yes, but I think it's only fair that you don't make up your mind yet. I know you have a wife and children. I know you've bought a house in Lisburn. I don't want you to make a mistake. I think before you make any final decision it's important to get to know the set-up, see the offices...."

As his voice trailed off, I thought I knew what the problem was. Word in the business was that *Scene* had not lived up to initial expectations. The amazing launch circulation that so excited everyone was achieved, in retrospect, not because 35,000 people wanted to buy the magazine, but because the generous Irish were only too willing to make 35,000 donations to a worthwhile charity. *Scene's* first commercial issue, I'd heard, reached no more than 21,000 sales, which dropped, in subsequent issues, to around 18,000, where it levelled off. Clearly this meant the radical idea of selling a magazine door-to-door simply hadn't worked when the charity element was removed. So *Scene* reverted to conventional distribution through the magazine wholesalers, which changed profit calculations on the cover price. This, in turn, meant it was now as reliant on advertising as any other magazine. While 18,000 copies was still a respectable baseline and a perfectly sound platform on which to build a more impressive circulation, it was probably not be enough to attract the level of advertising needed for a really healthy bottom line. Admittedly, the copies I'd seen were packed with ads, but I had no idea of the magazine's overall costings, so there might still be a financial shortfall. In summary, there was still a question mark hanging over the magazine's future, which left Morton in an embarrassing position. On the one hand, he thought my editorial skills might help the magazine succeed. On the other, he felt guilty about asking a young married man with responsibilities to bet a secure career on something that might not go the distance. I decided to bring it all out in the open. "How's *Scene's* circulation?" I asked. "Somebody told me it's sitting about eighteen thousand."

"Nowhere near," Morton said. "It's around nine and a half, but we keep that fairly quiet."

There was, in fact, little reason to keep that fairly quiet since the figure was no more accurate than my original estimate of 18,000. Those involved with *Scene,* I discovered later, lived in a fantasy world. But at the time I remained unsuspecting. "You seem to have plenty of advertising," I prompted hopefully.

"Most of it is fake," Morton said.

I'd never heard of fake advertising before, but Morton explained the theory. *Scene's* costs were based on an eighty-two-page magazine. The aspiration was that approximately one third of its content (twenty-seven pages) would be taken up by advertising which, at established rates, would cover costs and return a massive profit. Unfortunately, advertising agencies were suspicious of the new magazine and its uncertified circulation claims, so that paid advertising remained no more than a trickle—usually less than half a dozen pages. Which left an additional twenty or so scheduled advertising pages to fill. The obvious way to fill them, until sales improved, was with editorial, but, as Morton sourly pointed out, editorial cost money. So fake advertising was included instead. Much of it featured blue-chip companies in order to raise the tone of the publication and persuade advertising agencies to follow the lead of the big boys. There was also some expectation that if you gave a prestigious company a free ad, they might be so impressed they would pay for the next one. The whole thing had been dreamed up by Norman Ames and was the dumbest idea I'd ever heard. I began to wonder about Norman Ames.

"I can't understand the bastard at all," Morton said when I brought up the name. "You've probably heard he's sacked quite a few of the staff since the magazine started. That's one of the reasons I want you to be careful. He has complete control of the way the magazine is run. If he decides to sack you, I won't be able to overrule him." It was ominous stuff for a man who'd just been offered a new job. Morton must have caught my expression because he added quickly, "As against that, he's very loyal to the

The indefatigable Norman Ames.

Me as editor of Scene.

staff he respects. To give you an example, I criticised Walter Pfeiffer to him once and Ames threatened to resign because of it. That's the way he is."

It looked as if I might be getting into a tricky, complicated situation, but I *still* didn't care. "What's the next step?"

"I think you should meet Ames—I'll arrange that," Morton said. "Then possibly you could go down to Dublin for a couple of days, just as a visitor: get the feel of the people and the office. Then if you're still interested, we can work out the details. We'll be prepared to help you with moving expenses and there'll be a substantial rise in salary. There'll have to be— you'll need a lot more money to live in Dublin."

Helen took the news with her characteristic lack of excitement, although she was quite pleased by the prospect of moving out of our red-brick semi, which she hated. (We had neighbours who rattled their dustbins in the middle of the night.) A week or two later, on a wet Saturday afternoon, I drove to Morton's home for the meeting with Ames.

Ames, when he arrived, turned out to be a plump, youngish, well-groomed individual with a cultured English accent and an air of self-confidence bordering on arrogance. He was wearing a light grey business suit with a white shirt and conservatively patterned tie. The relaxed atmosphere changed immediately he walked into the room. I noticed at once that the habitually informal Jim Morton and Courtney Hutchinson both addressed him as 'Mr Ames' and he reciprocated in kind. Morton introduced him to me as 'Mr Ames.'

"Hello, Norman," I said as we shook hands.

Considering Norman had driven all the way from Dublin, the meeting was short and a bit surreal. I expected a discussion on my impending appointment, hopefully with salary details, but everyone strenuously avoided the subject. Instead they talked in a unfocused way about the magazine. Morton opened the topic by asking Ames about advertising bookings for the current issue. Ames said he was "extremely optimistic." Morton cheered up at once and asked if the number of ads had actually gone up. "No," said Ames coolly. "I simply have an intuition about it." I waited for him to smile to show he was joking, but his face remained impassive. I glanced from Morton to Hutchinson and back again. They seemed to be taking intuition seriously.

The conversation meandered for a while before Ames fetched an enormous folder from his car and we adjourned to the dining room to examine artwork and paste-ups for the next *Scene* issue. Staring at them I began to realise how little I actually knew about magazine production, but it didn't matter because the others seemed to be feeling their way as well. At one point, Ames mentioned he was attempting to introduce more sex into the magazine. Irish censorship regulations meant this had to be done with subtlety, so that for the forthcoming issue he had decided to sneak it under the radar in the guise of a fashion feature. "Walter Pfeiffer has taken some magnificent erotic pictures," he said and produced several examples. We leaned forward to look and both Morton and Hutchinson began to nod enthusiastically. The photographs were indeed magnificent, but about as erotic as a barrel of sauerkraut. I began to wonder if Norman Ames might have weird hypnotic powers.

After he left, I chatted for a few moments with Jim Morton, who seemed visibly relaxed now that we were on our own. "There's one thing you should know," he told me soberly. "When you get down to Dublin you'll find there's a lot of plotting and scheming: they'll break their arses to get you involved in it." I promised I'd be careful.

The following Sunday evening I took the *Enterprise* to Dublin. It was a curiously cloak-and-dagger journey: Morton had insisted no one in the office should know where I was going, nor, on my return, where I'd been. The *Scene* staff had not been told who I was, nor would they be until I had formally agreed to the appointment. I was to be introduced as a visiting executive from a Northern company which was considering taking out some advertising. "So wear a suit," Morton told me.

Norman Ames was waiting at the station when the train pulled in. He was a lot less formal than he had been in Morton's home and immediately invited me for a drink. We ended up in a tiny, crowded pub in the heart of Dublin where I quizzed him about *Scene* (which he claimed resulted from an overpowering desire to make money) and its staff (whom he made sound like an interesting collection of eccentrics.)

When the pub shut, he drove me to Wellington Road to inspect the magazine offices. To my surprise they turned out to be an imposing Georgian terrace house in a residential district. Norman—and it was very definitely first-name terms now: with the drink softening my critical faculties I'd decided I rather liked him—explained that he'd rented the accommodation as a private house since neither the premises nor the district was zoned for business use.

"Isn't that illegal?" I asked, frowning.

"Yes," he said.

We went inside and he showed me the two huge office rooms on the ground floor, one labelled *Reception*, the other used by *Scene's* advertising manager. Upstairs was a studio, darkroom (converted from a bathroom) and Norman's own office, an imposing space with an enormous, polished desk. "I'll be turning this over to you when you move down," he said, as if my position with the organisation was settled. The room off my prospective office was piled high with magazine bundles. There were parts of a bed, complete with mattress, propped up against one wall. "We keep the bed as a subterfuge," he explained. "This whole upstairs is leased as a flat. The idea is that when the landlord calls, I live in the flat and just happen to like office furniture in the living room."

"How do you explain the studio and the darkroom?" I asked.

"I am an exceptionally keen amateur photographer," Norman said.

I had not quite fallen in love with Norman Ames at this stage, but I was certainly feeling his confessional charm. Unlike Morton, who had always played his cards close to his chest, Norman seemed prepared to tell me anything. I decided to bring up the question Morton had raised about his sacking so many staff. Norman gave a hollow laugh. "You're presumably considering your own position, but I don't think you have anything to worry about. If you go into it, I think you'll find the men I've sacked have all been art directors. So far as I'm concerned, the appearance of the magazine is everything. And unfortunately for our art directors, I happen to know something about that: I've had art training and I've studied magazines for years. But I'm an absolute novice when it comes to editorial. You may say I've been editing the magazine up to now, but in fact all I've done is buy talent. I can't write myself so I get material from people who can and tie it all together. Morton has probably told you I've been pressing him for an editor for months and that's why. When you start here, I propose to turn over that entire end of the magazine to you. You'll find I won't interfere, because I can't. I haven't the talent or the know-how to interfere." He looked at me with the innocent expression of a child.

The following morning, I walked to *Scene* offices from my Baggot Street hotel and was introduced briefly to the staff before Ames disappeared somewhere, leaving me alone in the enormous office that I would apparently inherit from him if I agreed to join the staff. There was a knock on the door within minutes and Mary Anderson came in.

In later years, Mary became a leading light in Ireland's Women's Liberation Movement, but at this time she was very young, somewhat unconfident, and working for *Scene* as a secretary-receptionist: we'd been introduced when I made my little tour. She looked nervous as she closed the door, asked if I was about to become the magazine's new editor—so much for Morton's secrecy policy—then delivered a message from the staff feature writer asking if I would meet him privately in the Pearl Bar that evening. I'd been in the office less than an hour and the plotting and scheming had already begun. I told Mary I was booked on the northern train later that morning, so regretfully I had to decline.

That afternoon I stuck my head around the door of Morton's office and told him I would definitely accept the offer of *Scene's* editorial chair. It was only afterwards I realised I'd just nuked any chance of continuing the Thursday injections that had kept me going for the last three years.

Despite the upheavals, I managed to hold to my magical training. The Helios Course in Practical Qabalah turned out to be markedly less Qabalistic than the Inner Light studies I'd already undergone. There was less theory and more emphasis on magical technique. I remember a preliminary exercise based on the work of a British psychic named Olive Pixley during which you imagined yourself gently bathed in a snowfall of rose-petals made from light. By now, I was beginning to realise how big a part the imagination played in occult practice; and to appreciate how strong an influence it could have on one's mood, health and well-being. The calming effect of those imaginary rose-petals had to be experienced to be believed.

For the first few weeks of my new job I stayed in the Lansdowne Hotel, a small, family-owned concern much beloved, I was told, by commercial travellers who, like myself, only found their way home to wife and family at the weekends. The manager was a woman named Rivers (or possibly Flood: I am having trouble remembering some details) who put the fear of God into me. She had the disconcerting habit of sniffing disapprovingly before unleashing some devastating comment like, "I suppose you'll be going out *drinking* tonight?" One night I did and woke fully-dressed the following morning to find the wash-basin in my room was full of vomit. I could not bear the thought of Miss Rivers finding out about it. When running water exaggerated the problem and a wire coat-hanger failed to clear the blockage, I used my tooth mug to bale the hideous mixture into the waste-bin which I then emptied in a bathroom down the corridor. Anything rather than face Miss Rivers.

My accommodation was the cheapest the hotel had to offer, a single room little larger than a wardrobe, and I was anxious to find somewhere permanent to live so that Helen and the girls could come and join me. But *Scene* was proving such a roller-coaster ride that I had little time to search. Norman tried to persuade me that seeing one's partner only at weekends was actually good for a marriage, but Helen was having none of it. Eventually she took matters into her own hands and arrived with me in Dublin early one Monday morning. "Now you don't have to worry," she said as disappeared on her mission. By lunch time she was standing in my office with a big grin on her face announcing that she had achieved in a few hours what I had failed to do in weeks—found us somewhere to live. She'd made arrangements to view first thing next morning.

I'd assumed Helen would have searched for a largish apartment in

Dublin, which was what I'd tried to do. Instead she'd decided we were all far more suited to rural living and found somewhere near a village called Kill, several miles outside the city off the Naas dual-carriageway. "It's a converted apple store of an old country place," she explained in the car. "The rent is reasonable and it sounds absolutely lovely." The owner was a retired Army Major called Pierce Synnott. Helen had somehow elicited the information that he'd been Lord Mountbatten's secretary during the Second World War.

The 'old country place' turned out to be Furness House, a stately home guarded by two stone lions on a 300-acre estate. It dated to 1730 and the whole environment took my breath away. I noticed a scruffy old gardener and asked him grandly where I might find Major Synnott, only to discover he *was* Major Synnott. He led us through a courtyard and opened up the Apple House, a recent conversion that was eccentric, fully furnished and delightful. The front door led directly into the living room. A corridor beyond gave access to a kitchen and a small sitting-room I mentally earmarked as a study. Upstairs was an enormous bathroom and two good-sized bedrooms. As accommodation for a couple with two young children, it was close to ideal, but Major Synnott unwittingly clinched the deal when he remarked casually, "You'll have the run of the estate, of course. There's a Bronze Age rath across the fields and an interesting twelfth-century church through the woods." I suddenly realised I could not think of a more idyllic setting for my children to grow up in.

But quite a few of our children weren't human, so Helen asked anxiously, "How do you feel about pets? I'm afraid we have rather a lot of cats." Major Synnott took out a snuff-box and sniffed a hefty pinch up each nostril. His eyes watered as he put the box away again. "Expect they'll keep the mice down," he said shortly. We walked into the main house and signed the tenancy agreement there and then. Major Synnott offered us a celebration whisky and seemed astonished when I told him 11 a.m. was a little early for me. "'Fraid I'm a martyr to the stuff," he said. Two weeks later, we were in residence.

Furness turned out to be as magical as my Helios course, often in a very literal way. One of the first things I did after we moved in was to explore the Bronze Age rath Major Synnott had mentioned. The monument, which topped a high hill some distance from the house, consisted of a circular earthwork surrounding a tall megalith at the base of which was a cyst grave. The grave had been excavated during the 1930s, when archaeologists discovered it contained the remains of a woman and a wolfhound. Although the whole place was commonly referred to as a ring-fort, there was no indication of permanent habitation. Traces of ritual fires suggested a ceremonial function. Since the rath was open to the public, the archaeologists put a waist-high metal fence around the cyst grave and the central stone to protect them. I found the whole site almost unbearably atmospheric and visited it as often as time and weather permitted. I also developed a habit of talking about the place to anyone who would listen.

One Hallowe'en, Helen and I played host to old friends from Northern Ireland, a young married couple named Jim and Judy Henry. Jim, a sturdy, broad-shouldered man, worked as a motor mechanic, but was well known throughout Ireland as a rally driver. (I first met him while I was still editor of the *Ulster Star,* when he made page-one news by winning the Circuit of Ireland in a souped-up Mini.) I'd kept in touch with him by letter since leaving Lisburn and now he was anxious for sight of the rath I kept mentioning. I undertook to take him, but rain had set in for the day and there was no sign of a clearance until well after eleven that night. Jim asked if I was still game for the visit.

We equipped ourselves with torches, but by now the weather had cleared to moonlight occasionally interrupted by passing cloud, so we anticipated no real problems finding our way. Since neither of our wives fancied a muddy walk, the trip was confined to Jim and myself. We arrived at the rath shortly before midnight.

There were two natural entrances to the earthwork, one guarded by a fairy thorn which carried an interesting local legend. According to the story, an old woman gathering firewood during the early years of the twentieth century had snapped off several branches from the thorn. The fairies took exception to the desecration and the woman was found dead beneath the tree next morning. I told Jim not to break any branches as we walked past.

Inside the earthwork, the ground sloped upwards like an inverted saucer to meet with the standing stone in the middle. We walked across to lean on the metal fence and stare up at the megalith. By now the sky had cleared completely and the whole place was flooded with bright moonlight. After a moment, Jim said suddenly, "I don't think this place likes me."

I said, "Would you like to go back to the house?" He nodded and we began to walk towards the entrance. As we did so, a herd of approximately twenty tiny horses galloped around the top of the earthwork and disappeared down the slope on the other side. None was larger than a cocker-spaniel. All were pure white and unmarked. They looked perfectly solid in the moonlight.

I discovered Jim staring at me. "Did you see what I just saw?" he asked.

We ran for the entrance and emerged into the field only seconds later, but there was no sign of the little horses and after ten or fifteen minutes of futile searching, we started back to the house. Comparing notes on the way, we found we had both seen the same thing, but while my horses appeared in total silence, Jim said he had heard the sound of hoof-beats. By the time we reached home, we had more than half convinced ourselves we must have been mistaken. Tiny horses were impossible, so there must have been a trick of the light to make them look so small. Or possibly we'd seen some other type of livestock—sheep, perhaps, or even cattle. But when I asked Major Synnott the following day (without telling him why) he assured me there was no livestock at all—sheep, cattle or horses—in any of the fields adjoining the rath. I was so intrigued that some time later I returned to the rath by moonlight with several interested companions and checked the angle of sight to see if it optically reduced objects on the earthwork. It did not.

I was left with a mystery. It was not the only mystery I would find at Furness.

Between the time I said *yes* to *Scene* and the day I took up my new post, I went to see Dr Whitely one last time. He took the news phlegmatically and reckoned my course of treatment was 'probably about over anyway.' Since *Scene* came complete with a staff health plan, I broke the good news that the insurance company involved would pay him liberally for a confidential report on my condition. He wrote it on the spot and sealed it in the envelope the insurance company provided. I steamed it open when I got home to discover that my diagnosis was 'anxiety neurosis,' my current condition was 'in remission' and my prognosis was 'excellent.' Good old Dr Whitely had worked hard to ensure I got my health cover without any silly complications. Interestingly enough, he was right about my being in remission. I was so excited by the prospect of editing *Scene* that my head had no room for panic attacks.

During this same period there were two further developments. The first was that Norman Ames, who never fired anybody but art directors, fired the feature writer who had wanted to meet me for plotting and scheming in the Pearl Bar. "Technically speaking he resigned," Norman told me when I phoned for an explanation. "But I expect he would tell you I made it impossible for him to remain. He was quite useless, of course. To give you an idea: I asked him to take paste-ups of our entire last issue to the printers. He doesn't drive, so he took the bus. As he was getting off, a gust of wind blew the paste-ups out of his hand and blew off his hat. The silly fecker chased his hat."

"What am I supposed to do without a feature writer?" I demanded.

"Hire another one," Norman said.

Because I was focused on the feature writer, I missed the telling detail of the Dublin printer. When I finally arrived to start my new job, I was astonished to discover Morton Newspapers no longer had the *Scene* printing contract. Norman had given it to Beacon Press, a small letterpress house in Cabra. "I persuaded Jimbly Morton we needed letterpress quality for a glossy monthly and since he's only got offset..."

I never did hire another feature-writer, partly because Morton had warned me not to spend money—my entire editorial budget was £100 an issue—partly because it seemed simpler to write material myself. I quickly discovered the pace of life on a monthly magazine was far slower than I was used to on a weekly newspaper. Essentially you goofed off for three weeks and brought the publication out in the fourth. This was fun, but time sometimes hung heavily on my hands. Since I enjoyed writing, I took to dreaming up interesting features and producing them under a pen-name. It was a bad precedent—I finally found myself making up *Scene's* horoscope column—but it kept me out of mischief.

Shortly after I took up my new post, Diarmuid MacFeeley, the magazine's advertising manager stormed into my office. "I want you to sack Mary," he demanded. Although I'd met him briefly before, this was my first close encounter with Diarmuid. He was an extraordinarily good-looking young man—he'd once worked as a model—who dressed immaculately and took a serious attitude to life. Morton thought he was the best thing that had ever happened to *Scene* and our only hope of achieving worthwhile advertising revenues. I had been severely warned by both Morton and Hutchinson that I must keep Diarmuid happy at all costs.

"Why do you want me to sack Mary?" I asked.

He sat down and glared at me in outrage. "Do you know what she's just done? Do you? She's taken all my files, all my advertising files, all my private files, taken them out of my office, taken them outside onto the street and *thrown them up in the air!*"

"I'll have a word with her," I said.

When Diarmuid left, I pressed the intercom button on my desk and asked Mary Anderson to step into my office. She arrived looking sheepish. "I suppose Diarmuid has complained about me?" she said as I waved her to sit down.

"He says you took all his files and threw them up in the air." It was such a preposterous idea that I expected her to deny it, but instead she put her head in her hands.

"I couldn't stand it," she said. "Not one minute longer." She looked up at me. "The man's an idiot. Do you know what he does? He can't dictate. He doesn't know how. He writes all his letters out in longhand. But he doesn't give them to me, which would be the sensible thing. He calls me in and hides his draft on his lap and reads from it *pretending* to dictate to me. Just so he seems like a proper executive. He even puts in fake pauses and pretends he's considering the next sentence when it's there on his lap all the time. He thinks I don't know what he's doing. It's such a dreadful waste of time. I have better things to do even if he hasn't."

I blinked. "So you just…threw all his files up in the air?"

Mary said, "Are you going to sack me?"

I had no desire at all to sack Mary. She struck me as intelligent and talented. More to the point, while officially employed as receptionist and general secretary, she had recently started to contribute snippets of editorial to *Scene on the Town*, after quietly confessing ambitions to become a writer. Her pieces were a sight better written than the stuff I had from some of our contributors, and I had ambitions of my own to turn her loose on full-length features in the near future. "I'll have a word with Mr Ames," I said.

Norman had a large, comfortable car which he leased from a local dealer in return for free advertising in the magazine. (There were clearly hidden depths to his policy of padding out the publication with unpaid ads each month.) Since I loathed Dublin traffic and he enjoyed driving, he soon routinely chauffeured me anywhere I wished to go. Our favourite escape was to the Beacon Press, where we were treated as important customers and given coffee. On our way back, I brought up Diarmuid's problem with Mary.

"It's up to you, of course, but if you're happy with her, I'd keep Mary on," Norman said.

"What about Diarmuid?"

"He may not be with us very long," he told me enigmatically.

I couldn't draw him any further, but it sounded suspiciously as if the man who only ever sacked art directors was searching for another victim. He had also, I quickly discovered, forgotten his resolve not to get involved with editorial. We held a weekly meeting ostensibly so I could tell him, editor to publisher, my plans for magazine content. In fact these meetings—and many an unnecessary business lunch and car trip—were a vehicle for him to put forward his own ideas. To be fair, he never pulled rank or insisted on anything, but when he was really interested in an idea, he would sell it to me endlessly until I (usually) gave in from sheer exhaustion. Some of his suggestions were stupid, like his notion for an article entitled *Green Means Stop* about the Irish habit of halting at green traffic lights while driving through the red. Others actually excited me, like the time he suddenly announced he thought I should run an interview with Desmond Leslie.

Back in the early 1950s, Desmond Leslie collaborated with a Polish-American named George Adamski on a book called The *Flying Saucers Have Landed*. I picked up the paperback while I was working in the *Lurgan Mail*. The opening section, by Adamski, was a first-person account of how, in November 1952, he met a spaceman from Venus who had landed his flying saucer in the Californian desert. It was this account that generated the book's title and turned it into a best-seller, but despite affidavits from

[116]

several witnesses, I found Adamski's story unlikely. The second section, by Desmond Leslie, was something else. Without comment on Adamski's claims, Leslie produced an exposition of flying saucer sightings throughout history, tracing the phenomenon to ancient times, inserting the occasional esoteric reference and diverting to consider such mysteries as how the pyramids were built. His guided tour of the *Mahabharata,* one of India's two major Sanskrit epics, was especially interesting. Leslie interpreted it as an account of a prehistoric war that used flying saucers (called *vimanas),* laser weapons and atomics. More to the point, he quoted from his sources, allowing readers to see for themselves the passages on which he based this unorthodox interpretation. Leslie wrote with a light touch and a relaxed style. Where Adamski sounded like a nut, he came across as a serious author. His ideas about a technically advanced prehistoric civilisation fascinated me to such a degree that, many years later, I wrote four books of my own on the subject. But I knew nothing of Leslie himself. On the basis of his literary voice and a few hints dropped within the text, I believed him to be a retired army colonel living somewhere in England.

The four books Desmond inspired me eventually to write were **Martian Genesis**, Piatkus Books, London, 1998; **The Atlantis Enigma**, Piatkus, 1999; **The Secret History of Ancient Egypt**, Piatkus, 2000; and **Atlantis and Other Lost Civilizations**, Faber and Faber, London, 2006.

"Is he visiting Ireland?" I asked Norman.

"He's living in Dublin," Norman said. "I've been in touch with him and he's quite amenable to an interview. If you're interested, of course."

I didn't even pretend to be irritated at the editorial interference. "I'm interested," I said.

"Will you send Hilary or do the interview yourself?"

Hilary was Hilary Weir, a staff trainee prone to disappearing for entire afternoons at a time. When I challenged her about it, she told me she had been attending sessions of the Dáil to sharpen her sense of civic responsibility.

"I'll do it myself."

"Be careful what you ask him," Norman told me casually. "He knocked down Bernard Levin on TV."

Although it seemed as unlikely as Adamski's Venusian, I quickly discovered it was true. Levin had apparently written a bad review of a stage performance by Leslie's wife, the actress Agnes Bernelle. Shortly afterwards,

Desmond Leslie: a student of Theosophy, extraterrestial life,
and musique concrete.

Leslie walked out of the audience at one of Levin's TV talk shows, invited
him to stand up and punched him in the face. A surprised Levin fell over
but was able to continue the show minutes later.

"The irony is," said Norman, who always claimed he disliked gossip,
"he's now left his wife for another woman. That's why he's living in
Dublin."

I don't know how Bernard Levin felt when Desmond towered above him, but he certainly put the wind up me. Standing in the doorway of his Terenure flat, he looked like a giant; and at 6′ 4″ he very nearly was. I decided to avoid controversial questions. The flat had a temporary feel about it. He showed me into a large living area with cables snaking across the carpet to link into a featureless black box lying in the middle of the floor. A statuesque blonde, herself easily six feet tall, rose to greet me. "This is Helen," Desmond said. "My other wife."

"He has two," Helen told me confidentially and grinned. "Would you like a glass of wine?"

The wine took the edge of any formality, and we were soon chatting like old friends. I didn't quite know what to make of Desmond. He had a rolling, plummy, English accent and the same turn of phrase that had marked him as a retired Colonel in his book, but from his conversation he seemed to be Irish and there was nothing of the military about him. He wore large, black-rimmed glasses and walked with steps so tiny I wondered if he might suffer from a disease of the legs. Helen was easier. "Desmond rescued me from the orgy set in Chelsea," she told me cheerfully. Desmond nodded benignly. "She was a very naughty girl." I noticed, with some trepidation, that there was a school cane hanging from a hook in the ceiling.

Desmond told me he was a composer and we listened to some of his compositions on tape. He specialised in *musique concrete,* an abstract form for which there was something of a fashion in intellectual circles at the time. I listened without appreciation or understanding, but, mindful of the fate of Levin, kept criticisms to myself. "Did you hear that?" Desmond asked as a very curious sound insinuated itself into the piece. "I got that by farting in the bath."

Sometime in the middle of the afternoon I realised I'd been drinking too much wine and asked if we could do the interview. It lasted three and a half hours and took some interesting turns. We began, predictably, with flying saucers, but diverted when I asked him how he reconciled Adamski's Venusian story with the findings of the recent space-probe which showed the planet had a sulphuric acid atmosphere and a surface temperature hot enough to melt lead. Desmond told me that 'as a student of Theosophy' he had never believed the physical plane of Venus would be habitable, but that sentient human life existed there 'on the etheric plane.'

I pricked up my ears when I heard the word *Theosophy,* and thereafter— apart from one brief interlude when Desmond claimed to have invented Patrick Moore—the interview concentrated on such esoteric matters as

[119]

the Stanzas of Dzyan, the Christian Mysteries, levitation, mediumistic dematerialisation and the Ark of the Covenant, which Desmond believed to be "a highly sophisticated piece of electrostatic equipment." I was in my element and could not get enough of it, but I was also aware that much of what interested me most would be obscure in the extreme to *Scene* readers, so I reluctantly brought the focus back to flying saucers. If one came down in Phoenix Park, I asked, what would the reaction be. "Depends who saw it first," said Desmond. "If it was Dev, he'd trip over it. If it was the Papal Nuncio, he'd spray it with holy water. If it was the American Ambassador, he'd probably try to buy it." It was the perfect sign-off for my feature.

"Would you like to stay for supper?" Helen asked as I switched off my recorder.

"Yes, please," I said.

I can no longer remember the meal, except that it was followed by some very runny brie—the first time I had tasted this delicious cheese. While we were eating, I asked casually, "What's that black box in the middle of the floor?"

"It's a flying saucer detector," Desmond said.

"And the cane hanging on the hook?"

"Ah," Desmond said. "That's to keep this one—" He nodded towards Helen. "—in her place." He looked at me sleepily. "Would you like a demonstration?"

Before I could answer, Helen jumped up and bent over. She was wearing a leather mini-skirt and looked very fetching. Desmond took the cane from the hook and whacked her soundly across the bottom. "Ow, that hurts!" Helen protested.

"That's the whole point," Desmond told her.

They returned to the table and Helen passed me the brie.

My wife Helen had gone North to visit her parents. I tucked in the children and went to bed early, tired and alone. As I was falling asleep, I found myself standing, dressed only in pyjamas, on the lonely country road that led to the Furness estate. There was a cold wind rustling the leaves on the trees. I had no idea at all how I got here, no memory of leaving the house. It was as if I was in my bed one second, outside the next with nothing in between. It was a frightening experience.

There was a sound like a metal spoon dropped on a stone-flagged floor and I was back in bed, my heart thumping.

I sat up, switched on the light and tried to work out what had happened. At first I was convinced I must have walked outside, in which case I was suffering from amnesia—a frightening prospect, but not entirely out of the question, given my psychiatric history. But then a much more reasonable explanation occurred to me. When I believed I was only in the process of falling asleep, I must actually *have* fallen asleep and dreamed I was standing outside. Then I'd awoken, found myself back in bed and here I was.

It has been my experience that when something particularly weird happens, people instinctively search for the explanation that makes them feel most comfortable. I was no exception. The dream rationalization was nonsense, of course. Sleep research has shown there is a lengthy period between falling asleep and dreaming: it simply does not happen instantaneously. But I didn't know that at the time, and if I had, I doubt it would have made much difference. I needed reassurance, and the dream theory provided it. I turned out the light and went back to sleep.

A week or two later, I awoke in the night needing a pee. I lay for a minute, not really wanting to leave a warm, comfortable bed, then the pressure got too great and I slipped out quietly to avoid waking Helen who was fast asleep beside me. Our bedroom was at the end of the upstairs corridor. The bathroom, down a single step, was off the same corridor, a yard or two on the right. I walked around the bottom of the bed, reached the door and could not open it. I remember standing for a moment, puzzled, wondering if the door was locked. I certainly hadn't locked it and I couldn't imagine why Helen would have done so. There was moonlight streaming through the window behind me. The door had an old-fashioned brass knob in place of a handle and as I reached out to try again, I saw my fingers pierce its surface as if it wasn't there at all. I stood staring stupidly. My hand had actually penetrated the doorknob as if it were made from jelly.

I stepped back in bewilderment and glanced over to the bed. A part of my mind still insisted the door must be locked and I was contemplating waking Helen to ask her what she'd done with the key. But what I saw put that nonsense out of my head. There was a man lying on his back beside her in the bed. He was bearded, some inches above average height and seemed to be asleep. It took a shocked moment to realise he was me.

It's difficult to describe what I was feeling then. One emotion was definitely bemused fascination. I'm reminded of the first time I heard my voice recorded and played back. It didn't sound like me—or at least it didn't sound the way my voice sounded in my head—but it kept saying the things I'd just said into the mike. "That's not me!" I exclaimed. "That can't be me! Is that *really* me?" My feelings towards the body on the bed were much the same. It didn't look the way I thought I looked, yet I knew it must be me. I had walked across the room but somehow left myself in bed. At the same time, I still had a body with me. I could see my hands and arms, my pyjama-clad torso and legs. I was aware of the carpet underneath my feet. In other words, I was standing by the bedroom door, wide awake and feeling as I always felt, solid and real. And yet there was a second 'me' lying supine beneath the sheets.

What happened next was counter-intuitive. There are so many things I should have done in such peculiar circumstances—panicked, decided I was dead, examined the body in the bed, pinched the me that housed my consciousness—but I did none of them. My overriding concern was the pressure of a full bladder, which I could still feel physically and urgently as I stood beside the door. Some part of me must have decided that however I felt, that was my real body in the bed and it would be pointless attempting to urinate without it. So I walked back and lay down, aligning myself carefully. I wriggled for a moment until I synchronised with the body in the bed. Then I got up properly and hurried to the bathroom.

The bedroom door remained tight shut. This time I walked directly through it.

I repeated the sequence—back to the body, get it up, head for the bathroom—several more times. On one occasion I found myself standing by the bathroom loo, aimed and ready, before I realised I was *still* without a physical body. But finally I succeeded.

Once I had managed to urinate, I returned to my bed and lay awake for an hour or more trying to evaluate what had happened. Unlike my earlier experience when I found myself outside on the road, I could not dismiss this as a dream. While dreams may be confused with waking reality while you are dreaming, they have a distinctive signature that is easily recognisable in retrospect. I knew without a shadow of a doubt I had not been dreaming. I had been fully awake for the past fifteen or twenty minutes. During that time my consciousness had moved out of its usual seat behind my eyes. Somehow I had left my body. Curiously, I had little difficulty accepting a shift of consciousness in principle—it had already happened to me during my treatment with Dr Whitely. What really threw me was that I had functioned in something I could only call a second body, which felt just as solid, just as physical as the one I left behind in the bed. Yet it clearly was neither since I could pass through doors like a ghost. There was a dichotomy between what I felt subjectively and what I knew from rational experience. As far as I was concerned, it was the physical world that was insubstantial as I stood by the bedroom door, but I knew it was nothing of the sort. The problem remained unresolved as I finally drifted back to sleep. Before I did so, I remember wondering if anyone else might have had a similar experience.

It transpired that a great many people had. The first one I found out about was a sickly American named Sylvan J. Muldoon.

In 1915, when Sylvan was 12 years old, his mother took him to a Spiritualist Association camp in Clinton, Ohio. He found the experience scary and woke up in a state of paralysis during his first night. He felt powerless and his whole body began to vibrate at a great speed. There was a pressure on the back of his head and something akin to a blackout. When able to see and hear again, he found himself floating horizontally several feet in the air. Something rotated him so that he was standing on his feet. He managed to turn and discovered "there was another 'me' lying quietly on the bed." Muldoon described the two bodies as identical and claimed they were joined together by a nebulous cable (which he called the 'silver cord') that seemed capable of infinite extension. His first thought was that he had died in his sleep.

The young Muldoon went in search of his mother and found her asleep in her room. He tried to shake her awake, but his hands passed right through her. Much the same thing happened when he tried to attract the attention of others. He could not touch them and they could not hear or see him. He wandered about weeping for about fifteen minutes before the silver cord finally tugged him back into his physical body. He insisted he had been fully conscious throughout.

Experiences of this type continued well into adulthood. Muldoon was what my mother would have called 'delicate'—someone prone to frequent illness. During these bouts, he regularly drifted out of his body and wandered around like a ghost, passing through walls and other solid objects exactly as I'd done on my trip to the loo.

So far as I can discover, there was nothing in print about this curious phenomenon when Muldoon was growing up. But there was some research going on. A French experimenter named Charles Lancelin became interested in the 'animal magnetism' techniques of the eighteenth-century healer Franz Anton Mesmer and used them, so he claimed, to extract a second body from its physical shell. Lancelin's work attracted the attention of a psychical researcher named Hereward Carrington, who summarised it in two books, *Modern Psychical Phenomena* and, more fully, *Higher Psychical Development.*

In 1927, Dr Carrington received a letter from Sylvan Muldoon stating bluntly that he had forgotten more about second bodies than Lancelin ever knew. Although born in the Channel Islands, Carrington had emigrated to America at the age of 19. He paid a visit to Muldoon and found the young man seriously ill in bed. Nonetheless, he carried out a series of experiments that convinced him Muldoon was telling the truth. They later collaborated on a book about Muldoon's experiences, which I bought soon after I had mine. In it, they consistently referred to the phenomenon as 'astral projection.'

Curiously enough, I was already familiar with this term through my esoteric studies with SIL and Helios. There was even mention of *astral*—which means 'pertaining to the stars'—in Levi and several other sources. But what I'd read bore little resemblance to what Muldoon described and I had experienced. Any reference I'd seen to astral projection suggested it was a technique designed to give access to spirit realms or dream worlds. Carrington seems to have made the same connection, for he was careful to write in his introduction to *The Projection of the Astral Body:*

"I should like to draw the reader's attention particularly to the fact that no wild or preposterous claims are anywhere made in this book as to what has been accomplished during these 'astral trips.' Mr Muldoon does not claim to have visited any distant planets—and return to tell us in detail their modes of life; he does not claim to have explored any vast and beautiful 'spirit worlds'; he does not pretend to have penetrated the past or the future; to have re-lived any of his past 'incarnations'; to have read any 'Akashic Records'; to have travelled back along the stream of time

[124]

and reviewed the history of mankind or the geologic eras of our earth. He asserts merely that he has been enabled to leave his physical body at will and travel about in the present, in his immediate vicinity, in some vehicle or other, while fully conscious."

Muldoon himself remarked in a letter, "I have never had a conscious out-of-the-body experience when I was not here on the earth plane, just as much as I am right now. I wouldn't know where to look for the higher planes!"

Clearly there was a mystery here and I resolved to investigate it. The decision was to involve me in some fascinating experiments. It was also to lead to the publication of my first book.

The interview led to friendship. I became a frequent visitor to Desmond Leslie's Terenure flat. We spent hours discussing Theosophy, magic and religion. All three were intimately entangled in Desmond's head. He still considered himself a Roman Catholic, albeit one with unorthodox ideas, but told me the Catholic Mass was a magical ceremony that had lost its way. The problem, as he saw it, was that priests (except for Jesuits) no longer had the visualisation training that would allow them to work the rite with real magical power. "I have only ever seen it done properly in the Liberal Catholic Church," he said thoughtfully. "When those towering archangelic forms came roaring in, it sent a shiver down my spine."

"How come you mentioned Jesuits?" I asked curiously.

He looked at me in surprise. "Haven't you read the Spiritual Exercises of St Ignatius? They're exactly the same training a magician receives."

I hadn't, but I soon did and discovered he was right: when you stripped away the Christian elements, the *Spiritual Exercises* bore a striking resemblance to the training I was undergoing with Helios.

It was a relief to find someone with whom I could share my esoteric interests so openly. Despite her Spiritualist leanings, Helen did not really approve of magic (which she considered dangerous) so I avoided discussions with her. Norman, to my surprise, had proved sympathetic when I made a tentative confession, but only really wanted to talk about how magical visualisation might get him money. Desmond, by contrast, was open to everything that interested me, plus a few more besides, and had many more years' experience in the field. At the time, I sometimes found him credulous and simplistic. Now, looking back, I am astounded to discover how profoundly he influenced my thinking on a wide range of subjects and how much he knew about them.

During our discussions, I learned he had more time for Spiritualism than I had—like Helen he was a member of the White Eagle Lodge. Despite my visionary experience in the séance with Eileen Boyd, I had never witnessed any objectively spectacular phenomena. Desmond, however, claimed he had at a séance conducted by 'the materialising medium, Harris.'

The materialising medium Harris was Alexander Frederick Harris, a Welsh Spiritualist who died in 1974, six years after my conversation with Desmond. Harris was brought up a conventional Christian and remained so until his sister Connie died. The grieving family attended a séance held by the Scottish medium Helen Duncan, who conjured up Connie's spirit

Longstone Rath: where I met the miniature horses.

form. The young Alec was so impressed he decided to develop his own spiritual gifts and eventually claimed to have succeeded in materialising Connie himself.

For commercial séances at his home in the Whitchurch area of Cardiff, Harris permitted himself to be tied hand and foot to a chair in an open cabinet. The room was lit by the same sort of red photographer's light I'd seen used by Mr Sludge. Spirit forms materialised within the cabinet

[127]

and walked into the room where they would talk with sitters. This was the type of set-up popularised by America's Davenport Brothers in the mid-nineteenth century. Since one of them admitted to Harry Houdini that their séances were fraudulent—essentially an escape act masquerading as Spiritualism—it was not a set-up that inspired confidence. Certainly it inspired little confidence in Desmond: "When the so-called spirits appeared I could hardly believe Harris had been getting away with such a crude deception. They clumped about the place in hob-nailed boots. They were obviously accomplices dressed up."

He decided to expose the fraud. Although sitters had been warned before the séance that they must not under any circumstances try to touch the spirits, Desmond leaped from his seat and grabbed one by the arm. "I was never so surprised in my life. The creature simply dissolved under my hand and disappeared."

Helen Strong, who was listening to the account, nodded. "That's right—I watched it happen."

Since it seemed a good time to swap phenomena stories, I told Desmond of my encounter with the miniature horses at Longstone Rath. He listened without comment until I had finished, then said, "But, dear boy, don't you know what those were?" I didn't and said so. "Those were *faerie* horses," he told me soberly. "They're associated with the raths of Ireland and also with Japan."

On one occasion while searching for a reference book, he pulled an old photograph from a drawer. "That's Castle Leslie," he said. The photograph was blurred and seemed to show an old country house. Since he always claimed to be broke, I assumed the designation 'castle' was another example of Desmond's humour, but it subsequently turned out there really *was* a Castle Leslie—and a 1,200-acre estate—immortalised by Dean Swift in four lines of doggerel:

Here I am in Castle Leslie
With rows of books upon the shelves
Written by the Leslies
All about themselves

"You must come and see it sometime," Desmond said. Then added a little bitterly. "If I ever get things sorted with Aggie."

Desmond eventually did get things sorted with Agnes Bernelle, his first wife—by the brutal expedient of locking her out, according to their daughter Antonia—and I got to see his castle. But before that happened my free time filled itself up with concerns no less eccentric than the Leslie clan. I was still fascinated by my out-of-body experience and had begun to wonder if it might be triggered artificially. What I had in mind was the use of hypnosis. Who I had in mind was Denise Alexander.

Denise was an 18-year-old shop assistant I'd met when she was baby-sitting for some friends of mine in Lisburn, a young married couple named Jill and Dennis. I can no longer remember how I found it out, but she was one of the best hypnotic subjects I had ever known. She was also an attractive, outgoing girl who was game for anything so that when I called her to ask if she was willing to take part in an experiment—I believe I actually called it an experiment in psychical research—she agreed at once.

The arrangements I put in place were simple enough. I wanted to structure something that not only separated consciousness from the body but did so in a way that would provide objective proof. Consequently I asked Jill and Dennis to compose a note and leave it prominently on their mantelpiece on the day of the experiment. I emphasised that only they should know the contents of the note, but that they should send it to me by registered post when the experiment was concluded. Once the note was in place, I proposed to hypnotise Denise at my new home in Furness and send her second body to Lisburn—a distance of about 100 miles—to read the note. If she succeeded, this would surely provide proof that out-of-body experience was neither a dream nor an hallucination.

Jill and Dennis wrote the note and left it in place before vacating the house: they had planned a week's holiday. Arthur Gibson, my friend with the home-brew emporium, closed his shop in order to drive Denise to Furness. By then I'd discovered he was profoundly interested in esoteric phenomena: he had some experience of Spiritualism and, during his years in India, studied both hatha and mantra yoga. I hypnotised Denise—who passed into trance with her accustomed ease—then suggested she was leaving her body and flying back to Lisburn. She responded positively and moments later confirmed she was in the town. I told her to go to Jill and Dennis's home (which she knew well from her baby-sitting activities) and enter their living room.

These experiments and my out-of-body experience were the inspiration for the first book I ever published: *Astral Doorways*, Aquarian Press, London, 1971. The work is still in print, re-issued by Thoth Publications, Loughborough, in 1995.

When deep trance subjects hallucinate, either spontaneously or in response to suggestion, they typically develop REM, the rapid eye movements characteristic of dream sleep. Denise's eyes were flickering wildly now. There was no doubt she was experiencing herself as standing in our friends' living room, but whether this was a subjective vision or an objective reality remained to be seen. I was a little concerned that Jill and Dennis might have forgotten to leave the note, but when I asked Denise if she could see a letter on the mantle, she told me promptly that she could. I asked her to read it.

"I can't."

"Yes, you can, Denise. Go to the mantelpiece and read the note."

"I can't."

"Why can't you read the note?"

"It's too dark."

That brought me up short. It had not occurred to me that when Jill and Dennis left home, they would naturally switch off all lights. Night had now fallen so that if Denise was in their living room, she would be standing in the dark. I was not at all sure what to do about this: it was something I should have anticipated and organised in advance. But I was reluctant to abandon the experiment and tried to solve the problem with suggestion. I told Denise it was growing lighter in the room. She agreed that it was. I asked if she could now read the note. No—it was too dark. I asked her to go to the doorway and switch on the electric light. She accepted this suggestion too. Were the lights now on? The lights were now on. Could she read the message? No—it was too dark.

I was running out of options when an idea struck me. Instead of asking her to read the note, I asked her how many words it contained.

"Five," Denise said promptly.

"What colour is the paper it's written on?"

"Blue."

"Is it lined or unlined?"

"Lined."

"Is it typed, handwritten or printed?"

"It's hand printed in block capitals."

"Can you read what it says?"

"No, it's too dark."

I brought Denise out of trance and thanked her for her cooperation. Arthur said suddenly, "I'd like to have a go."

One evening before I left Lisburn, Arthur turned up at my door, demanded a cup of tea and asked my help. He was suffering from stress due to problems in his marriage and wanted to know if hypnosis might help him to relax. I assured him that it would, and we made arrangements for a series of weekly hypnotic treatments beginning the next day. While people vary widely (and quite unpredictably) in their response to hypnotic induction, I had never at that time met anyone who did not respond at all. My experience was that some ten to twenty per cent of subjects could achieve deep trance. Another forty per cent or more passed into a medium trance level and the remainder, without exception, showed indications of light trance, even though in many cases they were unaware of it themselves. Since even light trance is sufficient to produce a profound degree of relaxation, I was certain I could help Arthur. But when Arthur arrived next day, I discovered I could not hypnotise him at all. For the first time in my life, I had met someone who had no reaction to hypnosis whatsoever. With huge regret I told him I could do nothing for him. The only thing I could suggest was that he find another hypnotist. Since hypnosis seemed to involve a very personal interaction, I thought there was a possibility someone else might succeed where I had failed.

So when Arthur asked to 'have a go' I reminded him tiredly that I couldn't hypnotise him. Arthur said thoughtfully, "Would you try again? I've a feeling it might work this time." I sat him down, went through my standard induction and watched him fall into the deepest trance I'd ever seen. At first I couldn't believe it and began to run tests. Poor Arthur became in turn hypnotically rigid, insensitive to pain, amenable to post hypnotic suggestion, then amenable to bizarre post-hypnotic, a term that denotes the hypnotist's ability to trigger full-scale hallucinations in the subject *after* he has been awakened from trance. I even discovered he was capable of opening his eyes without affecting his trance level. (He looked so creepily like a zombie that I quickly told him to close them again.) After half an hour, I realised I had a subject who was even more suited to experimentation than Denise.

I would have liked to send him off to read the note, but unlike Denise, he was not familiar with Jill and Dennis's home, or even the district where they lived. Since I could not think of a way to guide him there, I dreamed up a new experimental procedure on the spot. The first thing I wanted to do was discover whether he was capable of separating out his second body, so I laid him on a couch and suggested he could take a trip anywhere in the world he wanted to do. Then I left him in his deep hypnotic sleep for fifteen minutes.

[131]

When Arthur awoke, he had no memory of being hypnotised or any of the immediate preliminaries. Nor did he report leaving his body in the way I had on my notorious bathroom trip. Instead, he told me that he had just flown to India, by plane on a commercial flight. He was able to describe the plane and the flight in great detail, right down to details like the meal served him by the hostess and the fact there had been little or no turbulence. He landed in Bombay and went sightseeing.

As he described his experiences, Arthur grew confused. He kept looking around the room, staring at Denise, then staring at me. He suddenly stopped the account to say, "I'm back in Ireland, aren't I?" When I confirmed that he was, he became agitated and asked how he had got here: he could remember the flight out to India quite clearly, but not any flight back. It was as if he had been pulled back instantaneously; or, even more disturbingly, as if there was something wrong with his memory. I reminded him he had been hypnotised, but he flatly refused to believe me. He reminded *me* I had once told him he was incapable of being hypnotised. I finally convinced him by drawing his attention to the time. He knew when he had left Ireland on his flight. Now he saw less than twenty minutes had elapsed, far too short a period for him to make the trip, let alone take a tour around Bombay. Gradually he came to accept what had really happened, although aspects of his experience continued to puzzle him.

Arthur had, of course, lived in India for some years and was familiar with Bombay. As we discussed his trip, I quickly realised it was no typical out-of-body experience and put forward the possibility that he had entered some sort of dream state in which he drew on old memories to create a subjective version of the city. Arthur agreed this seemed the most likely explanation but was confused by two factors. During his dream of Bombay he had visited a familiar restaurant and discovered it had been totally redecorated. Later, while walking through the Old City, he came across a wall where none had been before. Why, he asked me, would his memory play tricks on just these two points when everything else about the city was as he remembered? I had no easy answer.

"It was all so *real*," Arthur repeated, over and over.

Then he wanted to do it again.

I was equally keen. But I wanted to try something more controlled than another free-form trip to Bombay. I put him back into trance and this time suggested he was stepping out of his body, passing through my front door and making for the main house. Arthur, who was perfectly capable of talking without adversely affecting his level of trance, confirmed that this was exactly what he was doing. I told him to go inside.

Although I was familiar with the interior lay-out of Furness House, Arthur was not. But that didn't stop his describing it with total accuracy. A few weeks later he phoned me at the office. He was still obsessing about his Bombay trip; and with good reason. He had written to a friend in the city and asked him to check some things out. As a result, the friend had written back to confirm the restaurant had indeed been redecorated and the new wall Arthur saw was actually in place. A day or two earlier I received the note from Jill and Dennis. It was hand-printed on blue, lined paper and contained precisely five words: *HOPE YOU GET THIS NOTE.*

Scene settled into a routine. Norman finally found an art director he liked, a young advertising artist named Jim Fitzpatrick. "He's brilliant," Norman told me enthusiastically. "You just show him what you want and he copies it exactly!" Fitzpatrick had three additional benefits. He was able to illustrate articles as well as lay them out and his psychedelic style made the magazine look hip and modern. He was a workaholic who produced material fast and on time. And since he was paid on what he produced, he was constantly suggesting creative new ideas. One day he suggested *Sharona.*

Norman liked to say our new art director was 'influenced by Lichtenstein,' the great American pop artist. In fact, Jim just liked comics. He knew *Barbarella* as a comic strip when the rest of us thought of the Jane Fonda movie. He introduced me to a curious production called *The Adventures of Phoebe Zeitgeist* published by Grove Press in America, which also brought out *Evergreen Review. Evergreen,* a literary magazine, was available in Ireland. *Phoebe,* due to censorship regulations, was not. When Fitzie smuggled in his copy, it was easy to see why. The current adventure of Phoebe was concerned with necrophilia, prominently labelled: 'The Love that *Cannot* Speak its Name.'

"We could do an Irish version," Fitzie said. "Maybe not necrophilia, but sex. Set it in Ancient Ireland or somewhere, for cultural merit. Give the heroine an Irish name like Sharona. You write the script, I'll draw."

"What about the censor?" I asked cautiously.

"He'll only ban one issue and that would be great publicity. But somebody has to report it before the censorship board can even consider it and consideration can take months, depending on their backlog, so we might get away with half a dozen instalments before we have to stop."

He seemed to have a worryingly intimate knowledge of Ireland's censorship process, but in truth I liked the idea. When I mentioned it to Norman, he liked it even more. "We'll run it in full colour," he said.

"That'll cost a fortune," I told him.

"Can't bring out a decent magazine without spending Jimbly Morton's money," Norman told me cheerfully.

Sharona never did appear in full colour due to time constraints, nor did it attract the attention of the censor, despite our best efforts. But it did upset our printers. Beacon Press was run by two brothers, Gerry and Phil Price. Phil was the technical man, who looked after the actual printing.

Jim Fitzpatrick: a surge of creative ideas.

Gerry was the business head, who looked after much of the customer liaison. It was Gerry who alerted us to as an outrageous *Sharona* insertion. "Have a look at the seventh frame," he told Norman.

Norman called me into his office after he put down the phone. "Have a look at the seventh frame," he told me.

I had a look at the seventh frame. It was a fairly typical Fitzpatrick spectacular: an Ancient Irish army led by a scantily dressed (but perfectly respectable) Sharona marching beneath a symbolic and heroic banner. "What's wrong with it?" I asked.

"This may help," said Norman, handing me a pocket mirror. I held the frame up to the mirror. The symbolic design on the heroic banner suddenly resolved itself into the single word *FUCK*.

The magazine was already printed and distributed, but to our irritation, nobody else noticed and there was none of the controversy that might have generated extra sales. We were desperately in need of extra sales which would, according to Norman, produce extra advertising revenue. There was a scramble that amounted to panic for extra advertising. While every other department was instructed to economise, the advertising team had actually expanded. Diarmuid had taken on an assistant, an old advertising hand named Carlos Kenny, returning to employment after a protracted period of illness. But *Scene,* despite everyone's best efforts, continued to operate at a loss. Norman took the situation philosophically. "Do you know," he mused over an Italian lunch paid for out of petty cash, "the other day Morton asked me where his money was going. I thought of taking him to the front door, putting my arm around his shoulders and saying, 'Mr Morton, I want you to look at the blue sky and the cherry blossom. That's where your money is going—to build a better world!'"

As the man signing the cheques, Morton was considerably less phlegmatic. One afternoon he phoned to ask if I would visit him at home next Saturday. He didn't volunteer a reason, but as he emphasised that my visit must remain a secret, I assumed it was trouble. The intuition sharpened when I saw Courtney Hutchinson's car in the driveway and peaked when I discovered Ann Morton, Jim's wife, was to be part of the meeting. This was moral support big time. Morton himself was reclining like a Roman on his couch, still in pyjamas and dressing gown, sipping Coca-Cola. He fixed me with a gimlet eye. "Herbie, I've asked you to come here to discuss—very frankly, very earnestly, very seriously—the *Scene* set-up. We're not happy with it."

I grinned at him. "I had an idea you weren't."

Morton was in no mood to grin back. "Until now, while we haven't been happy, we've done nothing about it. Oh, we've moved staff around and we've sacked people and we've cut a few corners—necessary corners—on the economic end, but all this has been concerned with the magazine itself, the physical magazine." He sat up and set down the Coca-Cola to emphasise his next point. "But the magazine itself isn't the problem. Between us, you and I, we can ensure the editorial is okay. Now that Beacon have taken over the printing, I don't think we'll have any more problems about print quality. We've got a new designer who's probably the best in Dublin—"

"And the most expensive," Courtney Hutchinson put in gloomily.

"—and the most expensive," Morton agreed. "But you have to pay for quality and we're prepared to pay for good layout. So the magazine isn't the problem. But the company is. The company is losing a lot of money, a *lot* of money. If it goes on losing money, that will be the end of the magazine. And that's something none of us wants." He stopped to allow me to nod encouragingly, then said, "What we want from you is to know where the trouble lies."

[136]

I was treading on dangerous ground, and I knew it. "That's a tall order," I said.

"All right. Are we agreed the trouble isn't editorial?"

It was a rhetorical question. I was in charge of editorial. "I could hardly disagree about that."

"Fine," said Morton, "but everybody else says *Scene* is a first-class magazine, so the trouble isn't editorial. Is the trouble circulation?"

"Partly," I said.

"No," Morton said firmly, "because we lie about our circulation. And we're believed. The agencies think we're selling 20,000 copies every month and they book space on that basis. If we were *actually* selling 20,000 there would be no difference in the revenue coming back from advertising."

"But there would be a difference in the profit coming from sales," I put in.

Morton looked at me in surprise. "We don't make a profit on sales."

I blinked. "Don't we?" I knew the profit calculation had dropped since the door-to-door experiment, but I assumed there was still a healthy margin.

"No. I thought you knew that. We never have done and now we're being printed by Beacon we lose on every copy sold. So the problem isn't circulation, whatever you thought. All right then, is our problem the basic concept of the magazine—is that concept bad?"

"No."

"No," he agreed. "Then is the problem the administration or the management? Are Courtney and myself at fault? Or the team in Dublin? Or…" He paused for a beat, then spat out furiously, "…is there some one single bastard screwing up the whole business?"

He was gunning for Norman, of course. I put on my blankest expression and said, "You mean the advertising manager?" If there was one absolutely fireproof person in the entire organisation it was Diarmuid MacFeeley.

I was gratified by Morton's stunned expression. "Why would you say that?"

I opened my eyes wide and said disingenuously. "I suppose if we're not getting enough advertising, you would naturally think it might be the advertising manager."

He realised I was jerking him around and got to the point. "Ivan is very much against Norman Ames," he said. Ivan was Ivan Hanak, the in-house accountant of Morton Newspapers and titular business manager of *Scene*. He drove to Dublin once a week with a float of petty cash and a look of grim determination on his face. *Scene's* books seldom balanced and Norman's profligate attitude to money drove him batty.

"I know," I said. "But I don't think Norman Ames is the problem." By this time I'd grown extremely fond of Norman, whose enthusiasm for life went a long way towards keeping my anxiety neurosis at bay, but my comment did not arise out of loyalty. It occurred to me Norman *couldn't* be the problem since he no longer did very much except drive me around Dublin and complain about the Irish.

"You're wrong," Morton said bluntly. "Ames is the problem and we're convinced of it. Am I right, Courtney?"

"Oh, yes," said Courtney without a second's hesitation. "Sack the bugger. If it does nothing else, it'll save us his salary."

"And a bloody good saving too," Morton said.

I was wondering why they'd bothered to invite me to the meeting, since they had clearly decided on their course of action in advance. "Listen," I said. "Can I make one thing clear. I want to go on record as saying that if you sack Ames it won't make any difference at all to *Scene*. After he goes, you'll still have your problem and you'll still have to find out what it really is."

"Noted," Morton said. Then, to Courtney Hutchinson, "Then that's settled. We go down Monday and sack Ames."

I made a brief stop at a country phone box after I left Lurgan and called Norman. He took the news with an eerie calm. "What are you going to do?" I asked him.

"I expect I'll think of something," he said. "How are Helen and the kids?"

I got up early on Monday not to miss the fun. Watching from my office window I saw Norman arrive around 10.30 a.m. Morton's Rolls Royce pulled up half an hour later. Word went round the office at once there was an important meeting going on. Around 12.30 p.m. my internal phone rang and Norman's voice said tonelessly, "Can you come down? We're in the advertising office."

I went down. The office door was open and the three of them were standing inside. Norman was wearing his impassive Buddha face. Courtney Hutchinson looked confused. As I closed the door behind me, Morton said, "Herbie, we have had a very lengthy and very earnest discussion about the future of *Scene* and we have come to some important conclusions about the running of the magazine. We want you to be the first to know about them. From now on Mr Ames is in sole and complete control of everything here. He will have full and final responsibility and authority for every department. Including advertising."

As the Rolls Royce pulled away, Norman offered to buy me lunch. Over cannelloni and a passable Chianti, I asked him how he did it. "I simply persuaded them I was indispensable," he said.

On the way back, I discovered Norman had fired Diarmuid MacFeeley. "When did you do that?" I asked him, astonished.

"Just before we left for lunch. You may recall you waited at the door while I went back."

"I thought you went back for a pee." He had disappeared for perhaps two minutes.

"I didn't need a pee," Norman said.

"What did you say to him?"

"I'm terribly sorry, Diarmuid, but you're fired."

I let it sink in for a moment, then said, "Why?"

"We're not getting enough advertising. Advertising was Diarmuid's responsibility. It seemed the obvious thing to do."

"So who's going to sell advertising—you?"

"Good God, no," Norman told me. "I've promoted Carlos."

As my working life became increasingly surreal, life at Furness grew more magical. I foolishly told my landlord, Pierce Synnott, about my experience of the faerie horses and he excitedly insisted I repeat the story to members of the local archaeological society when they visited Longstone Rath. (I can still remember the utter blankness on their faces.) Thereafter, I became one of his curios. He made a point of introducing me to all his house guests, and since he was a man of extraordinary social connections, I met some interesting people. Among them was Hilda Morgan.

The name meant little to me as we shook hands, but Hilda Morgan turned out to be Hilda Campbell Vaughan, the distinguished Welsh novelist and poet. Her literary career began in 1925 with the critically acclaimed *The Battle to the Weak* and ended, thirteen novels later, with *The Candle and the Light.* When I met her she had more or less retired from writing—'Except for a little poetry, dear.' She was also, she said, still missing her husband, Charles Langbridge Morgan, an equally distinguished playwright and novelist, who died in 1958. With such a high-powered literary background, Pierce reckoned, without irony, we would have a lot in common. Despite the considerable imbalance of this viewpoint, Hilda and I did hit it off extremely well, although we talked less about literature than we did about ghosts. She was a handsome, grey-haired woman with a gentle voice and upper-class English accent that carried not the slightest hint of her Welsh origins; and in a very short time I decided I adored her.

One Sunday afternoon she was eating cake in my living room when she said, "I had rather an unusual experience yesterday. Would you like me to tell you about it?"

When I first arrived at Furness, Major Synnott mentioned two features of the estate—the rath where I subsequently saw the faerie horses and the twelfth-century church. The rath had been my first interest, but I wasted no time in exploring the church as well. What I found was the roofless shell of a wholly charming little building, a highly unusual blend of Norman and Saxon styles, with several interesting architectural survivals. It nestled beside the remnants of its ancient graveyard in a clearing in a wood. Beside it was a narrow stream and another, very curious, feature: a stone-lined pool some four feet deep and perhaps fourteen feet square. It was colloquially referred to as the 'monks' swimming pool' and though bone dry for decades, there was still clearly visible a system of channels and locks that would have allowed diversion of the stream to fill it.

On the day before our conversation, Hilda had taken herself off for an afternoon walk to the rath, which she found as appealing and atmospheric as I did. Her route back took her into the wood and past the ruined church. "You know that odd little pool, of course—I believe Pierce calls it his 'monks' swimming pool' even though it doesn't have any water. Well, as I approached it *did* have water and there was a wood nymph sitting on the edge, bathing her toes."

"A what?"

"A wood nymph, dear."

"How did you know she was a wood nymph?"

"Well, she was wearing a short green tunic that left her legs bare and she was very pretty."

"And there was water in the pool?"

"Definitely. She was sitting with her feet dangling in the water."

After a moment I asked, "Did you say anything to her?"

Hilda looked a little shocked. "Good gracious, no—it wasn't my place to speak to such a spiritual creature."

"So what did you do?"

And Hilda, whose genteel upbringing had taught her the important things in life, said, "Well, it was almost four o'clock, so I went on down to the main house to take tea."

The estate's propensity to trigger visions eventually caught up with the arch-cynic Major Synnott himself, who tended to treat any account of the supernatural as an opportunity for humour. I answered a thunderous knocking one morning to find him on my doorstep looking so pale and upset I thought for a moment he must be ill. But he declined my offer of a whisky (which convinced me something must be *seriously* amiss) caught his breath in a chair and blurted out that he had just taken Penny and Holly, his two terriers, for their morning walk. I waited, wondering what on earth was coming.

"We were walking through the woods by the church," he said, "when the dogs raised a rabbit and took off after it. I shouted at them—didn't want them to get caught up in a hedge—but they ignored me. Then I heard a sound and turned around and there was a little brown man sitting on a tree stump behind me."

"Brown man?"

"Brown clothes. Brown boots. Sort of thing workmen wear. Cloth cap. Or was it a hat? Brown anyway. Just sitting there, looking up at me."

I suppressed a smile. "What did you do?"

"'Fraid I got rather excited and shouted at him in Irish—*Erin go Bra* or some such nonsense. Waved my arms about a bit. Trouble was, that attracted the attention of the dogs and they came running back, barking. I was afraid they might frighten the little man and I turned round and shouted at them to stay away. When I turned back, he'd disappeared."

There was a long silence between us. I was finding him hard to read. I believed Hilda Morgan absolutely when she told me about the wood nymph, which is not to say I necessarily believed a wood nymph had been physically there. The detail of the water in the empty pool suggested a visionary experience, like my view of the parkland overlaid on Eileen Boyd's séance. By now I'd read enough literature on the paranormal to be convinced that certain places and/or situations were capable of triggering visions in sensitive people. Clearly Furness was one of them. But I wasn't sure I trusted Pierce. He found my interest in the supernatural immensely entertaining and was not above attempting a practical joke. As against that, he still looked like death.

Eventually I said, "You're telling me you saw a leprechaun?"

Pierce suddenly realised that was exactly what he had been telling me and stomped out, muttering to himself. He never mentioned his experience again, either to me or, so far as I could find out, anyone else.

While those around me were experiencing spontaneous visions at Furness, I was quietly getting on with my own esoteric experiments. Jim and Judy Henry visited again, and I took the opportunity of inviting Judy, who was an excellent hypnotic subject, to attempt an astral projection to the ruined church which, at that stage, she had not seen. She agreed, reported finding the ruined church and gave a reasonable, if limited, description of its surroundings. But it was a description that included a great many inaccurate details: that is to say, details of features that had no physical counterpart. Interestingly, Arthur Gibson had provided two inaccurate details of his own in his description of Furness House interior: he 'saw' a guest who was not present and he placed a distinctive fire-screen in a different room to where it actually was…although, curiously, in a room where it had once stood. So was Judy actually projected to the church? My guess at the time was that she was not. But then Judy offered to lead us to the place she had seen and did so in pitch darkness, even though the pathways were far from obvious even in daylight. A few days later, while still our guests, Jim mislaid Judy and sought my help in finding her. We wandered the estate calling her name and finally found her sitting in the old church. She was facing a wall and deeply in trance.

It was about this time that I expanded the scope of my hypnotic experiments. I was interested in the theory of reincarnation and had come across a technique known as *regression*. Regression began as a legitimate psychiatric tool to enable patients to recall repressed traumas. Typically the psychiatrist would place the subject in trance and suggest he or she was travelling back in time to re-experience their childhood. When the suggestion was accepted, a little careful guidance was usually all that was needed to unearth the target trauma.

Experimentation showed that regression was genuine: that is to say, it produced actual memories rather than fantasies. When regressed to an early age, subjects typically adopted the limited vocabulary of that age and might even begin to speak in a childlike tone. Personality changes occurred. Behaviour patterns become those of the suggested age level. If a drawing was requested, it showed a childlike technique. Handwriting changes often conformed precisely to handwriting samples produced by the subject when he was actually of the age suggested. In one experiment, a twenty-years-old woman regressed by stages, switched the chalk to her left hand when it was suggested she was six years old. She was, it transpired, born left-handed, but forced to use her right hand once she entered the educational system. The phenomenon of changed handedness has been seen quite frequently in regression experiments and has arisen spontaneously in cases where the subject had no conscious memory of ever being left-handed. In such cases, parents or older relatives usually confirmed the regression results.

Once the technique has proven its usefulness, a nineteenth-century French practitioner named Albert de Rochas embarked on controversial waters by using it to search for traumas experienced by patients while still in the womb. Since memories sometimes arose before the nervous system of the foetus was formed, many of de Rochas's colleagues refused to accept them as genuine. But this did not stop him experimenting further by regressing a patient *beyond* the womb. The patient—and several others who followed her—reported what appeared to be memories of past lives. In the twentieth century, a British psychiatrist named Alexander Cannon showed the phenomenon was widespread by regressing some 1,400 of his patients into what appeared to be past life experiences. I was also aware that several less academically respectable researchers had used hypnosis for past life research and could hardly wait to get started myself. All I needed was a suitable subject—ideally one who lived locally so that any past lives could be fully explored and, if possible, be confirmed by historical research. One possibility was Sheena Power-Smith, whose family home was literally five minutes' walk from Furness. Sheena's grandmother, Molly Ellis, had something of a reputation as a psychic, and like most of the Power-Smith family, Sheena herself was interested in esoteric matters. When she discovered I was searching for someone to take part in a regression experiment, she volunteered at once.

The experiment proved only a limited success. Sheena was a reasonably good hypnotic subject and regressed satisfactorily, but her only recall was of a life as a Tibetan hermit—something impossible to pinpoint in terms of a date, let alone verify with historical research. It seemed I would have to wait for a more evidential subject before I went much further with my study of reincarnation.

In the meantime, I decided to expand my astral projection experiments. And this time, instead of using the hypnotic techniques of psychical research, I was determined to try a purely magical approach

With Diarmuid gone, the staff of Scene consolidated into a tightly knit little group of plotters and schemers of which I was happy to consider myself a member. Norman, Walter, Fitzie, Carlos and I all liked one another, all admired one another, and all considered ourselves capable of making the magazine a success if only Morton would give us a great deal more of his money, then leave us alone. In fact he did neither, and between us all we ran the magazine aground.

The problem was we didn't know what to do with it. Everyone in the group held with Norman's theory that the secret of success was a higher circulation. Even Jim Morton bought into this idea eventually. But the financial haemorrhage made him impatient—unsurprisingly, since Scene was no longer being underpinned by Morton Newspapers Ltd., but by his own personal money. The impatience communicated a sense of urgency that made us silly. On any given issue of the magazine, we would debate endlessly, then decide on a circulation-building approach. But if it didn't work immediately, we switched to another. Thus Scene metamorphosed month by month from a general interest magazine to a half-assed man's magazine to a fashion magazine to a woman's magazine to a glamour magazine to a travel magazine and finally, in a moment of extraordinary desperation, to a homes and gardens magazine ('Ireland's Guide to Better Living.'). We even printed one issue with two covers and half the content upside down relative to the other half. Carlos was particularly happy with that one, pointing out that if newsagents could be persuaded to display both covers, we potentially faced a doubling of our circulation as people bought duplicate copies under the impression they were buying different issues.

The result was that readers never knew what sort of magazine they would be getting one month to the next. Neither did advertisers. When the woman's magazine issue came on stream, I forgot to tell Carlos who arrived in triumphantly waving an advertising order for Jockey Y-fronts. In desperation, as the crisis deepened, Jim and Ann Morton left their comfortable home in Lurgan to take a flat in Dublin so Jim could devote his entire time to Scene. There was no doubting his commitment.

A few weeks later, I walked into Norman's office without knocking and caught him trying to hide something underneath his desk. "What are you up to?" I demanded at once.

"I thought you were Jimbly," Norman said as he pulled out a draughtsman's board and laid it on his desktop. "What do you think?"

On the board was a paste-up of a classy magazine cover, but the magazine was not *Scene*. The masthead announced it as *Executive,* Ireland's New International Business Magazine. "What is it?" I asked.

"Insurance," Norman told me tersely. "I'm no longer certain *Scene* will make it with all this interference."

"So you're planning to launch a new magazine?"

"There's room in the market," Norman said. "All we've got is *Business and Finance* and that's a weekly. *Executive* will be an aspirational business magazine for up-and-coming middle management. Power dressing...where to buy silk suits...male cosmetics—that sort of thing."

"Who did the mock-up for you?" It was far too good for one of Norman's cut-and-paste jobs.

"Fitzie. Did it free in return for shares in the new company. When it's incorporated. You'll be editor, I'll be publisher, Walter will take the photos, Carlos can sell ads. Should be a lot easier for him with a targeted publication."

"I don't know anything about business journalism."

"That doesn't matter," Norman said.

"Why didn't you tell me?" I was slightly miffed that he'd handed out shares without handing them in my direction.

"I wanted to impress you with Fitzie's layout."

And so, as our publisher lost confidence, our backer threatened to pull his support, our circulation dropped like a stone, and our advertising revenues shrivelled, we decided to have a party.

I was at the meeting where Norman brought it up with Jim Morton. His rationale was that *Scene* did not have a sufficiently high profile among Dublin's advertising agencies, something that would be cured if we invited all the senior executives to a really memorable party. Providing it was done properly, it would be a sure-fire investment. He was certain that when the ad men got back to their offices, impressed by the magazine's sophistication, orders would come flooding in.

"What was that all about?" I asked him afterwards.

"I was bored," Norman said. "I just wanted to see if I could sell Jim Morton something."

Trouble was, he sold the idea too well. After an initially slow burn, Jim Morton took fire to a degree where he could think of nothing else. In another of the interminable strategy meetings, we wasted the better part of a morning trying to decide on a venue.

"We need," Morton explained, "a really novel setting. I'd been thinking of hiring the Gresham or the Shelbourne, but the agency boys are too used to those places. What we need is something novel, with atmosphere."

"How about the Old Cod?" Carlos suggested.

Morton looked blank. "What's that?"

"It's a restaurant. They have it in a cellar."

"A cellar? Now that's the sort of thing we need. Somewhere with bags of atmosphere. Has it got bags of atmosphere, Carlos?"

Carlos was impressed by Jim Morton. He was especially impressed by Jim Morton's car, which he referred to as the 'gold Rolls Royce.' "Oh, yes," he said. "It's all done up with fishing nets and that sort of thing. Food's good too."

"Sounds ideal," Morton said. "Would we have trouble getting it?"

Carlos shook his head. "No—I know the owner. Very decent bloke: he writes books."

The owner was a man named Eric Burdick, who distinguished himself by writing a novel called *Old Rag Bone* with the most depressing ending I have ever read. In an earlier issue of *Scene* we reported how he'd had the bottle to turn down a movie offer, only to be rewarded by a higher one. He was, as Carlos said, a very decent bloke.

"Ah," said Morton, "literary connections. This gets better and better. What do you think, Mr Ames?"

"I was thinking of the Martello Tower," said Mr Ames.

Despite my literary pretensions, I had never read Joyce and thought the Martello Tower was the new roof restaurant at the Intercontinental Hotel. It seemed surprising Norman would make such an unimaginative suggestion. But Morton's eyes lit up. "Great idea, Mr Ames, but we'd never get it."

I decided I had to be wrong about the Intercontinental. "What's the Martello Tower?"

"Joyce's tower—the place he used to live," Norman told me. "It's the setting for *Ulysses.*"

"Where is it?"

"Sandycove, Dun Laoghaire. Just past the Mirabeau. It's been preserved by the Tourist Board or somebody. They open it to visitors during the summer."

"Is it open yet?" Morton asked.

"No," Norman told him. "It's too early in the season." He sat back, looking supercilious. "I think it would be worth trying. Contrary to what you may expect, they're not averse to letting outsiders use it. We had it for a photo feature in the early days of *Scene*—no trouble at all."

"A party's very different to a photo feature," Morton said.

"I still think it's worth trying," Norman said.

As indeed it proved to be. When the approach was made to the authorities who controlled this slice of Irish history, they agreed without hesitation, but with certain conditions. They required a substantial donation to municipal coffers. They required special cases made to protect the priceless originals of Joyce's manuscripts from drunken revellers. Because of concerns about the safety of the flooring, they required that the guest list be confined to no more than eleven people.

"How many are we actually inviting?" I asked Norman.

"Forty-eight," he said. Then, as an afterthought, "And a piano-player with his own piano."

Life became one glorious round of party-planning meetings. Costs escalated, but for once Jim Morton didn't seem to care. "We'll have champagne!" he announced recklessly. "Nothing but champagne. We'll serve gourmet food. We'll hire well-known models to mix with the crowd, give it an air of sophistication." But as party night approached and his enthusiasm grew, even champagne, gourmet food, well-known models and a piano player were not enough for him. I had not the slightest intuition in advance, but my career and my esoteric studies were about to cross.

When my internal phone rang, it was Norman at his blankest. "I'm in a meeting with Mr Morton," he said. "Would you like to join us?"

I went downstairs to find Norman staring out the window—a bad sign since it usually meant he was trying not to laugh. Jim Morton wasn't laughing either. He fixed me with his sternest look. "Mr Ames has just been telling me of your occult interests." I glanced at Norman, who refused to meet my eye. "Yes?" I said cautiously.

"I understand you are familiar with the techniques of Spiritualism."

"I've been to a few séances," I admitted.

Morton leaned forward in his chair. "I am prepared to pay you, in cash, a fee of five hundred pounds, tax free, to raise the ghost of James Joyce as the centrepiece of our Martello party."

Clearly, bloody Norman had been feeling bored again. He turned back from the window and blinked at me like a contented cat. Five hundred pounds was a small fortune in the money values of the day, but it didn't even make me hesitate. "You're fucking mad, the two of you," I told them and walked out.

There are tides in the Unseen, according to my first mentor, Ernie Butler, and the success of any magical operation depends largely on their ebb and flow. Since there are five major tides in all—stellar, solar, planetary, lunar and terrestrial—the interactions might seem daunting, but the magical reality is that all extraterrestrial tides influence us by way of the Earth's magnetosphere, so if you understand what's happening there, you can generally afford to ignore the others.

To this day it's difficult to find much information about these tides in the standard textbooks of Western magic—the most you can usually hope for are 'tables of hours' which show fortuitous times for magical operations without telling you why—but the occult traditions of the Orient are a little more forthcoming. In the East, the invisible medium through which the various tides flow is called *prana*—a term that will be familiar to practitioners of yoga and which equates almost exactly to the universal *ch'i* of Chinese acupuncture theory.

To get your head around the theory, think of a vast energy field generated by the sun. Think of the planets, including our own, moving through it. Now think of the planets as having their *individual* energy fields, which influence the universal field and are, in turn, influenced by it. As you know, the Earth continually revolves on its own axis, completing a single revolution in approximately twenty-four hours. At the same time, it orbits the Sun, completing a single revolution in approximately 365.25 days. In combination, these movements set up centres of stress in the pranic and magnetic fields that surround our planet.

I like this sort of thing and am quite capable of droning on for the remainder of the chapter about the various tides generated by these stresses, but for the purposes of my memoir, you only really need to know about one: a steady, positive current that flows perpetually from east to west. According to the Oriental tradition, this tide comprises five different components, known collectively as *tattvas* and individually as *Prithivi, Vayu, Tejas, Apas* and *Akasha*. The terms equate somewhat to the old Western esoteric ideas about the Elements: *Earth, Air, Fire, Water* and *Ether*. But only somewhat. In the West, the Elements were believed to be component aspects of physical matter, often extended metaphorically into areas like medicine and astrology, where they became symbolic of certain *properties*—fiery, earthy and the rest. The tattvas are component aspects of the east-west energy flow, which share, at least to some extent, the same symbolic properties as the Elements. The *Akasha* (Ether or Spirit) element is strongest—and purest—at sunrise, but the tide is a composite of all five elements so that *Akasha* eventually wanes to allow *Vayu* (Air) to become dominant. *Vayu* follows the same pattern, waning to allow *Tejas* (Fire) to dominate. The cycle continues through *Apas* (Water) and *Prithivi* (Earth) until it returns to *Akasha* and the whole thing starts up again.

The concept of *tattva* tides was imported into Western magical practice by the Golden Dawn, which also began to experiment with certain symbols associated with them. The symbols are deceptively simple: an indigo or black egg for *Akasha,* a blue circle for *Vayu,* a red equilateral triangle for *Tejas,* a silver crescent for *Apas* and a yellow square for *Prithivi.* But basic or not, W.B. Yeats maintained that if you pressed one against your forehead, it would trigger inner visions…and those visions would share the elemental quality of the symbol, even if you didn't know which symbol you were using in the first place.

I wanted to have a go at that (when I wasn't calling up the shade of Joyce) but I wanted even more to use the symbols as gateways to the Astral Plane.

My earliest introduction to the term 'Astral Plane' was the occult fiction of Dennis Wheatley. One of his books, *The Ka of Gifford Hillary,* concluded with a thrilling astral chase in which both villain and hero changed form frequently in their attempts to murder and elude each other. As I recall, Wheatley went to no great pains to explain what he meant by the Astral Plane. It was just some sort of immaterial reality where his protagonists went following an 'astral projection.' But clearly the sort of astral projection Wheatley talked about wasn't anything like my bathroom experience, nor like the descriptions given by Sylvan Muldoon. According to Wheatley, once you came out of your physical body, you entered a spirit world with some very peculiar laws of physics that allowed you to fly and change shape at will. If this was even remotely close to occult reality, you can see why I desperately wanted to get there. Although Ernest Butler casually mentioned tattva gateways to the Astral in his book *The Magician: His Training and Work,* he neglected to explain how they worked. Now, however, I had progressed far enough in my magical training to have discovered the secret for myself.

The technicalities were relatively straightforward. The first thing I did was make myself a set of five tattva cards: *Prithivi, Vayu, Tejas, Apas* and *Akasha.* Each card was four inches square and plain white. I painted the relevant symbol on one side using acrylics I borrowed from Helen, then sealed them, on her advice, with clear varnish. They were my first magical implements, and I was delighted to find the little deck looked suitably impressive. (It would have been more impressive still—and considerably bigger—if I'd gone on to make composite tattvas. It was, apparently, possible to use gateways in which one symbol was superimposed on the other, but the literature I consulted suggested these could lead to 'astral complications'—the last thing I needed on my first trip.)

I had a moment of hope when Helen advised me on the artistic technicalities, but she backed off immediately when I suggested she might like to take part in the magical experiments. So I made a silly joke about sending out a St Bernard if I wasn't back in an hour and retired to my study alone.

I began by trying out the Yeats experiment of pressing a card to my forehead. Sure enough, the silver *Apas* made me think of the sea, but since I already knew it symbolised water, this was not the most impressive of demonstrations. I tried selecting a card at random, then pressing it to my forehead without looking at the symbol, but this was only a limited success: the thoughts that arose sometimes seemed appropriate to the card, sometimes not. It quickly occurred to me there was also a problem in deciding what constituted an 'appropriate' thought stream. If I thought of the moon, for example, did this relate to *Prithivi* because the moon orbits the Earth, or *Vayu* because the moon is up in the air, or *Apas* because the moon influences the watery tides; or is thought of the moon a complete miss, having nothing at all to do with any of the tattvas? Even an absolutely positively definite hit might not mean much, since there was a one in five possibility it would occur by sheer luck. I grew increasingly irritable about these unexpected difficulties, but eventually soothed myself with the realisation that I was embarking on a magical operation, not an experiment in psychical research. In any case, the forehead business was something of a diversion. What I really wanted was to reach the mysterious Astral Plane. I decided to stop messing about and get on with it.

In order to use a tattva card as an Astral gateway, I was instructed to make myself comfortable, relax as fully as possible, then stare fixedly at the symbol on the card until it developed a halo effect. On a whim I picked *Tejas* then sat in an armchair, positioned a reading lamp to illuminate the card, relaxed as best I could—my heart was thumping with excitement—and stared at the card. Despite my high stress level, the halo effect did indeed develop, and in a relatively short time. Although I did not know it then, much of the astral gateway technique relied on optical reflexes and was entirely automatic.

When the halo arose, I flipped the card so I was looking at the back. After a second or so, the optical reflex cut in again and I was looking at the *Tejas* symbol in its complementary colour, a curiously luminous green. I transferred my gaze to the white ceiling and the glowing green triangle appeared there as well, but much larger.

Now came the tricky bit. I closed my eyes and *interiorised* the symbol. That's to say, I drew it in, so to speak, until, instead of watching the optical reflex (which, of course, appeared external) I was watching a *mental picture* of the symbol. Having interiorised it, I was then required to exteriorise it again, pushing it outwards and enlarging it, so that I was imagining a six-foot-high green triangle shimmering in the air directly in front of my chair. After my years of visualisation training, this did not prove particularly difficult. I waited until the gateway stabilized, then attempted the projection: the idea was to move imaginally out of my body and through the triangle.

The result was disappointing. When I passed through the gateway, I found myself standing on a basalt apron in a barren volcanic landscape, battered by extremes of heat and watching ruby lava flows cut glowing streams across the ground. Directly behind me, the green triangle gateway hung unsupported in mid-air, ready for my return. I took a few tentative steps, examined the environment more fully and saw that it conformed in all its aspects to the fiery character of *Tejas*. I turned and walked through the gateway, back into my study. As I did so, I remembered a curious exchange that took place when I was being interviewed as a potential initiate of the Society of the Inner Light:

"I think that's about all we have to ask you," said the young Secretary whose name I can no longer remember.

"Do *you* have any questions?" Mr Chichester asked.

He meant, of course, did I have any questions about the Society, but I was not at all sure at that point whether I would be accepted for initiation and was determined not to pass up this opportunity to quiz a high-grade magician. "What's the Astral Plane?" I asked him promptly.

Chichester managed to look taken aback and scornful at the same time. Eventually he said, "It's an old term for the realm of the visual imagination."

I hadn't really understood him at the time, but I certainly understood him now. My first heart-pounding astral trip, my first wholly magical 'astral projection' had been little better than a day-dream, no better at all than my training visualisations. Was that it? Was that all there was? Were tattva cards just an excuse to go wool-gathering?

It never occurred to me I might be doing something wrong. It never occurred to me that the experiences of others might not be identical to my own.

Soon after I first met him, Norman Ames introduced me to his fiancée, an extraordinarily attractive Irish girl named Una Brennan. As we exchanged initial pleasantries (and marvelled at the coincidence of our names) I could not shake off the feeling I'd seen her somewhere before. Then I remembered. The pilot issue of *Scene* had run a photo feature headed *Ireland's Designing Woman* about the foremost children's-wear designer in the country. The face that stared out from the printed page was the same face that was smiling at me now.

Una, whom Norman called *Win* (as do I to this day), had rheumatic fever as a child and spent eight years bedridden before getting up to start her own business. She had a talent for classic design and her company soon began to export children's-wear to the United States. As a result, she made selling trips to New York two or three times a year where she would charm buyers from Saks Fifth Avenue and similar stores. Win usually made these trips on her own, but on one of them she was accompanied by Norman. The cover story was moral support. The reality was that he was trying to raise money to launch *Executive*. While he was away, Jim Morton sold *Scene* to the Creation Group.

The first I heard of this development was when Morton arrived in the *Scene* offices trailing Hughie McLaughlin, Creation founder and managing director. Hughie was not a particularly small man, but he had the look of an elf about him. Rumour had it that he ran out of money in the early days of his business and had to face an irate works staff demanding to know when they would be paid. Hughie arrived at the meeting leading a greyhound, which he tied to the nearest press. "See that dog?" he told the assembled men. "If it wins tonight, you'll have your money in the morning." Morton announced the sale with an economy of words and made the introductions.

"I want you to stay on," Hughie told me at once. "Come round and see me one of these days and we'll have a bit of a chat. Just drop in—you know where we are—I'm always around the place somewhere." He distracted himself by staring at a calendar above my desk, which showed a young woman in a bikini: not exactly hard core, but racy enough for Ireland at that time. Then he pulled his eyes away and said, "When's this fellow Ames due back?"

"He'll be away at least another week," I said to Morton's visible surprise. I had inside information on Norman's movements.

[154]

"Well, be sure to tell him to come and see me," Hughie said. He looked briefly back at the calendar girl then said, "I'll have to run on, Jim. Nice meeting you, Herbie. Don't forget to drop round for a chat."

Jim Morton, who was clearly relieved to get *Scene* off his pocketbook, took me out for the best celebratory lunch money could buy (his words) and we ended the day in the Intercontinental Hotel, replete with food and saturated with liquor. When we parted, I found a phone box and called Win who'd arrived back in Ireland the day before, leaving Norman in New York talking to financiers. "Listen very carefully because I'm drunk. Jim Morton's just sold *Scene*. Can you get in touch with Norman?" As it turned out she couldn't. Norman had departed for Boston without giving her his new address.

While we waited for him to get back or get in touch, I paid a call on the Creation Group for my little chat with Hughie. He told me he was planning to amalgamate *Scene* with *Creation*, a glossy monthly woman's magazine edited by his wife. "Have lunch with me and you can meet her," he said.

Nuala McLaughlin was one of those highly polished women who have a major relationship with their hairdresser. She and Hughie seemed to argue all the time; until, that is, they crossed the road together and held hands as unselfconsciously protective of each other as children. On the far pavement, the hands were released and the arguments started up again. After lunch, Nuala disappeared to have her hair done, leaving Hughie and I alone together in the restaurant. "I want you to keep her under control," he told me. "You'll be listed as joint managing editors, but between me and you, you'll be the boss. She doesn't care about editing anyway, so she won't give you any trouble. Stick in a bit of fashion to keep her happy. Most of the time you won't see her. Are you all right with that?"

I left him feeling dazed.

After that, things happened simultaneously quickly and slowly. I could get no sense at all out of Hughie about the technicalities of magazine production. One day he wanted to leave the printing with Beacon Press, the next the magazine was to be printed at Creation Group HQ. He changed his mind twice about amalgamating *Scene* with *Creation*. My fellow managing editor seldom appeared in the office before 2 p.m. and left soon thereafter for her hairdressing appointment. On one rare occasion when we shared a cup of coffee, she told me to 'leave Hughie to her' after I tried to unburden my problems. As a result of their pillow talk, he called me in a few days later, told me Morton had been paying me 'nothing at all' and promised me a raise of £1,000 a year—an unheard-of sum in those days. But when I tried to engage him about the magazine itself, he wandered off to solve some problem with his printing presses. As a result, we missed the deadline for the next issue. Nobody seemed to care.

Since the *Scene* offices had turned into a mausoleum—Norman was still in the States, Walter was out building up his freelance business, Carlos was desperately looking for another job, Mary and Hilary were long gone, Diarmuid had been sacked—I spent a couple of uncomfortable weeks checking in at the Creation Group each morning, chatting with Hughie's secretary (who was a darling), failing to get hold of Hughie, wandering the corridors, then going home just after lunch. It sounds like money for old rope, but it was driving me absolutely batty. One day I bumped into Fitzie and we went for an early afternoon drink. "You're looking for another job, aren't you?" he said.

Until that moment I hadn't realised I was, but I heard myself say "Yes" without a moment's hesitation.

"Don't take this wrong," Fitzie said. "I know you're an international magazine editor and all that, but there's a job coming up as a trainee junior copywriter in Wilson Hartnell. I can put in a word and get you an interview. It might not be what you're used to, but *Scene*'s not going to last and it will tide you over until something better comes along."

"Get me an interview," I said.

While I was waiting, I started to make preparations for leaving *Scene*. One of the things I did was put together a collection of every issue of the magazine, reckoning that a full collector's set might be valuable one day. Somebody else was thinking much the same way because very soon afterwards I got a call from a representative of Trinity Library. By law, every Irish publication is obliged to deposit one copy of each issue with the Library and Norman, of course, hadn't bothered. Since I no longer cared enough to be diplomatic, I explained to the worried academic that *Scene* appeared to be on its last legs and in my view his chances of getting copies now were slim. The news sent him into paroxysms of anxiety, and he pleaded with me to let the Library have a set of back issues, invoking their historical importance. In the end, I gave him mine after he pointed out that they would be treated as important documents, would not get lost and, as the donor, I would have privileged access to them should I ever need them in the future. He proved to be a lying toad. I made five email attempts to get access to them when I began to write this memoir and was roundly ignored each time.

Norman came back from the States and arrived on my doorstep at Furness carrying a bottle of champagne he claimed had appeared in his car after the *Scene* party in the Martello Tower. I filled him in on what had been happening and asked him what he was going to do. "See a solicitor," he said. "I'm not familiar with the law in these things, but it strikes me that Morton can't simply sell out without consulting his fellow directors, and this fellow director was in the States at the time." Then we opened the bottle and celebrated the fact he'd found some dim-witted American industrialist prepared to invest $20,000 in *Executive*. I would have broken the man's arm for the cheque, but Norman had played it cool. "We might manage a little better from Morton," he told me, smiling. I thought it was a joke and smiled back.

Just short of a week later, the phone rang while I was rattling around in the Wellington Road offices. I recognised Jim Morton's voice immediately. "Herbie? Do you know anywhere you can get in touch with Ames quickly?"

"I imagine so," I said. "What's the problem?"

"Something very nasty, Herbie. But I don't want to go into it on the phone. If you *can* get in touch with Ames, tell him I'm calling a board meeting of Scene Ltd for three o'clock tomorrow afternoon and I'd like him to be there."

I hung up and called Norman who promised he'd be there, then, pig in the middle, called Jim Morton back. "How come you can call a Scene board meeting when you've sold *Scene* to Hughie McLaughlin?" I asked him.

"I've only sold him the magazine," Morton told me absently. "The entitlement to publish, subscription lists, booked advertising—that sort of thing. Scene Ltd, the company as opposed to the magazine, is still technically in existence. Did you get hold of Ames?"

"He'll be there tomorrow," I said.

"I want you there as well," Morton said quickly.

"I'm not a director."

"No, but you have shorthand. I want you to take a verbatim note of everything that happens at the meeting. If somebody *farts* I want it on record. You don't think Ames will object to you, do you?"

"I doubt it," I told him gravely.

It was the most exciting development in weeks, and I was back in the office after lunch in loads of time for the meeting. Carlos, who had a fine-honed instinct for trouble, was already there. Jim Morton arrived with Courtney Hutchinson just minutes later. They were both carrying briefcases.

[157]

"Our old friend Ames seems determined to put everybody in the shit," Morton said as he sat down.

"What's happened, Mr Morton?" Carlos asked anxiously.

Morton leaned forward soberly. "When we were negotiating the sale of *Scene* one factor that took some attention was the future of the people involved. I'll not pretend it was our first consideration, but it was an *important* consideration. We wanted to make sure, if at all possible, that you and Herbie wouldn't be left without a job. We managed it. Now old buddy-buddy Ames has gone out of his way to put your jobs in jeopardy." He paused for effect, then hit us with it: "He's seeking an injunction against Hughie McLaughlin to prevent his publishing *Scene* in the future."

"Of course he won't get it," put in Courtney Hutchinson quickly. "Hasn't got a leg to stand on."

"That's hardly the point," Morton said. "The point is now his toy's been taken away from him, he's quite prepared to try something that could land his old friends Herbie and Carlos out in the street. The trouble is McLaughlin can't publish until the court straightens things out. Depending on how long that takes, he could have second thoughts on the whole deal. And that's not good news for anybody."

I had a suspicion there was more on Morton's mind than staff jobs. "How can Hughie back out of the deal?" I asked innocently. "Surely the whole thing's signed, sealed and delivered?"

Morton would never have fallen for it, but Courtney Hutchinson was upset enough to take the bait. "The money hasn't been paid over yet," he said.

There was a bit more discussion before Norman arrived as Dublin clocks were striking three. Carlos let him in then made himself scarce. Norman walked into the office looking like a totem pole in a Chester Barrie suit. He nodded courtly at Morton and Hutchinson, then spotted me and looked momentarily puzzled.

"Afternoon, Norman." I said. "It is my duty to warn you that anything you say will be taken down by me and may be used in evidence against you."

Morton grinned bleakly. "Ivan can't be with us, Mr. Ames. I am proposing that Herbie be elected temporary secretary for the purposes of our meeting to take notes of decisions. I assume you have no objections?"

"None at all," Norman said, sitting down.

I found a notebook and came back to my seat. Morton went round behind the blue steel desk and sat down. "As chairman of the board of directors of Scene Ltd. I now formally call to order this meeting. There is one item on the agenda. To discuss what action, if any, the board of Scene Ltd. wishes to take with regard to one, Norman Ames."

The aforesaid Norman Ames coughed slightly, and Morton stopped, looking up at him. "If you don't mind," Ames said frostily, "I would prefer to adjourn this meeting until I have had the opportunity to consult with my solicitor."

"Are you moving that as a formal proposal, Mr Ames?"

"No," said Norman. "I'm simply saying that I had no prior indication of the nature if the agenda and consequently I would prefer to withdraw and consult my solicitor. I would be perfectly prepared to meet you again tomorrow."

"Mr. Hutchinson and I have gone to considerable trouble and expense to be here today," Morton said coldly.

"I appreciate that. Nonetheless, I feel in the circumstances I should be permitted to consult with my legal adviser."

Morton clearly had had enough of the play acting. "Mr. Ames, I formally move that this meeting of Scene Ltd. carry on now. Have I a seconder?"

"Seconded," said Courtney Hutchinson predictably.

"I'm afraid, Mr. Ames," said Morton triumphantly. "I will carry on this meeting whether or not you are with us. Now, do you still propose to withdraw?"

I thought I caught the ghost of a grin on Norman's face. He was obviously seeing the funny side. But all he said was, "Very well."

Morton sighed and sat back in his chair. "I think for Herbie's benefit I should explain that in formal terms, the board of Scene Ltd. is an entity divorced from the individuals who comprise it. Consequently it is perfectly legal for the board of Scene, as an entity, to consider action with regard to one Norman Ames."

I'd never been in a board meeting before. It excited me and I wanted to talk so I could feel part of it. "In other words," I put in, "Norman Ames is considered a separate entity as opposed to a director of Scene Ltd?"

"That's right," Morton said. "We are at the moment dealing with a Mr. Norman Ames. He could be any Norman Ames as far as the board of Scene is concerned."

Unlike Norman, I couldn't stop myself grinning. "How much of this do you want me to take a note of?"

"Just decisions, Herbie. We haven't made any decisions yet."

I ignored the instruction, of course: one reason why I have such clear recall of the meeting now, after all these years. Morton swung round to face the other two. "As Chairman, it is my duty to report to the board that a Mr. Norman Ames has sought an injunction against Hugh McLaughlin and Creation Ltd. restraining them from publishing further issues of *Scene*. That is my report. Does anyone move any action with regard to this matter?"

Hutchinson, who had obviously been well rehearsed, said, "I move that Scene Ltd. be not involved in any legal action pending between a Mr. Norman Ames and Creation Ltd."

I second that," said Morton. "Is there any amendment?" He looked at Ames, who grunted. "Did you move an amendment, Mr. Ames?"

"No," Norman said.

"Then I declare Mr. Hutchinson's motion carried. I should like to move a further motion that the board of Scene Ltd reserves the right to seek an injunction against a Mr. Norman Ames restraining him from interfering with the operation of Scene Ltd."

"Seconded," said Hutchinson.

"Any amendments?" Morton asked. This time Norman didn't even grunt. "In that case," said Morton, "I declare the motion carried. Thank you, gentlemen. Thank you, Herbie."

Norman looked surprised. "Is that all?"

"Yes," Morton nodded.

Norman stood up, nodded briefly to them both and turned to the door. As he was leaving, he said, "Nice seeing you again, Herbie." The office door closed, and we waited in silence for the outside door to slam. When it did, Morton said, "I've always wondered what that man was and now I know—a French letter full of shit."

There were a few further formalities and one more hideous, hybrid issue, but that, essentially, was the end of *Scene.*

[160]

It was another Northern Irish friend who started me wondering about the nature of imagination. Sam Gordon was an engineer in his early twenties. He came to visit for a few days, managed to get himself laid by one of my neighbours and volunteered for an astral gateway experiment. He was able to use the cards reasonably well, but like myself experienced little more than a peculiar daydream. Since he proved to be a good hypnotic subject, I hit on the idea of having him work with the cards while in trance. This dramatically increased the reality tone of his experience, although not to the extent where he might confuse it with waking reality. He told me it was more like a visit to the cinema: all the colour and sound was there, and you were deeply immersed in the action, but a part of you remained an observer.

I can no longer remember which card Sam used as a gateway, but fortunately I was sensible enough to ask him for a written account of his trip, which he posted to me a few days after he went home. He called it *A Journey from One Place to Another* and the account read, verbatim:

> I am in the desert. There are sand dunes. The journey begins with me on a half-horse, half-donkey animal. I feel half-priest, half-soldier. The street is fairly narrow with Arab-like traders on each side of me. They are selling brass and copper goods, but not to me.

> On my pure white mule, dressed in scarlet and gold and wearing a cardinal's hat, I pass under three arches and then out of the town and into the desert.

> In front of me and to my left is a great pit. I cannot see to the bottom of this, but there is grass and red areas low down. I keep well away and continue on my trip.

> The ground rises towards the horizon. The wind starts up and I am in the middle of a sandstorm. I have an idea that while the storm is on, I'll make time, so I beat the mule with my whip. Soon I realise this is not good at all and I leave the beast alone.

> The storm stops. Below me is a shallow valley with a stream running down the middle of it. To my side, sand and nothing else. On the other side, an area of darker sand supporting some

vegetation. The sand is darker because it is in the shadow of a great white cloud.

In this darker region is a walled city. That's where I'm going. The walls are a muddy grey.

I go down the gentle slope to the river and cross at a wooden bridge. A soldier (Spanish type and armed with a lance) comes my way. Almost half way across the bridge, he steps close to one side and lets me by. I give my mule a chance to munch a few blades of grass, then we have to be on our way.

Guards are at all the gates and doorways, but the mule takes me on. Anyway, everybody clears out of my way (or the mule's) and we step into a white palace or the like after climbing a lot of steps.

On my right and left are two rectangular swimming pools, but I take little notice. There is a greeny tint about the floor here. There are also a few people, but again I take little notice.

I climb many white marble steps. There are red carpets and curtains about. I think I can see the throne, but I am looking for the king. But my journey ends.

I would imagine you are as unimpressed by the account as I was. It seems, on the surface, to stand somewhere between a dream and a fantasy—a stream of consciousness whimsy any one of us might construct given a little encouragement and too much time. Certainly there was nothing in it that related particularly to any elemental tattva Sam may have used. The sand dunes and the desert might be representative of Fire, but the sandstorm was a mix of Air and Earth, while the stream and the swimming pools were obviously Water. If I had handed him a compound tattva, I might have been (moderately) excited, but at that time I had not made anything other than the five basic cards. Sam's journey from one place to another read like a brief subjective daydream. The only thing of any interest was the fact that his experience had terminated so abruptly, and for no apparent reason. It seemed to me that Sam had brought it to an end himself. But he was, at the same time, still in trance and remained so until I brought him out of it. As such, he should still have been amenable to my original trigger suggestion. The trip's conclusion was a puzzle; but only a very small one. While I was not prepared to write off the experiment as a total failure—Sam had visited some internal movie theatre after all—I could hardly see it as a shining success either.

But shortly after he came to visit, Sam joined the Merchant Navy and four months later wrote to me in a state of high excitement. He had landed at some port of call in the Middle East, taken shore leave and found himself, to his astonishment, in an environment that matched, detail after detail, aspects of his vision. This is not to say the environments were identical. For Sam, and indeed for me when I matched his two accounts, it was as if what he had 'seen' in trance was a mix of the physical environment he visited in the Middle East, superimposed on purely fantasy elements. I was reminded of Arthur Gibson's ghostlike projection into Furness House. Arthur had seen the house as it actually was, but somehow overlaid a fantasy figure not present in reality while at the same time subtly changing a small detail of the house as it actually was.

Sam's letter got me thinking about the nature of imagination. Specifically, I began to wonder if there might be more to Chichester's comment—that 'Astral Plane' was an old term for the visual imagination—than I had previously considered. Like most of us, I was culturally conditioned to think of imagination—the curious ability so many humans have to visualise Donald Duck—as a purely subjective faculty, a sort of picture-making mechanism built into our heads. The pictures themselves were nebulous, consciously created, unconsciously triggered or externally suggested, but all the time purely mental constructs bearing no more profound relationship to reality than a photographic image does to the thing it represents.

But perhaps Mr Chichester's astral definition meant I should be looking further than the daydream. It occurred to me that Mozart heard symphonies in his imagination before he wrote them down, that *War and Peace* flowed through Tolstoy's imagination before it streamed onto the printed page, that every worthwhile work of the creative arts had its taproot in somebody's imagination. It occurred to me imagination was the same mechanism that creates the vividly immersive worlds of our sleeping dreams, the transcendent visions of the mystics.

And now the evidence I was gathering seemed to suggest there might be more to it than that. Arthur's out-of-body experience, which may or may not have involved some sort of energy body, certainly *had* involved an overlay from his own imagination; and might even have been a particularly vivid manifestation of his own imagination from start to finish. But if the latter, it showed that Arthur's imagination was capable of accurately imaging details of a physical environment he had not previously seen. And if the former, it showed his imagination could intrude on aspects of the physical reality he was visiting while in an extruded state.

Furthermore, if I accepted Sam's account of his Middle Eastern port, it appeared that *his* imagination had linked with an objective physical environment, incorporating it into his visionary experience. Or alternatively, his imagination may have been capable of mocking up partial 'memories' of an environment that lay four months in his future.

Sam himself leaned towards this latter possibility and put forward a suggestion that would allow us to test it experimentally.

I interviewed for the junior trainee copywriting job in Wilson Hartnell Ltd and was apologetically offered a starting salary that was close to double what I was being paid to edit *Scene*. Hughie McLaughlin took my departure with good grace and brought out no more issues, combined or otherwise. He once mentioned he had bought *Scene* 'for buttons' and I half suspect he may simply have wanted to kill off competition. Certainly he never showed much heart for publishing the magazine.

Like many journalists, I looked on the advertising industry as parasitical, unprincipled and bursting at the seams with pseuds. I viewed my new job as a sell-out of my creative principles and vowed it would be as temporary a stop-gap as I could make it, even with its massive salary. In the event, I discovered I'd come home. I loved advertising more than weekly journalism, more than feature writing, more than editing. Most of the attraction was the people, who were highly intelligent, sparky, irreverent and creative. Two of them, my copy chief Brian Martin and the agency's creative director, Nick Van Vliet, were even interested in the occult.

I took to the work like a duck to water. The initial arrangement was that I would undergo a six-month trial, passing all my work through Brian, after which (if I proved satisfactory) I could drop both the *trainee* and *junior* from my job description, achieve permanent status and receive a pay rise. In actuality, the process took two weeks. Brian decided he was fed up rubber-stamping my submissions, told management I was a natural, increased my income to unimaginable proportions and took me out for a celebratory lunch with Nick Van Vliet. The conversation must have turned to matters weird and wonderful because all three of us skived off for the afternoon to Nick's place where he introduced me to the *I Ching*.

The book he took down from the shelf was in Dutch, but that didn't matter because the *I Ching* is not a work you read like a novel, but an oracle you consult. Nick consulted it on my behalf, promising translations on the fly. He asked me for a single, serious question, then manipulated a bunch of dried yarrow stalks in a sequence of sub-divisions and tallies that went on for fully twenty minutes. When he had finished, he consulted the book and gave me the answer to my question. I no longer recall either, but the impromptu consultation was the start of a love affair. I asked if the book might be available in English. Nick recommended the Wilhelm/Baynes translation, which I bought mail order that same evening. In those pre-internet days, it took almost three weeks to arrive, but I have the copy still, sharing shelf space in my library with the version I wrote myself a very great many years later.

The Magical I Ching was brought out by Llewellyn Publications in the US to mark the new millennium. Their reader seemed surprised to discover my version of the oracle actually worked.

Tradition claims that the *I Ching* is the oldest book in the world. It is certainly the oldest of the Chinese classics. There is controversy about its origins. Academic theory holds it developed out of a prehistoric practice of augury in which bones were heated and the cracks interpreted. I prefer the traditional explanation which begins with the Emperor Fu Hsi staring up to the sky in order to contemplate the mode of heaven, then down to the ground to examine the matters of earth. 'Thus,' says an ancient text, 'did Fu Hsi obtain the measure of all things.' How he did this was to create specific symbols for concepts that were ancient even in his day. From time immemorial, the Chinese had seen the universe—including the world they lived in—as governed by change, moving in a perpetual cycle from potential to actual and back again. Within this cycle, at any given time, events always comprised a duality: a part that was changing and a part that stayed the same. The part that changed was characterised as *yang*. The part that stayed the same was seen as *yin*. What Fu Hsi did was represent *yin* and *yang* as broken and unbroken lines, *yin* expressed as – – and *yang* as —. In so doing, he laid foundations for an oracle.

You can see how it might work at a very simple level. Suppose you decide *yang* means yes (which indicates things will change) while *yin* means no (which suggests they'll stay the same). All you need now is some way of generating the broken or unbroken line appropriate to your situation. Once you have it, your oracle will give answers. The Chinese had the interesting idea that random events partook of the essence of the moment when they occurred...as did any question asked at that moment. Thus tossing a coin might help you generate the relevant line; or, in the days before coinage was invented, heating an old tortoise-shell until it cracked would do the same job: an unbroken crack represented the answer *yes*, a broken one gave the answer *no*. Or nearly. The Chinese mind is subtle—too subtle to think in terms of simple yes or no. Change is the essence of every event, and nothing is absolutely certain. So when you ask your simple oracle whether or not you should embark on a specific course of action, the answer was never strictly *yes*, but rather *time for action*, never strictly *no*, but rather *not yet*; and either one could, would and must change in relation to the ebb and flow of change itself. Furthermore, there are obviously a great many questions that do not lend themselves to simple yes/no answers, nor even time-for-action/not-yet answers. So the Chinese began to extend their basic *yin/yang* principles of change. The word for change itself, which embodies the *yin/yang* duality, was *I*. When written down, the component parts are represented by the ideogram for 'sun' combined with the ideogram for 'moon.' So as well as meaning *time for action,* the unbroken *yang* line could also mean the sun—which allowed it to represent sunlight, daytime, wakefulness, action and heat. Conversely, the moon character *yin* might represent darkness, night-time, sleep, rest and coolness.

Once you start to think like an Ancient Chinese, it's surprising how far you can take this. If one unbroken *yang* line means 'heat' then two such lines must logically mean 'very hot' (heat upon heat). By extension, the same two symbols could be taken to mean the very hot season of the year—summer. Two *yin* lines would stand for winter, of course: cold upon cold. And you could generate the remaining seasons just as reasonably. Spring is a time when the cold of winter gives way gradually to the heat of summer, so the broken *yin* line would reach upwards to a second, unbroken *yang* line, while a reversal of the symbolism gives you autumn.

So the single lines of Fu Hsi's original invention first became double lines then, by 1150 BCE or thereabouts, evolved into treble *yin/yang* lines (trigrams) as the oracle sought to answer increasingly complex questions. At this point, a provincial governor named Wen Wang got hold of them. He was in jail at the time, incarcerated by a jealous Emperor, and consequently had both the time and the motivation to improve on Fu Hsi's creation. As a result, the trigrams grew to hexagrams. Wen's son, the Duke of Chou, pitched in to add extensive commentaries and the oracle became known as the *Chou I,* or *Changes of Chou. Chou I* is the old name for what we now call the *I Ching.*

The full *I Ching* comprises sixty-four six-line *yin/yang* figures known as hexagrams with a judgement on the question asked and an image of the overall situation attached to each one. Each line of each figure has the potential to change into its opposite, producing a new hexagram in the process, thus modifying and enlarging the original answer. The result is an oracular system of considerable complexity.

"Does it work?" I asked Nick while he was counting my oracle.

"Difficult to say," he told me.

Carl Jung was less reticent. He asked two questions of the coin oracle and made this comment on the answers:

> Had a human being made such replies, I should, as a psychiatrist, have had to pronounce him of sound mind…Indeed…I should have had to congratulate [him] on the extent of his insight…[22]

But he went on to warn, 'The *I Ching* does not offer itself with proofs and results; it does not vaunt itself, nor is it easy to approach.' He certainly had that one right. When my copy arrived, it might as well have been Nick's Dutch edition. The language was flowery, obscure and often totally opaque. Yet despite the difficulties, I was drawn to the oracle like a magnet. I went out and harvested some yarrow, then dried the stalks in the bottom oven of our Aga. I taught myself the counting ritual, which was simple enough, though time-consuming. I learned how to use three coins as a fast track to the same result. Yet the result was not always—indeed not often—comprehensible. What, for example, was I to make of: *A jug of wine, a bowl of rice with it; Earthen vessels simply handed in through the window—there is certainly no blame in this?* At the same time, a single piece of advice turned up again and again: *Perseverance furthers.* I did not know it at the time, but I was experiencing one of the most curious of all the phenomena associated with the *I Ching*—its ability to present you with the answer you need…even when it is not the answer you request. I persevered. Some oracles seemed relevant, some did not. Some were clear, some obscure. Gradually, very gradually, I came to realise what was going on.

The first thing I figured out was that the *I Ching* was not a method of fortune-telling, even though it is used for that purpose throughout the Orient. Its structure did not lend itself to direct questions like *What numbers do I need to win the Irish Sweep next week?* And when I tried subtle workarounds (like asking for omens on each horse in a race, for example) the results were inconclusive or confusing. Eventually the oracle presented me bluntly with hexagram 4:

'It is not I who seek the young fool;
The young fool seeks me.
At the first oracle I inform him.

22   C. G. Jung Foreword to *The I Ching*, Richard Wilhelm/Cary F. Baynes trans. (London: Routledge & Kegan Paul, 1969.)

If he asks two or three times, it is importunity.
If he importunes, I give him no information.'

Then, with a smile on its invisible face, the *I Ching* added, *'Perseverance furthers.'*

Oddly enough, it was the answer that gave me the clue. Until this point, I had approached the oracle as a mystery. Now I realised I was communicating with a *person*, a spiritual intelligence of Chinese origins who had far more experience of the world than I had and consequently far more wisdom. He had no interest in the Irish Sweep or which stupid horse would win at Cheltenham. His eyes were fixed on distant horizons. He was concerned with morality, with destiny, with right behaviour and right paths. I visualised him as a Chinese sage.

I knew how the sage decided on the answers to my questions. Although technically he worked with *yin* and *yang*, what he actually examined was the current state of that other great Chinese duality, *Heaven* and *Earth*, the realm of spirit and the mundane world. Each time I asked a question, he sought to determine how far, and in what way, the two realms were in harmony. That was his sole secret; but it was enough. It allowed him to determine which circumstances were fortuitous and which not. It allowed him to see beyond superficial appearances and offer guidance for the long haul that sometimes ran contrary to short-term benefits. It allowed him to compare the questioner with his evolutionary goal—the *superior man*—and show how a true warrior-sage should act. It allowed him to point out pitfalls, give warnings about actions and inaction. Above all, it allowed him to predict with a real degree of confidence how things were likely to turn out if his advice was followed.

But the sage had one drawback: his vocabulary was limited. While the questions he might be asked were infinite, he could only frame his answers within the limitations of his sixty-four hexagrams, their moving lines and their developments. Furthermore, his hexagrams and their meanings had all been constructed against his own cultural background: which is to say they reflected the concerns and constructions of Ancient China. Consequently some answers were necessarily approximate—the best he could do with a limited vocabulary—and many (perhaps most) answers were obscure because I was unfamiliar with his terminology.

At that time, it never occurred to me there was anything I could do about the limitations of the *I Ching's* vocabulary. The oracle was the oracle, embodying millennia of wisdom, and there was no way I was qualified to extend it. But I did have a way of familiarising myself with the terminology. I began a project that was to take two full years to complete. Each morning, without fail, I asked the *I Ching* the same question: *What are the influences on my day?* Then I threw the hexagram and made a note of the result. Each evening, without fail, I compared the answer I was given with the events I had experienced. In this way, very slowly, I began to understand what the oracle meant when it used particular expressions. Over two years I gained a working knowledge of my sage's vocabulary— not a perfect knowledge, to be sure, but the more I used the oracle, the better understanding I obtained.

My increasing familiarity with the *I Ching* went hand in hand with constant visualisation of the sage. Eventually it became second nature to picture the spirit of the oracle as standing before me each time I consulted him. The exercise produced two interesting developments.

When the French explorer Madame Alexandra David-Neel was camped in the mountains of Tibet, she was visited by an artist she knew vaguely from her time in Lhasa. The man arrived with a weird companion. Behind him loomed a shadowy shape, as if he were haunted by a spirit. I suspect from her various books that Madame David-Neel was quite prepared to believe in ghosts, but she found something particularly odd about this one. When she inquired of her artist friend, she discovered the 'creature' was a Tibetan deity with whom he had a special affinity. For years he had visualised and meditated on the deity, painted its traditional representation scores of times. As a result, he had created a mental image of the entity so powerful that it could, under certain circumstances, be seen by others. Such mental images were known and accepted in Tibet, where they were called *tulpas*. Several years after I began my visualisations of the spirit of the *I Ching,* a psychic asked me who the old Chinese man was standing by my left shoulder. Later, two others—one of them my present wife—independently asked the same thing. I would speculate that they thought they were seeing spirits, but my own belief is that my constant use of the oracle produced a *tulpa*. The image took material form when my wife discovered a wooden Chinese figurine in an antique shop. "That's the figure I can see standing behind you," she told me. The wooden figurine now watches over me in my library as I write.

The second interesting development was that my visualisation solved the problem of the oracle's limited vocabulary. When the written word produced answers I could not understand, I eventually realised I had the option of calling up my *tulpa* figure and asking him directly.

[170]

Once when Nick and Bea Van Vliet were in holiday in Sweden, Bea was on a sightseeing tour when she noticed a family of trolls squatting by the side of the road. Over dinner that evening, she mentioned it to Nick and couldn't understand why he did not believe her. It transpired that Bea thought trolls were a race of Scandinavian pygmies and it took an encyclopaedia to persuade her she'd seen something paranormal. I met Bea later in the afternoon of the *I Ching* consultation. She was a plump, dark-haired woman in an eye-popping mini-skirt, wife of Nick, mother of Oscar and, as it turned out, a remarkable psychic. She and Nick promised to visit early in the New Year.

During Christmas week, Helen and I spent some of our new-found advertising wealth entertaining friends; and of an evening, a group of us embarked on an experiment known as *pathworking*. The technique is often referred to as a 'guided meditation' but might be more properly called a guided *visualisation*. There are two main types, both involving a group leader. In the first type the group leader describes a (usually archetypal) journey which the rest visualise carefully and in detail as the story unfolds. In the second, the leader sets the scene, then permits the group to decide where they wish to go within it and what elements unfold. Within this second type, individuals may be required to follow their own visualisations silently, eyes closed, before returning to an agreed point on the leader's command; or, alternatively, the group may work as a unit, describing and agreeing on their visualisations as they go along. I was introduced to pathworking in the Society of the Inner Light, which used a specific form as a standard introduction to certain of their rituals. Our pre-Christmas experiment used the first of the two main types of pathworking with myself as leader, and was based on an aspect of the Qabalistic Tree of Life. Afterwards some members of the party took a moonlit stroll to Longstone Rath.

Early in the New Year, Nick and Bea arrived, had lunch and demanded a tour of the rath. As we strolled towards it across the fields, they peppered me with questions about its prehistoric history and use. Since I was conspicuously short of answers, I suggested—not entirely seriously—that somebody should try psychometry.

In psychology, *psychometry* is an alternative term for *psychometrics*—the science of measuring mental capacities and processes. In Spiritualism, psychical research and some forms of magical practice, it carries a very different meaning. In this secondary sense, the term was coined by an American scientist named Joseph Rodes Buchanan in 1842. Professor Buchanan developed a theory that all things gave off an emanation so that 'the past is entombed in the present, the world is its own enduring monument.' In any experimental investigation of the theory, the idea is to discover facts about an event, or person, by touching inanimate objects associated with them. I was introduced to the practice by Helen's medium friend Eileen Boyd, who told me to hold some object like a ring or a watch to my 'third eye'—i.e. the centre of my forehead—relax, clear my mind, then describe whatever mental pictures might arise. I turned out to be quite good at it. Nick Van Vliet turned out to be even better—and a good deal stranger.

Nick entered the rath alone and climbed the metal fence while Bea and I stood by the entrance. Then he stood embracing the stone, with his forehead pressed against it. After a moment he began to describe his mental visions as they arose. I was expecting a prehistoric landscape or something mythic, perhaps associated with my faerie horses, but clearly Nick was visualising nothing of the sort. In fact I was hard put to figure out *what* he was describing, except that it seemed tantalisingly familiar. After a moment, I suddenly realised why. He was describing the pathworking my friends and I had undertaken just before Christmas. To say I was surprised is putting it mildly—I had not told him of the experiment and he did not know my Northern Irish friends—but what I felt at that point was nothing to what was coming. As Nick continued with his description, Bea leaned forward and whispered in my ear to describe in detail what was coming next before he said it.

"How do you know that?" I hissed at her.

Bea shrugged. "I see it in my mind as he does."

I took the two of them back to my home and suggested we might continue the experiment by embarking on a Qabalistic pathworking similar to the one they seemed to have picked up at the rath. They were both enthusiastic, but as soon as we began, they became violently ill. We broke for a while, then tried again. The same thing happened. Later, one further attempt produced the same results. But Nick was determined and asked if there were any other gateways than the Qabalistic. With some reluctance, I told him about the tattvas. Both he and Bea immediately wanted to try them. I produced the cards, Nick tried to use the Earth square and got sick again. Bea took it from him, failed to make it work, but at least escaped the nausea. Then she tried the Fire triangle…

The Fire triangle proved to be Bea's breakthrough gateway and my first intimation that, for some people, the tattvas did a lot more than provoke daydreams. Once she went through, she all but lost touch with the rest of us and found herself in a dream world with such reality tone that she reported physical reactions to effort and emotion. She also met with a guide who had sufficient autonomy to hold a conversation with her. At one point she found herself in difficulties and wanted to return to normal consciousness but could not find the way. Almost instinctively I told her I would travel through the triangle myself and lead her out. She reported meeting me within her vision and together we returned to the gateway and passed back to the waking state without incident. For some reason, Bea's experience acted as a catalyst for Nick, who discovered he could use the Fire gateway without getting sick. He too had visions of a guide, who led him to a temple apparently dedicated to Anubis, the Egyptian god of the dead, and showed him a hieroglyphic inscription which he translated as *'This is the light.'*

Their experiences fascinated both Van Vliets, but had a particularly profound effect on Bea, who continued her astral journey in a sleeping dream that night and encouraged Nick to make their own set of tattva cards so she could continue to experiment. Within a short time, she had built up so much experience of tattva visions that I was moved to suggest another, somewhat different, experiment. I still had Sam Gordon's letter and report of his *Journey from One Place to Another,* described in Chapter Thirty-Three. Sam was convinced his astral trip had been predictive of the physical journey he later took as a sailor. In his letter, he suggested that if the astral trip were extended, it might predict further ports of call. Now it occurred to me I had found an ideal subject to attempt the experiment. Bea had never met Sam but was more than willing to attempt to predict his future.

Since the tattva gateways did not offer the control we needed, Bea gave me permission to place her in a deep trance—she was, predictably, an excellent hypnotic subject—and lead her step by step through the same visionary environment Sam Gordon had explored. When she reached the throne room, I suggested she continue the journey without further guidance. Bea did so without difficulty and met up with a richly dressed man who clearly wanted to show her something. She followed him into a long, arching gallery from where the man pointed to a brick pathway leading down to a Middle Eastern city situated in a deep valley.

As she watched, the sky darkened and the city changed. The original structures vanished and new ones emerged. Bea drew closer and was able to examine architectural features and wall paintings, which enabled her to recognise the location as Mexico. Sam was at sea while the experiment was conducted, but I received another letter from his next port of call.

It was posted in Veracruz, Mexico.

During my days with *Scene*, Norman suggested I should write a profile of Paul Goldin. I looked at him blankly. "Who's Paul Goldin?"

"Stage hypnotist," Norman said. "Should be right up your street."

I made a few inquiries and discovered Goldin was an extremely popular entertainer in Ireland. His shows at Dublin's Olympia Theatre were sell-outs and he generated endless Press publicity by persuading members of his audience to chase imaginary leprechauns. His performance was billed as 'one step beyond hypnosis' but most of it sounded standard hypnotic stuff: volunteers came up on stage and made fools of themselves. Goldin had just arrived back in Ireland to begin a new run. I called him at his hotel and set up an interview appointment.

The man who walked across the lobby was neatly dressed and relaxed. I took to him at once. He moved onto first-name terms from the off, expressed a willingness to answer even the most probing questions, then threw me completely by asking how much money he would be paid for the interview. With Morton's economy measures in full swing, it looked as if the feature was dead in the water, but when I explained it 'wasn't magazine policy' to pay for interviews, he simply shrugged as if the matter were of no importance and invited my first question. I asked him about his family background, and he told me he was the son of a French surgeon who had followed his father's footsteps into medical school until he realised he did not want to spend his life cutting up patients and switched to psychology instead. He did his Master's at Berkeley University in California and was now living in Hawaii, but planned to move to Ireland in the near future to establish a Dublin Institute of Applied Psychology.

I long-fingered the Institute in order to ask him about his stage show. I'd discovered that public displays of hypnosis were illegal in Ireland and was wondering how he avoided being closed down. "I don't use hypnosis," Paul said blandly.

With volunteers barking like dogs and post-hypnotic leprechauns, it sounded like hypnosis to me. "What *do* you use?" I asked.

"Operand conditioning," Paul told me.

Like most people I was familiar with the term 'conditioning.' Just before the turn of the twentieth century, a Russian psychologist named Ivan Petrovich Pavlov found that if he rang a bell while offering food to hungry dogs, they would eventually salivate at the sound of the bell even when no food was present. He concluded that the salivation response was now conditional on the bell rather than the food. By a glitch in translation, Pavlov's 'conditional reflex' became known in English as a 'conditioned reflex.' How it could make people see leprechauns was beyond me.

When I got back to the office, I looked up operand conditioning and discovered it was an obscure aspect of Skinnerian Behaviourism which held the consequences of a particular behaviour produced changes in the probability of the behaviour's occurrence—as, for example, the consequences of sticking your head in a fire would probably make it less likely that you'd do it again. I began to smell the heady scent of bullshit and wrote a tongue-in-cheek feature that repeated Paul's claims without comment but pointed out the basic research for operand conditioning had been carried out on pigeons. I expected him to be furious, but when the feature appeared, he rang with congratulations and invited me out for a drink.

"You don't *really* use operand conditioning?" I asked somewhere into the second round.

Paul shook his head. "No, but nobody's ever questioned it before. They're afraid to admit they don't know what it means."

"So you're a hypnotist?"

"Yes, of course. But stage hypnosis is illegal in this country, so I have to pretend it's something else."

"How do you get away with it?"

Paul grinned at me. "I did a private demonstration for the Archbishop of Dublin and told him I was using applied psychology. Once you have the Church on your side, nobody contradicts you."

"So you've been running hypnotic shows for years just by claiming you don't use hypnosis?"

"People don't understand hypnosis," Paul said.

"Not even psychologists?"

"*Especially* not psychologists. Professionals are the easiest of the lot to fool. Besides, there's a *bit* of applied psychology involved. Some of my subjects are exhibitionists. They come on stage to act the fool and I take the credit."

"This clinic you're planning to open," I said frowning. "Will that use hypnosis?"

"Operand conditioning," Paul said innocently. "Amazing what you can do with pigeons."

It was, although I lived to regret it, the beginning of a lengthy friendship. By the time I left the sinking *Scene* and settled into my new career with Wilson Hartnell, Paul had opened his clinic in Fairview under a variety of aliases including the Dublin Weight-Loss Centre, the Dublin Relaxation Clinic, the Dublin Executive Stress Clinic, the Dublin Smoking Clinic and the Dublin Institute of Applied Psychology. The two mainstays of his business were weight loss and smoking, with a sideline course in Mental Motivation which promised to get tired businessmen up and running. Several months later, he invited me to visit.

The Dublin Weight-Loss Centre proved to be a low-slung Scandinavian-style building set in its own grounds. It positively reeked of medical exclusivity, an impression reinforced when the door was opened by a wafer-thin young woman in a white coat. Paul emerged from the depths to give me the guided tour.

The reception desk was flanked by a bank of closed-circuit TV screens, something seldom seen outside of science fiction in those days. The waiting room was focussed on a massive television set that looped a commercial for the various courses presented by Paul himself. "This is our consultants' office," he told me as we entered an enormous workspace built around an intimidating glass-topped desk.

"Like...*medical* consultants?" I asked, impressed.

"Just sales people actually," Paul said easily. "You don't need qualifications to call yourself a consultant."

"But won't people think they're meeting some sort of doctor?"

"I suppose they might get that impression." He gave me the famous grin, then sobered. "Actually we do insist on a medical examination before anybody takes one of our courses. We have a panel of doctors who come in when we need them. I pay them three guineas per examination, and they sign a document taking full responsibility for anything that might happen to a patient during treatment."

I let it sink in for a moment. "So you could *kill* them and the doctor takes the rap?"

"In theory. We try not to kill people—it's very bad for business."

"How did you set that up?"

Paul shrugged. "I advertised for doctors. They don't make as much money as you'd think. Most of them are only too delighted to earn a little extra. We have a waiting list to get onto the panel."

There were three treatments rooms: darkened cubicles equipped with vibrating armchairs, closed circuit TV cameras and a state-of-the-art loudspeaker system. The deal was that you made an appointment with a consultant to discuss your problems. (If they involved weight loss, you were weighed first.) The consultant, who wore a nice suit, listened soberly and tried to look medical, then sold you on an appropriate course. If you paid your money up front, it worked out cheaper than pay-as-you-go, but either way you got a written guarantee: if you didn't lose weight/stop smoking/feel better by the end of the fourth week, you got your money back. Once you signed up for a course, you came in once a week and were escorted to a treatment room by one of the skinny, white-coated dolly-birds. Your first treatment included the three-guinea medical examination, after which you sat in the vibrating armchair at a light level that would have done justice to a photographer's darkroom. From this relaxed vantage point, Paul's silken voice put you into an operand conditioned trance and gave you non-hypnotic suggestions relevant to your problem. It sounded like a licence to print money. As a business proposition, I was very much impressed.

Paul took me back to the consultants' office before I left and pulled a newspaper from the desk drawer. "What do you think of that?" he asked, throwing it across. There was a small ad for the Centre ringed in Biro.

I read it through. "It's okay," I said.

"Think you could do better?"

"Yes," I said.

When I went back to the office, I drew up a display ad and got one of the designers to lay it out as a nixer. The illustration was a plump Victorian lady in a spotted bathing suit. Paul ran it in the *Evening Herald* three weeks later and it proved so successful that he offered me a directorship, shareholding and substantial pay-rise to manage his new company.

It took me all of fifteen seconds to agree.

Paul Goldin liked to pretend he had occult powers. He sold a self-published book exposing his own 'mind-power secrets' at his stage performances and in his clinic. He held a séance at the ruins of the Hellfire Club in the Dublin mountains and frightened participants with manifestations of weird sounds and ghostly whispers. He demonstrated an amazing talent for telepathy between himself and his wife, who showed again and again that she could pick up his thoughts, accurately and in detail, over great distances.

It was all nonsense, of course. He presented me with a signed copy of his book which proved to be a pastiche of American positive thinking and the sort of wishing-hard-will-make-it-so theories that were popular in self-help manuals during the late 1950s. The paranormal phenomena at the Hellfire Club séance were all achieved with the aid of a miniaturised tape recorder hidden underneath the table. "Nobody thought to search me," Paul remarked as we read the newspaper accounts together. His liking for gadgets was also behind his telepathic talent. The demonstration was stunning. While we were strolling through the grounds of his clinic, he asked me to write down a random sequence of thoughts, then speak them aloud so he could transmit them telepathically to his wife who was somewhere inside. When we returned to the building, she told me accurately and in detail exactly what I had been thinking. After which Paul showed me the tiny radio transmitter concealed in the fountain pen he'd loaned me to write down my thoughts…"It's CIA issue," he told me, possibly truthfully. "Spies use them a lot in the States."

All the same, there were two areas where my m0agical interests and his insights overlapped. One was his theory of the Witchdoctor Syndrome. He used the term casually while we were chatting about his stage show. I asked him to explain.

"You're as good a hypnotist as I am," Paul said. "I've seen you work. You have a good technique, a lot of experience, and you get results. But you don't get them as quickly or as easily as I do. That's because of the Witchdoctor Syndrome. With my stage show and all the publicity I generate, I'm obviously better known than you and people's expectations of me are far higher. I'm the great witchdoctor. They think I can do things other men can't. Frankly, a lot of the time I don't have to use hypnosis at all. I can do anything they *believe* I can do."

He was right about that. During one of the interminable 'farewell runs' of his stage show, he decided to stimulate advance bookings by announcing that he would demonstrate the art of levitation for his final performance. He issued several press releases and trumpeted the promise from the stage. By the time his final performance came along, he was guaranteed a packed house and peak expectations.

"What did you do—fake it?" I asked him when he told me the story. Stage levitation had been a feature of illusionist performances since the Victorian era.

But Paul shook his head. "Didn't know how. Besides, that needs specialist equipment, and I didn't have it."

What he did instead was put on an elaborate charade. First he announced that the promised levitation would take place as the climax of his show. Then he built up expectations by referring to it at intervals throughout the evening's performance. When the time came for the actual demonstration, he entreated the audience to remain completely silent, since the experiment he was about to attempt was known to be extremely dangerous. He then waffled on for some minutes to the effect that he was well known as a hypnotist and while he used no hypnosis whatsoever in his shows, on this very special occasion, he was going to put *himself* into trance. After which he lay down in the centre of the stage and folded his arms across his chest like a corpse. A stagehand scuttled across with a microphone so the audience could listen to his breathing and his heartbeat. Paul closed his eyes and the orchestra quietly struck up some eerie music.

Paul's breathing deepened and his heartbeat slowed as Paul passed into trance. A softly spoken announcement on the PA system explained that Paul was now about to attempt levitation, that silence must be maintained and that patience was requested, since this difficult feat could take anything up to fifteen minutes. In fact it took considerably less. As Paul knew well, Harry Houdini was the only performer capable of holding an audience for anything remotely approaching fifteen minutes while it waited for something to happen. After a suitably dramatic interval, the sound of Paul's breathing became ragged and his heartbeat, previously so slow and steady, began to elevate. The audience, who had no way of knowing they were actually listening to a pre-recorded tape, became increasingly anxious and restless. The orchestra raised the tension by ramping up the eerie music. As the apprehension reached its peak, Paul suddenly screamed, jerked upright, clutched his chest and collapsed. The heartbeat and breathing on the sound system stopped abruptly. The curtains swept across. An anxious appeal across the loudspeaker system asked if there was a doctor in the house. Minutes later there was an announcement that Paul Goldin had been rushed to hospital after suffering a massive heart attack brought on by the strain involved in levitation. A few days later, the newspapers announced he was recovering.

In fact he'd never been ill. The whole thing was staged to get him out of his promise to levitate and create extra publicity for his show. A private ambulance arrived ostentatiously, but drove him home rather than to hospital where, I imagine, he had a drink and counted his takings. But this example of carefully planned showmanship was not the interesting part of the story. That came later when the 'fully-recovered' Paul met up with several members of his closing-night audience. They told him soberly that just before his 'heart-attack' he had succeeded in levitating almost eighteen inches. They had seen it with their own eyes...

The whole of stage magic is, of course, predicated on persuading people they are seeing something different to what is really happening, but very few realise quite how far this can go. Years later, I discussed the phenomenon with Professor Arthur Ellison, then Vice President of the (British) Society for Psychical Research. He told me of an experiment he had carried out before an audience representing a broad range of professions. He began with a short talk in which he described recent scientific investigation into the power of the human mind—notably controlled visualisation—and asked his listeners' assistance in taking the study further. What he proposed was a cooperative attempt to levitate a vase on the rostrum table using the single-pointed concentration of everyone present. He then explained the visualisation techniques that had proven successful in laboratory experiments and gave the signal for everyone to begin their levitation attempt. After a few moments' concentration, the vase levitated some eighteen inches and hung briefly in mid-air before slowly sinking down again as audience concentration waned. Arthur concluded the experiment by asking each member of the audience to write down exactly what he or she had seen.

When he collated the reports, he found some interesting variations. As police often discover when interviewing witnesses at an accident or crime scene, people seldom agree on details. Some members of Arthur's audience thought the vase had levitated only a few inches, some exaggerated the actual height to more than three feet, some noted that it hovered briefly, some seemed to think it had dropped directly down. But the most interesting reports were handed in by two physicists, both known sceptics about psychical research, who stated categorically that the vase had failed to levitate at all.

The experiment was not what it seemed. Arthur was a retired professor of engineering and had little difficulty in rigging the vase to levitate and hover by means of a powerful electro-magnet. What he was trying to determine was witness reliability. The majority of his audience were interested in psychical research and accepted at least the possibility of mind-induced levitation. The two physicists were sceptics who *knew* it was not possible. Where suggestible members of Paul Goldin's audience persuaded themselves they saw levitation where none occurred, Arthur Ellison's two scientists were literally unable to see levitation when it did.

At the time Paul told me his story, I thought we were dealing with a purely subjective phenomenon—a contrived illusion in which expectation persuaded the senses to return false information. By the time Arthur told me his, my experience of magical practice had begun to make me wonder if his physicists might not be living in a different universe which interfaced only partly with that of the remainder of their colleagues. If that notion was correct, then Arthur's vase both levitated and failed to levitate simultaneously—an obvious impossibility.

But then magical philosophy accepts impossibilities and magical practice seeks to manipulate them. In the years ahead, my interest in the esoteric was to bring me in touch with a great many impossibilities.

The years 1971 and 1972 proved unusually eventful. I published my first book, packed in my job, lost my wife and children, was evicted from my home, met a ghost and received an *I Ching* warning about corpses in a wagon.

The book was *Astral Doorways,* a non-fiction opus I started writing at Wilson Hartnell and finished shortly after I joined Goldin's clinic. It was partly my attempt to make sense of occult teachings about the Astral Plane, partly a report of the experiments I had carried out with Nick, Bea, Arthur, Sam and all the others. Since I had long since been dumped by Curtis Brown—and singularly failed to find another literary agent—I bought a copy of the *Writer's and Artist's Yearbook* to search for a possible publisher. High up in the alphabetical listings was the Aquarian Press, then operating out of Vauxhall Bridge Road in London. Since it expressed an interest in esoteric works, I sent my manuscript and had an acceptance by return. (In my naiveté, I did not find this at all surprising.) John Young, the managing editor, explained that as a small family firm, they could not afford to pay advances. Any disappointment I felt was swallowed up by excitement. I realised that journalism and short stories never really counted. Only a book would hack it. I was about to become a published author.

Astral Doorways came out in February 1971 with a cover that featured the tattva cards, a frontispiece photograph of Longstone Rath, and several illustrations including some sketches of his visions made by Nick Van Vliet. In its first year of worldwide sales, it brought in a royalty of £72, less than I would have made from a single short story if you counted in foreign rights. John Young enclosed a charming letter with the cheque, expressing his hope for more handsome earnings in the future, but I didn't care: I was a published author.

When advance copies arrived, I spent hours re-reading the text, smelling the print, fingering the paper, stroking the cover, admiring my name on the spine. For all my studies and experiments, this was my most magical moment. I was a published author. I posted a copy to my mother and was devastated when she ignored it. I convinced myself the package must have gone astray and wrote to her. She wrote back in a week or two, acknowledging receipt. The book, she said, 'seemed very nice.' Others were more enthusiastic—*Astral Doorways* has been continuously in print for almost forty years now—but their appreciation somehow failed to touch me.

My first book, still in print after forty years.

Indeed, the question of appreciation is one that haunts me to this day. Readers—even reviewers—are often complimentary about my work; a few have even been kind enough to suggest something I wrote has changed their lives, but I find such comments difficult to hear. I feel the reaction is exaggerated, perhaps even ironical; and on the rare occasions when I do accept appreciation, the warm glow lasts for an hour or two at most, after which I manage to forget it ever happened. The reaction became so acute following publication of my *Faerie Wars* in 2003 that I decided on a magical solution and posted a copy to my father, who died in 1944. For reasons best known to the Post Office, the package eventually found its way to a British web-based company who recognised my name on the cover as a one-time customer and emailed asking for instructions. The company was MagicTricks.co.uk.

But despite the small personal setback with my first published book, I decided at once to write another. This one I called *Experimental Magic* and John Young liked it too. I quickly followed through with a third, little more than a booklet really, called *Five Keys to Past Lives*. It detailed five psychological techniques for investigating what purported to be re-incarnatory memories. In an orgy of creative enthusiasm, I began work on a fourth book with a very different slant from the others. The first three had all essentially been how-to books. The fourth was speculative history, investigating an area that had long fascinated me—the interest in magic shown by senior members of the Nazi Party. I called it *Occult Reich*. Despite the departure in style and content, John Young issued me another contract.

> Books are not necessarily published in the order they are written. **Five Keys to Past Lives** came out in late 1971. **Experimental Magic** was published by the Aquarian Press, now moved to Wellingborough, in 1972.

I was still writing short stories, of course. As a result, I built up long-dis-tance relationships with the fiction editors of various women's magazines. Among them was Janice James, an historical novelist who worked for *Woman's Own*. For some reason, Janice took a personal shine to me. She tried to interest TV companies in buying rights to my stories. She encour-aged me to write a comic novel. She came to visit me in Ireland. Most important of all, she introduced me to Murray Pollinger. Murray was the son of Laurence Pollinger, one of Britain's top literary agents. Murray had worked in his father's agency for a time but decided to branch out on his own. He was, said Janice, hungry for new clients and she had taken the liberty of mentioning my name…

Since I had nothing else to show him, I posted Murray a manuscript copy of *Occult Reich* with a letter explaining that it was already sold, but I was working on a new book about the fourth dimension. Murray responded by telling me that *Occult Reich* was fascinating but had been sold to the wrong publisher. Aquarian were esoteric specialists: what *Reich* needed was a mainstream house who could give it the distribution it deserved. He proposed that he persuade Aquarian to release me from the contract, then sell the book elsewhere. I thought his chances were slim but told him to give it a try. John Young proved the perfect gentleman. He accepted the argument that he was not the ideal publisher for *Occult Reich* and released me from my contract without penalty or quibble. Murray promptly sold the book to Futura for a stunning £1,000 advance and subsequently shifted North American rights to New American Library for a good deal more.

Futura, a London publisher brought out *Occult Reich* as a paperback original in 1974.

It was an excellent start and it set me thinking. Since I was a child, I wanted to be an author. I wanted to get up in the morning, walk to my study and write books. When I went into journalism, I thought it was much the same thing; or at least a step in the right direction. In the event it proved nothing of the sort. Advertising was no better, and with my move into the weight-loss business, I had ceased to be a full-time writer altogether. Despite my published books, I was a million miles away from my goal of becoming a professional author. The prospect of leaving honest employment terrified me, but I talked it over with Helen, who was totally supportive, then told Paul I was resigning from his company. He wished me well.

I set up a regular column—*A Man's View of a Woman's World*—with the Irish weekly *Woman's Choice* (ironically published by Hughie McLaughlin) and negotiated a fee that exactly covered my rent at Furness. I increased my output of short stories to such an extent that I saturated the market. There were only a few woman's magazines in Britain at the time and they each ran just one story per issue. As the manuscripts began to back up, I negotiated a serial that guaranteed me regular income for several months. I had a call from an advertising man named Frank Lalor, who was about to open his own agency and wondered if I might be in the market for some freelance creative work. I said yes and agreed a baseline retainer. I woke nervous every morning—a familiar feeling, but this time there was good reason—until the day arrived when I realised the roof was not about to fall in and I relaxed a little. At which point the roof fell in.

Helen announced that she needed to take a prolonged holiday, preferably near New Lands in Hampshire, the headquarters of her White Eagle Lodge. I found her the money (for which, irritatingly, she gave the credit to White Eagle) and she departed with the children 'so I could get on with my work undisturbed.' She had arranged to stay with a fellow Lodge member. Her last words were, "I'll be back in time for Christmas." In mid-December, a neighbour rang me with the news that Helen had bought a car, decided to remain in England and our marriage was over. A few weeks later, Pierce Synnott told me he needed my home to house an estate labourer and handed me formal notice to quit. I rented a gate-lodge on the edge of a country estate outside Dunboyne, in County Meath, moved in my cats and, in the fullness of time, saw my first ghost.

A perk of my rental of Hamwood Lodge was use of a walled garden that formed part of the main estate. In its original outline, the garden dated back, I believe, to the fifteenth or sixteenth century, but had been majorly refurbished in the 19th. It was a delightful spot and I enjoyed it enormously. Thus when my thirty-second birthday rolled around on a cloudless July day I decided to take time off work and do a little reading in the sunshine. At around 11 a.m., I equipped myself with a rug, my novel and a Thermos of fruit juice and repaired to the walled garden. Twenty minutes later, I was reading my book when a young woman appeared from the direction of the main house. She was about my own age, dark-haired and very pretty. For some reason she appeared to be wearing evening dress—or at least fairly formal, old-fashioned attire far more suited to the evening than a sunny summer's morning. I remember thinking there might be a fancy-dress party arranged at the main house and she was a guest trying out her costume.

She strolled across the lawn and when she was a yard or two away, I gave her a bright smile and a big *hello*—with Helen gone, I was a little starved of female company—but she ignored me. She walked past and continued across the lawn until she reached a low box hedge some ten to twelve feet from where I was lying. Then, while I watched her, she vanished. It was exactly like the transporter effect in *Star Trek:* she shimmered, then faded and eventually disappeared completely, leaving a momentary sparkling in the air. I was beyond shock. Hairs literally stood up on the back of my neck. I scrambled to my feet and ran the few feet across the lawn with some mindless idea she must have fallen down behind the little hedge. But she had not. After a moment, with thumping heart, I was prepared to accept I had seen a ghost.

(Or perhaps not. Years later I told the story to the American alien-abduction author Whitley Strieber during a radio interview. He suggested that I had witnessed a time-slip rather than a ghost: the young lady, strolling in the garden centuries ago, had walked through a rift in time, briefly entered my reality, then walked out again. Whitley seldom gets much thanks for this sort of speculation, and I took him less seriously then than I do now. Research has since convinced me that glitches in time, while rare, really do occur.)

[187]

I eventually wrote two books on the subject: *Time Travel: a New Perspective*, Llewellyn Publications, St. Paul, 1997 and *Time Travel*, Faber & Faber, London, 2006.

At the time, my ongoing magical experiments were largely confined to the *I Ching*. My idea of asking for an oracle each morning and comparing it with my experience each evening was producing excellent results. I hoped to learn the language of the Book of Changes and I was succeeding. Hexagram 11, for example, shows Earth (our material world) supported by Heaven. The title of the hexagram is *Peace*, and it promises success, but what it really means is harmony, a rare coming together of Heaven and Earth in which everything is as it should be, in its correct place, and life runs like a well-oiled machine. On the days I drew that hexagram, everything turned golden. Everything I attempted succeeded—and with elegance and ease. In Hexagram 12, *Stagnation*, the positions of Heaven and Earth were reversed; and so were the expectations for the day. Nothing worked properly, enterprises failed, there was neither ease nor luck (unless the luck was bad). On *Stagnation* days, your best bet was to stay in bed.

Peace and *Stagnation* were two very clear-cut oracles, instantly recognisable once you'd lived through them. Other hexagrams generally signalled much more subtle influences, but with close attention to my personal experiences, I came increasingly to know them; and with familiarity came error. It seemed to me that the *I Ching* spoke metaphorically and relatively, as—usually—it does. My error was the assumption that it never spoke literally. Then, one morning, I drew Hexagram 7.

Hexagram 7 is entitled *The Army*. According to the Wilhelm translation, its Judgment (that basic pointer towards what influences are in play) suggests 'The army needs perseverance and a strong man—good fortune without blame.' Thus my day, generally speaking, would involve a comparative degree of leadership, interaction with others, discipline and a perfectly benign outcome, probably without much effort on my part. But the Judgment is only one part of the outlook and need not even be the most important part. In some circumstances, the *I Ching* will note a tension in certain of its lines that will give them an influence superseding all other considerations. This means that against the background of what might normally be considered a fortunate situation, your particular reading could pinpoint specific factors that could lead to a negative experience.

On the morning I drew Hexagram 7, I had emphasised lines in the third and fifth places; and both interpretations had an ominous ring about them. The third line carried the explanation: *Perchance the army carries corpses in the wagon. Misfortune.* The fifth line had a more expansive meaning: *There is game in the field. It furthers one to catch it. Without blame. Let the eldest lead the army. The younger transports corpses; then perseverance brings misfortune.* Although the lines sounded ominous, I was not unduly concerned. I had learned that *I Ching* readings were associated with the mundane nature of my day-to-day situation, where disasters tend to be small and crises manageable. More to the point, I had learned the language of the oracle leaned towards the metaphorical.

By the time I drew this oracle, I was creative director of Frank Lalor's new agency, Lalor and Partners, and while remaining self-employed, I spent a great deal of time each week in the Fitzwilliam Street office and was due there that morning. Traffic proved exceptionally heavy, and by the time I reached the narrow, winding segment of road between Castleknock and Phoenix Park, I was in a line of vehicles that had slowed to a crawl. Oncoming traffic leaving the city was moving normally. As the car ahead of me stopped briefly, a pheasant rattled out of the hedge to my left and flew off over a field, catching my eye for a second. When I looked back, I saw an oncoming lorry, perhaps a hundred yards ahead, swing across the road as if making a right turn. Then people started getting out of their cars and I realised something was wrong.

I left my own car and ran down the road. The articulated lorry was skewed across, effectively blocking traffic. I could see the driver high up in his cab. His face was pale and he was staring blankly into space. In front of the truck was a small family saloon car driven by a middle-aged woman. Beside her in the front passenger seat was a younger woman, heavily pregnant. Their vehicle was partly on the verge. I asked the pregnant woman if she was all right, but she did not reply. Her driver said, "She's all right—somebody's gone for an ambulance." It was fairly clear that the lorry had struck their car, spinning it around and pushing it onto the verge. I wondered about the lorry driver and climbed up to the window of his cab. "You okay?" He nodded without speaking. As I climbed back down again, I saw the second car—a red Mini with a young male driver and two older female passengers. All three were dead.

In the year 2000, the American publishers Llewellyn brought out my own version of the oracle under the title *The Magical I Ching.* In Chapter Four I told the story of this tragic accident and analysed the prognostication I received about it. Some of the points I made are worth repeating now:

» The *only* mention of corpses in the whole of the *I Ching* occurs in Hexagram 7…[and]…during the two years I consulted the *I Ching* on a daily basis, I never saw another dead body. Nor have I seen one since.

» Immediately prior to the accident, a pheasant emerged from a hedge and flew out across the meadow to one side of the road. Pheasants are game birds—there was 'game in the field' as the oracle predicted.

» The hexagram as a whole referred to a situation that was inherently dangerous but could be contained by external discipline. This exactly describes driving a motor vehicle on modern roads.

» The *I Ching* specifically advised, 'Let the eldest lead the army,' suggesting that the eldest of the group take charge of the disciplines needed to meet these dangerous circumstances—in other words, the older person should drive the car. But of the three people in the Mini, it was the youngest who was driving. Did he insist on doing so at the start of the journey? We shall never know if this was the 'perseverance' that 'brings misfortune'. But we do know it was the younger driver who transported the corpses.

It may also be worth mentioning that on the only other occasion I drew Hexagram 7 with mention of corpses, I drove past a road wreck later that day.

My experiments with hypnosis continued; and led me into some strange—even frightening—byways. My interest was theoretical as well as practical and for years I had been reading everything I could find on the subject. It was inevitable that sooner or later I should stumble on reports of telepathic hypnosis. The first I came across originated from an unlikely source—the scientific records of the Soviet Union. It appeared that from around 1924—coincident with Stalin's rise to power—a group of scientists under the leadership of L.L. Vasiliev had experimented with telepathic manipulation of behaviour and induction of pain. Vasiliev himself claimed to have hypnotised a subject more than 1,700 kilometres away, causing him to fall into trance and waken on command.

A little research showed this was by no means the first example of telepathic hypnosis in Russia. In 1818, a professor of physiology at the Imperial Academy in St Petersburg documented experiments indicating that a 'magnetist' could induce trance at a distance simply by the con-centration of thought. Twenty-seven years later, another Russian, Andrey Ivanovitch Pashkov, claimed to have alleviated rheumatoid arthritis in a woman whom he hypnotised at a distance of 300 miles. Even the notorious Grigori Rasputin seemed to be operating in much the same area. Having demonstrated his ability to control bleeding in the young Tsarevich by a laying on of hands, he managed the same trick in a gypsy encampment miles from the Palace by the simple expedient of prayer.

But the most detailed and intriguing report came not from Russia, but from France. It concerned some high jinks at a dinner party in Le Havre in 1886. Among those present were Professor Pierre Janet, the prominent French psychologist, Frederick Myers, the founder of the British Society for Psychical Research, the psychologist Julian Ochorovicz and a local doctor named J.H.A. Gilbert. Dr Gilbert entertained his companions by telling them of a series of experiments he had been conducting with a Spiritualist medium he named as 'Léonie B.' She was such an excellent trance subject that he found he could hypnotise her simply by pressing her hand. But later he realised it only worked if he concentrated at the same time. This led him to the idea it was the thought that did the trick rather than the pressure on her hand. He put his theory to the test and found he could hypnotise Léonie by thought alone with no physical contact.

The others were intrigued by Gilbert's story and began to speculate whether it might be possible to hypnotise Léonie by telepathy there and then. Gilbert agreed to try and went off to his study to concentrate. The remaining five academics scurried off to surround Léonie's home, almost a mile away. As they hid in the shadows, Léonie suddenly emerged from her house with her eyes shut and walked briskly to her garden gate. Then, for no apparent reason, she stopped, turned and walked back in again. (The men subsequently discovered that Dr Gilbert allowed his concentration to waver and dozed off) They waited. Nothing happened and after a few minutes Janet was elected to find out what was going on. He walked cautiously up the path to the house, but as he reached the front door it was flung open suddenly and he was almost knocked down by Léonie as she came out, walking very quickly. (Dr Gilbert had woken up again.) The scholars regrouped and set off in hot pursuit. Although her eyes were again shut, Léonie somehow managed to avoid lamp-posts and negotiate traffic for fully ten minutes as she headed in the general direction of Dr Gilbert's home. But then she stopped dead and looked around with every sign of confusion. (Dr Gilbert had decided the experiment was a failure and started a game of billiards to amuse himself.) The watchers decided not to interfere, and after a short time Léonie fell into trance again and continued on her journey. (Dr Gilbert resolved to give the experiment another try, abandoned his billiards and began to concentrate again.)

With renewed confidence that something was happening, Gilbert went to his front door to see if Léonie was coming. As he opened it, she walked into him with such force that she knocked him to the ground. With her eyes still shut, she actually walked over him and ran through the house shouting, 'Where is he? Where is he?' Dr Gilbert picked himself up and called to her mentally. Léonie heard and answered him. Later, Professor Janet experimented with Léonie and found that he too could place her in trance from the other side of Le Havre just by thinking of her. And like Gilbert, he could call her to him.

Although Léonie's story had farcical elements, it clearly pointed towards the existence of an extraordinary power with implications far beyond the theory of hypnosis I had learned when I first began to study the subject. At the time I came across these curious reports, I believed hypnotic induction was essentially a question of persuading a subject to accept a particular suggestion, then stacking another, slightly more complex, suggestion on top of it. Typically, I would have my subjects fix their gaze on some object set above eye level, then after a few moments tell them that their eyes were growing tired and heavy. Since your eyes would naturally grow tired and heavy if you were forced to keep looking upwards, this suggestion was readily accepted. By accepting the first suggestion, the subject was then predisposed to accept my next (that it was now impossible to keep the eyes open) and so was led, step by step, into trance. But if a subject could be hypnotised telepathically—or even, as Gilbert initially discovered, simply by pressing her hand—it made nonsense of this cautious technique. I determined to find out for myself whether there was anything in the various reports. Fortunately I had a Leonie of my own to experiment with.

Leonie Carstairs was my next-door neighbour at Furness. She lived with her husband Ian in a self-contained, converted wing of the main house and absolutely adored to be hypnotised. More to the point, she was an extraordinarily reactive subject—she proved capable, for example, of reacting to a post hypnotic suggestion *eighteen months* after it was initially implanted. Her trance level was comparable to that of Arthur Gibson. If ever there was an ideal subject for a telepathic induction experiment, it was Leonie.

There is a potential problem with this type of experimentation. Ethically, of course, no one should be hypnotised without their knowledge and consent. But if you tell someone you are about to hypnotise them tele-pathically, the very suggestion (that they are about to be hypnotised) may be enough to induce trance. (Judy Henry, for example, would routinely fall off her chair entranced when I was working on an induction with somebody else.) I called Leonie, discussed what I was proposing to do and asked permission to make the telepathic attempt at a time of my own choosing, over a period of six months, without alerting her beforehand. Once satisfied that I would avoid dangerous situations—as when she was driving a car for example—she agreed.

In the event I made two attempts, both successful. On the first we were alone together, sunbathing in adjacent deck-chairs, both reading books. While Leonie was absorbed in her novel, I merely pretended to be absorbed in mine and mentally began the induction routine I had used with Leonie so often in the past. At the critical point, her eyes closed and her book slipped to the ground. I waited an arbitrary period, then mentally gave her the command to wake up. Her eyes opened at once, she picked up her book and continued reading.

Although I am now quite satisfied that the induction worked, I had some doubts at the time. I thought there was at least a possibility that Leonie, who was relaxed in the sunshine, had simply fallen asleep, then woken spontaneously a few minutes later. Although the odds against the timing seemed high, coincidences *did* happen. I decided on another, less ambiguous, attempt and carried it through, several weeks later, during a noisy drinks party at the Carstairs' home. I made sure Leonie was comfortably seated on a low couch, between two guests, then stood with my back to her at the drinks table and began the induction. Moments later there was a hubbub behind me, and I turned to find Leonie lying on the floor to the huge consternation of those around her. I took the opportunity to test for trance, reassured her worried friends, then brought her telepathically back to normal consciousness. She reacted exactly as if I had spoken aloud.

The implications of telepathic hypnosis are far-reaching and disturbing; and I have been cautious about experimenting with it since then. But I continued to use hypnosis to investigate another of my interests: reincarnation research. After the disappointing beginnings with Sheena Power-Smith, I eventually discovered a much more promising subject in Pan Collins, who was at the time senior researcher with RTE Television's *Late Late Show.*

I met Pan originally while giving a television demonstration of how hypnosis could be used to influence heart rate and other autonomic bodily responses. We got talking and discovered a mutual interest in the theory of past lives. Pan asked if it would be possible to regress her and since she claimed she was 'God's gift to hypnotists', I agreed to give it a try. The experiment took place in Pan's flat under less than ideal circumstances—there was a rock group practicing in the room next door—but she passed into a deep trance quickly and easily. I regressed her to a point beyond her birth, then asked her where she was.

"I am walking along a riverbank."

"Who are you?"

"My name is Cynthia Lambert."

"What year is it?"

"It's the year 1797."

Over the next half hour or so, I elicited further details of 'Cynthia Lambert's' life, including her marriage in a church off Sackville Street in Dublin and the name of the officiating priest. When she emerged from trance, Pan decided there was enough information for her to research whether Cynthia Lambert actually existed. The results proved frustrating. What is now Dublin's O'Connell Street was indeed known as 'Sackville Street' in the eighteenth century, but this was hardly evidential since Pan, like most educated Dubliners, already knew that. A check of parish records and the National Library unearthed various references to Lambert families, but with very few exceptions these followed only the male line—she was unable to find any specific reference to Cynthia. As against that, the church in which Cynthia Lambert was married really had existed on the site she remembered, although it had burned down during the late Victorian era. Furthermore, she had correctly identified the officiating priest.

I found the results of Pan's research convincing, if not actually conclusive, as did Pan for a time. But in 1979, she underwent another regression attempt with the British hypnotist and reincarnation investigator Joe Keeton, who took her back no further than early childhood, then terminated the session because he considered she was remembering the experience from an adult viewpoint. "So I think now that I have never been brought back to a previous existence under hypnosis," Pan wrote in her autobiography, *It Happened on the Late, Late Show.* "Because everything that I have said in any of these sessions could have come out of my own subconscious mind."

Later, however, I was to meet up with a subject whose experience of regression was vastly more detailed and even more evidential than Pan's. In a book I eventually wrote on the subject[23] I referred to her as Pearl D., a convention I propose to maintain here. She approached me originally about a recurring dream in which she tried to cross an ancient arena but collapsed and died on the sand before she could achieve her goal. She had no particular interest in ancient history, nor any explanation for the dream, but hoped I could shed some light on the puzzle. I couldn't; although it did seem possible a dream of this type might point towards an emergent past-life memory. I suggested we try an hypnotic regression. Pearl didn't believe in reincarnation but thought the regression experience might be interesting.

She proved a good hypnotic subject and regressed very satisfactorily, but the first few sessions produced nothing of relevance to her recurring dream. She *did* present what purported to be past life memories, but they were set in the late Victorian period and around the time of the First World War. Pearl herself believed they were fantasies.

Then without any warning, the ongoing sessions took a dramatically different turn. I was using a technique known as 'non-directive regression.' Basically this means the only key suggestion given is that the subject will travel back beyond the point of her birth, then stop. The technique is hit-or-miss in relation to a specific past-life story but is necessary in order

23   J. H. Brennan *Discover Reincarnation* (London: Aquarian/Thorsons, 1992.)

to ensure that the story itself has not been suggested by the regression instructions. Once you work on a specific story, of course, the subject may be validly sent back directly to that story in order to bring forth more details. On the occasion in question, the non-directive technique found Pearl seated beside a tiled mosaic pool, wearing a short linen tunic and surrounded by a large party of friends. Her name, she said, was Andreas and she was 20 years of age.

Unusually for this sort of work, Pearl's identification with the Andreas persona was total. While the sessions lasted, she was unaware of herself as Pearl and believed my questions to originate from a forest spirit. I quickly elicited the information that her mother was Greek and her father, whom she called Ado, the ruler of the country. This did not, however, make Andreas a princess. She lived in a country where the rule of law was paramount. A title—like that of princess—was only partly a matter of birthright and she had to prove her fitness by working with her father in the Law Courts.

Over a series of regression sessions, a comprehensive picture emerged. Andreas was a Mede, living in Xanthus, her country's capital city. She worshipped in a temple that contained a statue of Mithras (although acknowledging other gods) and had received a prophecy of an insurrection that was now taking place. The temple was a small, dark, sparsely-furnished building that might hold a maximum of about forty people—entry to the temple was open to men and women of any rank. There was a fire on the altar and a well set slightly above floor level. Andreas seemed to be psychic: at any rate she reported seeing pictures in the altar fire and hearing spirit voices. The voices told her that her father had been killed in the insurrection.

The earliest regressions found Andreas in her villa on an offshore island which was somewhat isolated from political events so that it was some time before the prophecy was confirmed. Her father had been murdered by his own brother, Pericles, who headed a rebellion of provincial governors then usurped the throne. Pericles' troops eventually arrived on the island. Andreas was seized, brutally beaten and imprisoned. Her underground cell was cramped, wet and filthy. Food was pushed through a hole in the door once a day. After eighteen months of darkness and malnutrition, she developed a lung condition and weakened to the point where she realised she was about to die.

During her period of incarceration, she did have one point of contact with the outside world: a young guard captain who whispered news of what was happening from time to time. One morning, guards came for her. When she was taken outside, she discovered it was already noon. She was blinded by the bright sunlight and unable to walk without help. The guards washed her and untangled her hair, then gave her a fresh tunic to wear. The young captain told her she was being taken to the arena under military escort. When she asked him why, he explained that her uncle's coup had never been particularly popular with the masses and now there was a strong groundswell of opinion against him. Suspicion was growing that he had murdered his brother, not simply replaced him; and there were rumours that Andreas has been assassinated rather than imprisoned as Pericles claimed. So Pericles had now decided to display Andreas in the public arena to prove she was still alive.

Ill though she was, Andreas realised at once the situation presented her with a unique opportunity. Under the laws of the country any public accusation had to be followed up with a full trial, whatever the rank of the accused. She determined to accuse her uncle of murder and treason, hoping that in the trial, the truth about her father's death would come out. Here, obviously, Pearl's regression experience interfaced with her recurring dream and explained why she was so anxious to cross the arena. During the regression in which she recalled her ordeal, she described her last painful attempt to reach the area in front of Pericles' official box where she could make the accusation—and, true to the dream, described how she died before she could do so. There was, interestingly, a brief out-of-body experience during which she surveyed the scene from a height of about fifty feet above the arena before the regression ended.

This was an extraordinary—and extraordinarily dramatic—story; one which I have often been tempted to turn into a novel. But it had one flaw. When I set out to validate its historical details, they turned out, one by one, to be false.

Clearly, the Andreas account was set somewhere in the period of ancient history, so there was no question of the sort of document search that Pan Collins carried out. In such circumstances, the best I could hope for was to find out whether Pearl's story was consistent with any set of genuine historical incidents; and whether the incidental details she gave matched the customs of the time.

I began with Pearl's remark that Andreas (and indeed her father) had been *Medes*. I was aware of a Biblical reference to the notoriously strict 'laws of the Medes and Persians' which tallied nicely with the information that in Andreas' country, the law was above all else. Her comment about fire on the temple altar sounded promising as well: whatever about a Median religion, fire worship was prevalent in Persia at the time and may well have crossed borders. But after that, the investigation nosedived. Medes were, of course, inhabitants of Media, a country that no longer exists, but once occupied what is now north-western Iran, roughly corresponding to Kurdistan, Azerbaijan and parts of Kermanshah. It was probably founded circa 625 BCE with the unification of various regional tribes under King Cyaxares, but while it grew into an Empire, little enough is known about it: no written texts have yet been discovered and very few artefacts. All the same, a look at a map was enough to show that ancient Media could have been nothing like the country Pearl described. Andreas lived in a maritime culture with considerable emphasis on overseas trade. Media was a largely inland region with only a tiny stretch of coastline fronting the Caspian Sea: it could never have developed as a maritime nation, nor is it described as such in the various external references that have survived. Worse still, the Median capital Xanthus simply did not exist, nor did *any* Median capital occupy the sort of geographical location Andreas described.

I was unhappy with the description of Andreas' religious practice as well. Although the fire on the altar might be a lucky hit, I was very well aware that Mithras was a military Roman god associated with bull sacrifice rather than fire worship. Perhaps more to the point, he had an exclusively male following—Andreas would not have been permitted to enter his temple.

There's a lesson to be learned from all this; but perhaps not the obvious one. The lesson is that where you finish up depends on where you start. I started with Media and ended up concluding that the story was a fantasy. Pearl, by contrast, started with Xanthus and opened up a wholly different can of worms. She first found, as I had, that there had never been a Median capital—or, indeed, any Median city—of that name. But then she decided to find out if there had ever been a city named Xanthus *anywhere* in the ancient world. It turned out there had. Xanthus proved to be the old name for Kinik in the Antalya Province of Turkey. Kinik is situated above the mouth of a river—now known as the Koca, then also called the Xanthus—as Andreas described during one of our regression sessions. The whole of Antalya Province is located on the Mediterranean coast of southwest Turkey between the Taurus Mountains and the Mediterranean Sea. It once encompassed ancient Lycia, a maritime culture with a long stretch of coastline and considerable focus on overseas trade: enemy countries sometimes referred to Lycia as a nation of pirates.

In 540 BCE, a bloody war left Lycia a vassal state of the expanding Persian Empire, colonised and administered by Medes. Sometime around 400 BCE, the current Lycian ruler (a Mede) was overthrown by his own brother, following a rebellion of provincial governors. The brother was named Pericles and he ruled for some eighteen years. Andreas seemed to have been right about her country's religion as well. Although Roman and martial in its later manifestations, the Mithraic Cult actually originated in Persia, where it involved fire worship and was open to both men and women. Archaeological evidence indicates that Mithraic temples were always very small and invariably incorporated a raised well in their structure.

In short, the regression of 'Pearl D' produced a story, set in a particularly obscure period of history, that was internally consistent and evidential in its detail.

I moved from Dunboyne to Dublin, then Killiney, then bought a cottage outside Monasterevin, which I rebuilt, extended and refurbished to create a thatched house so picturesque it was constantly photographed by Japanese and German tourists. In the process, I met the philosopher and master thatcher, Paddy Malloy, who once said to me thoughtfully, "Now you and I, Herbie, are not superstitious men. But all the same, don't you find yourself looking for the second magpie?"[24]

The second magpie has haunted me for most of my life. Are the omens real? At what point does coincidence become...something else? When you investigate magic—or engage in psychical research for that matter—you quickly come up against the Trickster Effect, named for the old Norse god Loki and his fellow Trickster deities worldwide. You will find indication after indication that magic actually works, then, just as you are teetering on proof positive, there is a giggle from Valhalla, life flips over, and you find indication upon indication that magic is all nonsense. After which—that giggle again—the positive evidence begins to accumulate once more. No one helped me gather more positive evidence than Dolores Ashcroft-Nowicki.

> At the turn of the Millennium, I ended up writing a book with her: *The Magical Use of Thought Forms,* published by Llewellyn, St Paul, 2001.

My first contact with Dolores came without warning or fanfare. I picked up my post one morning to find a letter with a Jersey postmark. In it, she explained she was a former Initiate of the Society of the Inner Light (SIL) and now director of studies of an organisation called *Servants of the Light* (a.k.a. SoL) which had grown out of the Helios Course in Practical Qabalah. She had enjoyed my *Astral Doorways,* come across my address as a Helios student and decided to write. I sent back a polite response, thanking her for the kind words about *Doorways* and asking her about SoL. She wrote back, I wrote back, she wrote back, and after a while she came across to visit. (There was no question of my reaching the Channel Islands. With my fear of flying, I could think of no circumstances that would ever persuade me to leave the island of Ireland.) The meeting was to prove another of life's turning points.

24   There's a superstition in Ireland that seeing a single magpie is a bad omen, while spotting two is good: *'One for sorrow, two for joy...'*

Meeting Dolores Ashcroft-Nowicki was to prove
another of life's turning points.

In the sort of weird coincidence that has plagued our relationship for decades, Dolores began writing her autobiography the same day I started this memoir. I can guarantee her book will make fascinating reading, but before you rush out to buy your copy, here is a brief flavour of the woman we are dealing with:

Dolores Ashcroft-Nowicki was ten years old when the Nazis invaded Jersey. Her parents promptly evacuated to mainland Britain and ended up in Liverpool. It proved a jump from the frying pan into the fire. Liverpool was a strategically important location in the Second World War. Over ninety per cent of all the war material brought into Britain passed through its eleven miles of quays; and the German's knew it. As a result, the city became their second most important bombing target after London. As Dolores settled into her new home, Liverpool suffered more than 300 air raids before the end of the year. More than 400 people were killed over just one three-day period due to direct hits on air-raid shelters. At the peak of the blitz, 681 Luftwaffe bombers were overhead and a total of 2,315 high explosive bombs were dropped. The north of the city suffered enormous damage and loss of life. Whole swathes of streets simply disappeared. The Huskisson Dock was destroyed when a German bomb triggered 1,000 tons of explosives in the hold of the *SS Malakand* at anchor there. The explosion was so violent that some pieces of the ship's plating were found almost a mile away. The British Government played down the damage for propaganda purposes, but by the end of the war more than 4,000 Liverpudlians had lost their lives, twice the number killed in Birmingham and three times that of Coventry. Many thousands more were injured. The 10-year-old Dolores spent night after terrified night in the air-raid shelter.

One night, listening to the crump-crump of the approaching bombs, she found herself…elsewhere. The shelter itself was at the back of the houses where her family had been billeted by the War Office. It consisted of a concrete base and four walls, just two bricks in thickness, with another layer of concrete for a roof. Inside were wooden benches and nothing else. During one particularly bad raid, Dolores was sitting with her head in her mother's lap, fingers in her ears; when the noise died away, her fear began to subside, and she could no longer feel her mother's arms around her. She lifted her head and found herself in an entirely different place. She was standing on a plateau surrounded by high, snow-covered mountains. Sparse, stunted bushes grew here and there and though she did not feel it, she knew it was extremely cold. Seated around a campfire in a silent circle was a group of orange-robed figures. One raised his head, smiled and indicated that she should take her place in the circle.

When Dolores told me the story of her vision many years later, she recalled that she seemed to stay for hours soaking in the silence, the peace and, above all, the companionship of those around her. Nothing was said and she eventually returned to consciousness in the air-raid shelter as the all-clear sounded. But she was to return to the plateau on other occasions when the bombing was particularly bad or her fear particularly high.

The last German raid on Liverpool took place on January 10, 1942, when the Luftwaffe managed to destroy the house where Hitler's nephew was born. On the final visit to her snow-bound plateau, Dolores was silently directed to observe the mountain background as if to fix it in her mind. She was also informed that it had once been part of her life and she was among friends who could be called on when the need was great.

(Over thirty years later, she described the strange outline of the mountains to her spiritual teacher, W. E. Butler. He got up to fetch a book from his library and opened it at a picture of high, snow-covered mountains. They were instantly recognisable. Butler explained that in this area there had been for centuries a Lamasery of a special kind, and that it still existed. She had, he told her, been given protection to safeguard the immature mind from excessive trauma and that she was by no means the only one under such protection.)

Dolores survived the war and took training as an actress at the Royal Academy of Dramatic Art. But alongside her career ambitions was a growing interest in magic. When she called at the old Aquarian Press store in Vauxhall Bridge Road to pick up a Tarot deck for her mother, there were some second-hand books on the shelves, and among them she discovered a Medieval grimoire. She was leafing through it when a hand fell on her shoulder. "You don't need that. You need this." She turned and the shop's proprietor handed her a copy of a little book entitled *Magic, Its Ritual Power and Purpose* by W. E. Butler, the same slim volume that had awakened my own interest in the Western Esoteric Tradition. Like me, it pointed her towards the Society of the Inner Light. But thereafter, it took her in a very different direction.

Dolores proved to be one of those people like Madam Blavatsky or Dion Fortune who seem larger than life until you get to know them... then *still* seem larger than life. We got on extremely well, but the second or third time she came to visit, she seemed oddly ill-at-ease. "I want to tell you something," she said eventually, "and I'm not sure how you'll take it." She looked out of the window for a moment, then turned back looking sober to the point of misery. "I don't know how to say this. You might think I'm mad."

"Try me," I said.

Dolores had an Indweller.

I looked at her blankly: it was the first time I'd heard the term and since she was obviously uncomfortable about talking at all, I did not want to stop her by asking for a definition. So I waited, and a peculiar story unfolded.

When Dolores and Michael, her husband, applied to train with the Society of the Inner Light, they asked if it would be possible to meet with W. E. Butler, who was then a member. Warden Chichester insisted they finish the course before they would be allowed to do so. As a result, their meeting was postponed for four years. But in 1969, Dolores walked down the laneway to Little Thatches, Ernie Butler's Tudor cottage, and met her mentor for the first time. He was 71, a small, unassuming man with diabetes, an impish sense of humour and an encyclopaedic knowledge of the occult. Although nothing seems to have been formally discussed, Dolores promptly took him as her guru. So, when they met a little later, did Michael. Michael was working for BEA at the time, so the couple had access to low-cost flights and used them frequently. Essentially, Ernie took over where SIL left off and became responsible for their continued magical training. During their discussions, Ernie sometimes mentioned someone called 'The Opener.' Dolores quickly realised he was talking about an Inner Plane being, a term that may need a little explanation.

Novelists are familiar with the phenomenon of the run-away character—the hero or heroine of a story who simply will not do what s/he's told and ruins a perfectly good plot by going his or her own way. Everyone is familiar with the experience of meeting people in dreams who are perfectly capable of holding conversations or taking actions as independently as they do in waking life. Despite this autonomy, most authors and dreamers cling to the idea that they create and control their cast of characters, albeit—and especially in the case of dreamers—at an unconscious level. Jungian psychology begs to differ. Jung held that there is a level of the psyche that is *not* created by the individual: he named it the *Collective Unconscious*. Within the Collective Unconscious are entities—called archetypes—that have, to all intents and purposes, an independent existence. These entities are capable of walking into a patient's dreams or fantasies and wreaking havoc, offering information or stimulating healing. Magicians like Dolores (and myself for that matter) are in there punching with the Jungians. But while Jungians think of archetypes as expressions of particular psychic patterns, magicians think in terms of much more rounded beings: spirits, angels, devils, even gods. And while Jung discovered only one Collective Unconscious, magicians believe there are multiple Inner Planes, each one existing within (or at least contactable by) the human mind, each one inhabited by various entities. And that's not to say such beings necessarily *live full-time* on the Inner Planes. They can sometimes have physical bodies—in the Himalayas or the house next door or orbiting some distant star—but their consciousness *functions* on the Inner Planes...as, to some extent, does yours and mine.

So Ernie Butler thought he was in contact with a spirit, perhaps a ghost, perhaps an angel, perhaps a guardian, perhaps a god, but in any case some form of being he referred to as 'The Opener.' It was clear to both Dolores and Michael that he considered this creature his spiritual Master, his teacher of the esoteric arts. For someone (comparatively) new to magical practice, the idea of learning from a shade who floats inside your head might have taken some getting used to, but Dolores was completely enamoured of Ernie and would never have dreamed of questioning anything he told her. But if there was ever the slightest hint of a lingering doubt, it dissipated one day on Haverstock Hill.

It was about a year after their first meeting. Dolores and Michael flew in from the Channel Islands to take Ernie Butler to a ritual meeting of the Society of the Inner Light. Butler was not a well man by this stage. His diabetes was progressive and age was taking its toll. His wife worried about him constantly and Dolores and Michael had slipped gently into the roles of minders. The trio arrived in London and had lunch together in an Indian restaurant. (Butler had spent several years in the Far East and still retained a taste for blistering curries.) Then, since it was too early for their meeting, they sat on a bench at the top of Haverstock Hill to admire the view and pass the time. Ernest was talking to Michael when Dolores abruptly became aware of a tall, male presence beside and slightly behind her right shoulder. The creature told her bluntly, "I want you to tell Ernest that you will take on his work after his death. Tell him I am The Opener."

It was an embarrassing message. Nobody wants to talk to a sick old man about his death and Dolores tried to avoid it. The entity insisted and kept following her until she agreed. Ernie took the news calmly but wanted to know the identity of the creature. Dolores knew all right but didn't know *how* she knew; and was in any case reluctant to say. Ernie proved as insistent as the mysterious Opener, and eventually Dolores gave in. "He's the Opener of the Ways!" she blurted. "He's Upuaut. He's Anubis." She meant the Egyptian god, who takes the form of a jackal or, sometimes, the form of a man with a jackal head. Ernie accepted that news calmly too. "You took your time coming," he told her.

Dolores eventually discovered there are four broad levels of contact with Inner Plane entities: 1. ESP—You need to be a natural psychic for this one. The contact is hit-or-miss, like a poor phone connection, and can produce intermittent communications but little more. 2. Mind touch—This usually requires an experienced receiver, although children are sometimes open enough for a mind touch to take place, in which case they frequently report playing with an invisible companion. In adults, the contact will usually take a traditional form—god-form, angel, guardian or the like. The adult receiver instinctively 'hears' and understands. 3. Overshadowing—Here the entity becomes the constant, or near-constant, companion of the receiver, hovering nearby (so to speak) within easy calling distance. 4. Indwelling. With this form of contact, the entity actually 'moves in' to the extent that s/he takes up a permanent piece of mind-space, like renting an apartment. For most entities, polarity is a prerequisite—a male entity can only indwell a female and vice versa. For all entities, compatibility is necessary: the receiver must have a persona that resonates strongly, perhaps exactly, with that of the entity. The relationship is non-exclusive—a bodiless entity is generally capable of indwelling several hosts simultaneously.

For Ernie, the contact with his Opener was a strong overshadowing. For Dolores, who had the requisite feminine polarity, it was an indwelling. Time passed. Ernie became increasingly ill until he was no longer able to maintain the contact in any form. In 1978 he died, leaving Dolores to carry on his work as director of studies of SoL, now a flourishing international esoteric school. By this point, Anubis was in permanent residence, pointing the way, offering new knowledge and advice.

Dolores looked at me anxiously as she finished her story.

I wanted to make sure I'd understood her properly. "You're in contact with a god from Ancient Egypt?"

"Yes."

"Who's living in your head?"

"Yes."

"Passed on to you by Ernie Butler?"

"Yes."

"Can he speak through you, like a Spiritualist medium?"

Dolores frowned. "Well…yes, I suppose. If I went into trance…"

"Have you done it in public?"

She looked shocked. "Brought him through in trance? Good heavens, no. Oh, no. No, definitely not."

"Have you told anybody else about this?"

"There's Michael, of course…" Dolores said uncertainly. "I mean, I don't exactly boast about it. You tell people you're indwelt by Anubis and they think you're mad." She hesitated, then added, "Do *you* think I'm mad?"

"No," I said. "I just want to talk to him."

I began to play Dungeons and Dragons.

It has been my observation that the smallest—and very often silliest—incident can have a profoundly significant influence on my life. In this case, the incident was a Christmas gift of the game—the original game, that is—published by TSR Inc. in 1974: three slim booklets and some funny dice in a box. I started playing as part of a five-strong group on St Stephen's Day. Towards the end of March, I woke one morning to the realisation that I had done no work for three months and was at impending risk of bankruptcy. Even then it hardly seemed to matter. My head was full of orcs.

For those of you who have never played Dungeons and Dragons or any other form of FRP (fantasy role play), I should explain that it's a far cry from Monopoly or chess. There is no board, no pieces, nothing but a group's imagination and a set of rules. Those rules allow you to create fictional characters whose strengths and weaknesses are initially determined by dice throws. Once named, the characters embark on imaginary adventures in a fantasy setting. One player, called the Dungeon Master, forgoes the pleasures of adventuring for the pleasures of God: s/he acts as the game's referee and storyteller, creating and maintaining the setting in which the adventures occur. During each session, the players listen to descriptions of their character's surroundings, peppered with additional information and potential choices, then describe their actions in response. The characters form a party that interacts with the setting's inhabitants (and each other), solves problems, engages in battles and gathers treasures and know-how which allow them to become increasingly powerful. The experience is addictive in the extreme; or at least so it proved for me. I even began to buy FRP magazines, most of which appeared to be aimed at—and quite possibly written by—12-year-old nerds.

But while enamoured, I was not blind. FRP struck me as one of the freshest, most fascinating game ideas of the century, but its implementation left a lot to be desired. Instructions were amateurishly explained and scenarios—the settings and adventures in which characters interacted—were badly written. I had a look at a couple of competing products, *Tunnels and Trolls* and *Runequest*, and decided I could do a great deal better. I searched the magazines for a suitable publisher and liked the sound of Yaquinto, a gaming company in Dallas, Texas. Then I put together a proposal for an FRP system based on time travel, emphasized my track record as a published author, and posted it off to 'The Commissioning Editor.' I got back a response from the president of the company. His name was Stephen J. Peek, another individual destined to change my life, although not in any way I would immediately have predicted.

Steve was impressed by my credentials, interested in the growing FRP phenomenon and enthusiastic to get into the market. He not only gave me the green light on *Timeship*, my original proposal, but suggested I might also like to consider creating a more traditional FRP system (with emphasis on the fantasy) called *Man, Myth and Magic*. Wearing his business Stetson, he had the idea that once Yaquinto established a popular system—be it time travel or fantasy—we could feed the product with limitless add-on scenarios and thus make a bundle of money. Steve liked to think big. He proposed that we plan for *Timeship* with one extensive included scenario to see how it went. His bright idea for *Man, Myth and Magic* was that we include the first four episodes of an adventure campaign in the box but sell the concluding five as separate scenarios. Then, having got the bit between his teeth, he thought it would be an excellent idea to launch the project with an additional adventure—say a trilogy set in Ancient Egypt—that could also be sold separately. Plus a third adventure about werewolves to find out whether horror role-play might prove popular. Suddenly, from not having done a thing for three months, I now had more work than I could handle. When I told him so, Steve proved sympathetic but unwilling to back off his master plan...or the ludicrously short timescale he'd set to carry it through. He suggested that if he wrote the three-scenario Egyptian adventure himself, plus an introductory module for the werewolf thing, this would leave me plenty of time to create the two game systems, the *Timeship* adventure scenario and all nine scenarios of the *MM&M* initial adventure. I thought what the hell and got down to work.

The total immersion in role play had an influence on my esoteric interests. Like Harry Potter in a later decade, FRP gaming, spearheaded by Dungeons and Dragons, had begun to attract censure from religious fundamentalists who maintained the hobby had the potential to open doorways to the infernal regions. For once, the fundamentalists might have been onto something. Occult theory holds that if you want to call up Inner Plane entities—angels, archangels, spirits, demons—you must first create an astral (i.e. imaginal) form sympathetic to the particular entity's nature. Given the right rituals, a little spiritual cooperation and a bit of luck, the entity will then animate the form you created and use it to communicate. As you can see, that isn't exactly allowing entities

Steve Peek: a powerful storyteller.

access into our world, except as far as the inside of your head, but it's certainly a step in the right direction. In a typical FRP game, imaginal forms are vividly created and some of them—usually the nastier variety at that—follow traditional patterns and thus might be suited to the evocation of a spirit entity.

It was the reality tone of the imaginal structures in FRP that intrigued me. There was something in the group experience of gaming that gave human imagination exceptional power. Whatever about using this to call up entities, it seemed a way to improve on the traditional form of pathworking. In fact, since pathworkings were supposed to form points of contact with archetypal worlds, it seemed a way to reach parts of the astral plane that might prove difficult using conventional esoteric methods. I began to experiment and eventually came up with the Atlantis Technique.

The Atlantis Technique is an amalgamation of hypnotic and FRP procedures. After initial exercises in sensitivity training, a session is carried out with group members seated in a darkened room, their eyes fixated on a single lighted candle, placed centrally on the floor. An elected Lore Master sets the scene for the inner journey.[25] The technique derives its name from the fact that I road-tested it across three different groups to

25   For a full exposition of the Atlantis Technique (although that name is not mentioned) see the experimental programme that forms part of my book *Time Travel: a New Perspective* published by Llewellyn.

investigate astral remnants of the famous lost continent, with the trigger description based on Plato's Atlantis accounts in his Timaeus and Critias dialogues. Although the groups experimented independently and without any consultation about results, there were some twenty-five points of similarity in their respective experiences, strongly suggestive of an objective vision. I self-published a booklet on the technique and its results for distribution among the esoteric community and was pleased to note that within a few years my ideas were increasingly adopted by esotericists searching for a variation on traditional pathworking.

But the Atlantis Technique was little more than a sideline to my fascination with FRP. Yaquinto published *Man, Myth & Magic* in a brightly coloured fantasy-themed box, then pumped out neatly-packaged, shrink-wrapped modules to feed the monster. It proved no competition for *Dungeons and Dragons* but sold well enough to encourage Steve to take the next step in our arrangement and publish *Timeship*. Probably because it was less of a me-too product, the initial market reaction was stronger. Enthusiastic players rang Steve's office at Yaquinto to ask questions about the game, and when he grew too busy to deal with them he instructed his secretary to tell them to call back yesterday. (They loved it.) Next thing I knew Steve had cut a deal with a start-up company in Texas called Five-Star Software and *Timeship* was scheduled for publication as a computer game. I was fascinated to learn that the very best programmer they could find to handle the conversion was 14 years old. Never one to miss a creative opportunity, I sold Five-Star on another, more exotic, project—a computerised Tarot reading. At that time I was capable of programming in compiled BASIC (a talent I have now lost along with calculus and long-division) and supplied them with bug-ridden code and simple, but acceptable, graphics. The complaints began rolling in within days of publication: they had to withdraw the entire issue while I battled to correct my mistake. From then on, to the industry's relief, I left computer programming to 14-year-olds.

Despite the mediocre performance of the boxed games and the disaster with the software, the relationship with Steve continued. He was interested in becoming a writer, and when he sent me some samples of his work, I discovered he was one of the most powerful storytellers I had ever read, interested in the sort of distinctively American, off-beat, often frightening themes reminiscent of authors like Stephen King and Dean Koontz. I encouraged him to put some effort into creating a body of work, but frustratingly, business pressures held him back; he would typically begin a book, become diverted by his game-industry career then, when time again allowed, lose interest in his original book and begin something else. The result was a series of unfinished works, notoriously difficult for a first-time author to sell to a publisher. We corresponded for a time, then Steve decided to visit Ireland and we met face to face. He proved to be a big man with a big voice, an encyclopaedic knowledge of sales and marketing and a playful nature that made him an ideal game business executive. As far as I was concerned, it was love at first sight and I offered him the hand of friendship. He repaid me by making me rich.

In those days before email and cheap trans-Atlantic phone calls, I opened my post one morning to find the briefest of letters from Steve. He asked if I'd heard about *The Warlock of Firetop Mountain*, a solo adventure in book form that had sold out of its first print run in less than a month. "This is the coming thing," said Steve. "You should get in on the ground floor and do it better."

I knew about solo adventures. Most FRP magazines included at least one per issue—short, multiple-choice stories designed for gamers unwilling or unable to form a group and role-play properly. The few I'd read were dreadful. The news about *Warlock of Firetop Mountain* had passed me by, but I bought a copy from my local bookshop. It was published by Puffin and written by two gamers, Steve Jackson and Ian Livingstone; and as Steve Peek said, it was selling like popcorn. Even my local bookshop confirmed the kids couldn't get enough of it. I read it through and came to the same conclusion I had about *Dungeons and Dragons*—great idea, but I could write it better. I called Murray Pollinger and told him I was about to embark on a gamebook project. "What's a gamebook?" Murray asked.

Up to this point in my career, I had never written a children's book—my output was almost entirely non-fiction for adults—and I was reluctant to invest too much time in an untried market. So rather than write a speculative gamebook, I put together a proposal for a series, taking great care to answer Murray's basic question and emphasizing my credentials as the creator of those two incredibly successful role-play boxed games, *Timeship* and *Man, Myth & Magic*. I figured, correctly as it happened, that few British publishers would bother to contact Dallas to check sales figures.

A perplexed Murray began to offer the proposal. A few weeks later, he reported back without any noticeable good news. "They just don't understand the concept," he told me.

"I've explained the concept," I said crossly. "Nearly the whole of the proposal is an explanation of the concept."

"They still don't understand it," Murray said.

But then, a few weeks later still, somebody did. Murray walked through the doors of William Collins & Co., having sent them my proposal, and a deputation from the children's department fell on his neck. They had noted the incredible sales of Puffin's *Warlock of Firetop Mountain* and were desperate to find somebody who would write a me-too product. But while writers were two a penny, writers with role-play backgrounds were not, so Murray's entrance in the lists must have looked like the appearance of an angel. He came back with a three-book contract. It was at this point I realised I had absolutely no idea how to write a gamebook.

In any sensible work of fiction, you begin by writing chapter one, following it with chapter two, then continuing in sequence until you reach an exciting, satisfying conclusion. Gamebooks aren't like that. They work in sections rather than chapters, some of them very short indeed. Readers plunge into the first section which, however, will typically end with several different choices: do you take the road ahead, explore the ruined castle on your right or fight the troll lurking under the bridge? Depending which decision you make, you are then directed to another section somewhere deep in the book...where you will find more choices to contend with. Furthermore, fighting that troll raises problems of its own—you need a game system that allows you to do so, with different tracking depending on the fight's outcome. All this is fun for the reader, who creates his own narrative as he bounces through the book, but it's a nightmare for the writer.

I've no idea how Jackson and Livingstone created *Warlock*, but I started my project by deciding on an arbitrary 150 sections for the adventure. I then wrote the numbers 1 to 150 underneath one another on a piece of paper. I stared at the piece of paper for a while, then took another one and typed the introduction. I had the idea of setting the adventure in King Arthur's Camelot and my gimmick was that Merlin the Magician would cast a spell to draw the reader back in time to help tackle whatever disaster might be facing the realm. So the introduction had Merlin speaking directly to the reader and explaining the situation, including the rules of the game. This led to an opening section, written in the second person singular, which described how the reader was now in Avalon and facing a bully called Mean Jake. Above the number 1 on my other piece of paper, I noted 'Reader in Avalon: meets Jake.' To ease the reader gently into the adventure, I decided on simple initial tracking: losing the inevitable fight with Mean Jake sent the reader to Section 1, winning to Section 2. Beside 'Reader in Avalon: meets Jake' I wrote 'Loses—1; Wins—2.' Then, back in the actual book manuscript, I wrote the text of Sections 1 and 2, both of which tracked to Section 3, which ran for several pages before optionally tracking either to Section 4 or Section 5. On my separate sheet, I briefly described the contents and tracking numbers of the sections I'd written.

If all this sounds hideously complicated, I can assure you it was, but I got the hang of it after a while and the book, called *The Castle of Darkness*, went remarkably smoothly. By the time it was finished, I had a title for my series (*GrailQuest*) a suitably sexless name for my hero/heroine (Pip) and a far better idea how to write the next volume. Collins published *Castle of Darkness* as an Armada paperback original in 1984, closely followed by the second in the series, *Den of Dragons*, a few weeks later. The timing was perfect. Mine were the second gamebooks of any sort in the market. Kids who'd had their appetites whetted by *Warlock* had nowhere else to go and began to buy *GrailQuests* in their thousands. Murray struck like a hawk and negotiated me another three-book contract, then another. I took to writing gamebooks at the rate of one a month. Murray got to work on overseas rights and sold the series to America, then Spain, then Denmark, then Japan, then France, after which I started to lose track.

GrailQuest did respectably well in most markets except the USA where it bombed so badly that only the first three volumes of the series were ever published there. In Britain, sales were happily measured in the tens of thousands. Then the Japanese brought out their lavishly packaged version of the series which rocketed into hundreds of thousands sales: my Japanese publisher requested my home address so he could send me a present. It struck me as a charming custom—one that British and American publishers would do well to follow—but the present never arrived. Nonetheless, I did not believe life (or income) could get any better than this. But it did. Gallimard brought out *GrailQuest* in France and subsequently sent me the largest royalty cheque I had ever seen in my life, and only the first of many. The gamebooks exploded into multi-million sales.

Steve Peek had done me a big favour.

Dolores reacted positively to my suggestion that I speak directly to her Opener, even though the idea had now expanded into a proposal that if I really quizzed him, it might produce enough material for a book. *"Interview with Anubis,"* I told her, waving my hands about enthusiastically. I didn't say so, but I had hopes it might outsell Anne Rice's *Interview with the Vampire,* which was the hot literary property of the day.

"Of course *he* will have to agree," Dolores emphasised, frowning uncertainly. "I don't really have much say in the matter."

"Ask him!" I demanded like a small child in a sweet shop. Ask him she did, and the Opener approved. We arranged to hold the formal interview next time Dolores visited Ireland. I bought myself a new cassette recorder for the occasion.

The interview took place in my study to the background of a barking dog who became so hysterical at one point that I wondered half seriously if he could sense the jackal. The first couple of tapes soon filled up with questions to Dolores about how she came to meet with her contact (essentially the material covered in Chapter Forty-One), and then we looked at one another, took deep breaths and decided that the time had come to launch the formal interview.

By this stage I had experimented hypnotically with Dolores. She was an exceptional subject, and, among other things, we had explored several of her past life memories together. But there was no need for a hypnotic induction now. Dolores sat back, closed her eyes and within a few moments was exhibiting the signs of trance. She turned her face towards me, eyes still closed. "Her-Bai," she said. I was talking to the Opener.

Psychologists refer to entities like the Opener as 'secondary personalities.' It is probably true to say most of them think of such personalities as expressions of the unconscious—fictional characters creatively animated by a level of the psyche of which the medium is unaware. But not Carl Jung. While Jung began his academic career by investigating the mediumistic abilities of his own cousin and concluding she was essentially talking to herself, he ended it in a very different place. Towards the latter years of his life, his experience led him to the conclusion that the 'spirit hypothesis'—which suggests secondary personalities may be the result of possession by an objective entity—provided a better explanation of the phenomenon than any other. I tend to agree, at least in certain cases; and with the proviso that the position is more complicated than a simple either/or. It seems to me that where an objective entity *is* involved, any messages it attempts to communicate is filtered through the psyche of the medium and may sometimes be distorted by the medium's own agenda. It was, however, difficult to see what agenda Dolores might have been following. What emerged from the interview with Anubis was a far cry from the classical Egyptian mythology she clung to when discussing her indweller in the waking state. Despite this, I confidently expect details of the interview to feature in Dolores's autobiography. In the meantime, here are a few highlights:

The entity speaking through Dolores had no concept of time. He was aware of his past in spatial terms with his life spreading through a continuum, any element of which he could visit (or re-visit) if necessary. What we call 'now'—an ever-moving present—was for him a question of focus. Interestingly, this is an experiential expression of the reality of our space-time continuum as expressed in Einstein's relativity theory.

Whatever the Egyptians believed—itself something he dealt with at length during the interview—Anubis was not a god, but rather what we might today call an extraterrestrial. The origins of his species were difficult to explain and involved a quirky definition of the term 'eternity.' For most people, *eternity* conjures up the idea of a long, long time. For the Opener, it was an encapsulation of time itself. I was reminded of the Hindu *Breath of Brahma* concept which describes the universe as created on the out-breath of a supreme deity, existing for many millions of years, then withdrawn from manifestation as Brahma takes an in-breath. Essentially the same idea appears in modern physics when scientists speculate that the universe (and time itself) came into being at the moment of the Big Bang and may at some stage in the future contract to nothingness, time and all, in a Big Crunch. The Opener's encapsulation of time seemed an amalgamation of these two concepts, Hindu ideas of rhythm and cyclical repetitions joining with the physicists' insight that time itself must form part of any ultimate universal creation and destruction. Within this definition of 'eternity' the origins of the Opener's species lay not in this Eternity, nor the previous Eternity, but in the Eternity before. In their original form, members of his race were giant (twenty to twenty-five foot tall) hominids inhabiting a planet with a less dense atmosphere than our own. Over aeons, they evolved first to a smaller stature, then out of their physical bodies altogether. This enabled them to survive the absorption of their universe at the end of the current Eternity.

There was a largely unstated—and somewhat Theosophical—background to the Opener's story. He and his kind lived in a hierarchical universe governed by even more highly evolved spiritual entities from whom they took direction at first unconsciously, later consciously. Ultimately, they found themselves in communication with a unity they called simply 'The One.' Within this context, the beings of the Opener's race saw themselves as teachers and guardians of less evolved creatures. ("It is our nature to teach, guide and inspire.") They functioned, in essence, to help the evolutionary process and attempted to coax other beings along the winding road to a truly spiritual civilisation. Among those 'other beings' was humanity.

The first contact between the Opener's species and humanity occurred at the time the first cave paintings were produced,[26] initially by a sort of telepathic influence, then, as suitable hosts arose, by the type of open indwelling Dolores experienced. Indwelling carried benefits for the specific host: it tended to increase longevity, psychism and sensitivity. Once indwelt, the host himself or herself then developed into a conduit for teachings, sometimes becoming a prophet or religious leader in the process. One example of this contact process was that it sowed the seeds of the Mediterranean Mystery Religions.

The Opener's first personal contact was with a host who, in a violent era, died at age 15. By this time humanity progressed to a point where it was becoming increasingly aware of its disembodied teachers and had begun to see individual entities—at least as imaginal figures—and even paint them. Imprinted humans—which is to say individuals who had been influenced by the watchers—began to move into Europe, but the Opener himself elected to remain in North Africa. It was here, some 3,000 years before the unification of Egypt, that he came to be identified with the jackal. He had contacted and supported an early host in the desert. When the man returned to his people (with the Opener in tow) they nicknamed him 'The Jackal' since jackals were the only mammals able to survive in the wasteland. The first 'Jackal' trained others, who carried the contact down the generations.

It seemed from the Opener's story that there was—and presumably still is—a sort of masterplan for human evolution, with entities like the Opener stepping in to nudge the process back on track whenever it threatened to go astray. One of the more interesting examples of intervention concerned the Christ story. According to the Opener, the drama of the slain and

26   The earliest European cave paintings date back 32,000 years. The earliest known rock paintings, at time of writing, are dated some 8,000 years earlier.

risen Christ—which is, of course, reflected in various mythologies down the ages—was effectively stage-managed by his kind and involved the indwelling of Jesus by a feminine entity. A controversial detail suggested that Jesus' mother, Mary, became pregnant not by immaculate conception, but as the result of intercourse with one of Herod's sons.

Although I tried to approach the interview and the Opener with an open mind, I cannot pretend I was entirely convinced at the time. The entity's expressed origins had the feel of science fiction—a literary genre I knew Dolores enjoyed as much as I did—and the new take on the genesis of Christianity seemed somehow inflated: the sort of story would-be gurus concoct to make themselves appear important. I was frankly doubtful about the *bona fides* of the Opener himself. Like the youthful Carl Jung, I wondered if he could be the product of his medium's unconscious. It even occurred to me that I might be witnessing a virtuoso performance by Dolores herself, who had once trained with the Royal Academy of Dramatic Art. I decided I could test the latter possibility at least and asked Dolores if she would permit me to monitor her brain-wave patterns while she was in trance. She agreed without hesitation. I set up the equipment and a curious picture emerged. In the waking state, her brainwave patterns were well within the standard range with no indication of any pathology or abnormality. Hypnotic induction produced a high alpha wave, which was exactly what I would have expected, given my experience of other hypnotised subjects. When she sank into her self-induced trance for the purpose of spirit communication, essentially the same brain-wave pattern emerged, confirming my suspicion that mediumistic and hypnotic trances were more or less identical states. Then something quite extraordinary happened. The Opener took over and the read-out changed to something I had never seen before: *two* brainwave patterns—one the expected alpha, the other a distinctive theta—broadcast simultaneously.

At that point I decided to rule out conscious fakery and put the question of unconscious creativity on hold. I suppose it stayed there, with varying degrees of agnosticism, until the night I met one of the Opener's kind directly and experienced my own indwelling.

Dolores made it a project to entice me out of Ireland. Somehow she was able to draw an astrological birth map without consulting an ephemeris—"How do you do that?" I asked. "I don't know," she said—and came to the conclusion that since I had both Sun and Moon in Cancer, I was a crab's crab and would go nowhere unless I had my house on my back. "What you need to do is think ferries and, most important, take your car," she told me. "You can't *really* have your house on your back, but your car is the next best thing."

I told her I would think about it, hoping she'd forget and go on to other things. I should have known better. A few weeks later she phoned with an invitation to attend her Advanced Magic five-day workshop in Devon. "Now we know how you can travel, it will be easy. I'll meet you off the ferry and we can drive down together. You'll be lionised. Everybody there has read *Astral Doorways*."

I told her I'd think about that as well, but deep in my black little heart I realised the *lionised* bit had struck a chord. As a writer, I led a reclusive existence. The *GrailQuest* success was now years in the past. My current books were produced and posted to publishers, then came out without launch parties or publicity. I received miniscule fan-mail. I was not well enough known for invites to speak at libraries or book fairs. I had never done a signing in my life. For me finishing a book was like throwing it into a Black Hole. The idea that I might be lionised—quite possibly by pretty young women—had a distinct appeal. I called Dolores back and accepted her invitation. The crab-shell of my car worked its magic. As a result, one sunny June day, I found myself on the edge of Dartmoor, staring at a magnificent Georgian building called Grimstone Manor in a place named Horrabridge.

Grimstone functioned as a conference centre and came equipped with goodies like an indoor heated swimming pool. The workshop participants were mainly SoL students, some from as far afield as Sweden. Dolores lost little time in giving me the celebrity treatment, and while her students resolutely resisted the urge to lionise, several of them were indeed familiar with my books. Early on in the proceedings, Dolores asked me to give a talk on astral projection. It was the first time I had ever spoken in public, but being Irish I managed to waffle for the better part of an hour. In the break called after I'd finished, a woman came up to me, asked for my advice, then launched into a fascinating story.

She was, it appeared, a schoolteacher. The previous year, her school organised a summer trip to the Peak District, but she was on a course at the time and decided not to attend. The decision turned out to be a mistake. The day of the trip was one of the hottest on record. As she tried to work on her course, she found her mind continually wandering to her colleagues and pupils who, she imagined, must be enjoying the cool breezes and delightful scenery of the mountains. The trip took place on a Friday. After the intervening weekend, my schoolteacher found herself discussing it with one of her faculty colleagues. When she expressed her regret that she had not attended, he looked at her in astonishment. "But we spent most of the afternoon together," he said. When she prompted him for details, he claimed that he had been in her company for much of the trip and they had engaged in several conversations.

"Do you think that was astral projection?" she asked me.

I did think it was astral projection. The daydreaming of being somewhere else was a classic precursor. Furthermore, there were several case studies in the literature of people seen in two places at once. There was even another schoolteacher—Mlle Emilie Sagee lost several jobs because her students claimed there were two of her. But while Mlle Sagee's phantom might sit in a corner and watch her at work, or even leave to stroll through the school grounds, this was the first time I had ever heard of a projection engaging in a rational conversation without the knowledge of the host. If the story was as my schoolteacher recounted it, the implications of her experience were profound in what they suggested about the structure of the human psyche. I began to realise the importance of getting out more, especially among people who had similar interests to myself. But at that point, I had no idea quite how important this particular outing would prove.

I wrote in more detail about the case of Mlle Sagee in *Discover Astral Projection*, Aquarian Press, London, 1989.

The sort of magical workshops in which Dolores specialised, tended, despite my little lecture, to be severely practical affairs. As part of this one, she required one of her SoL supervisors, a tall, softly spoken man named Ray, to write a mythic ritual which would then be staged by workshop participants. Ray's choice of subject was the marriage of Dionysus and Ariadne.

You may recall that according to Greek myth, Ariadne was a daughter of King Minos of Crete and half-sister to the Minotaur imprisoned in the labyrinth at Knossos. Her major duty was to prepare sacrificial victims of the Minotaur, who fed exclusively on human flesh. But when the young, handsome Theseus volunteered as a sacrifice, she fell in love with him and gave him a ball of twine so he could find his way out of the labyrinth. Theseus escaped and sailed off with Ariadne, but eventually abandoned her for another woman and threw Ariadne overboard. She washed up on the Island of Naxos where—from the frying pan to the fire—she was torn apart by followers of the god Dionysus. After death, her soul was carried to Hades where Dionysus himself was so impressed by her beauty and her willingness to be sacrificed that he took her in a sacred marriage. It was this sacred marriage that formed the inspiration of Ray's rite. When he gave out his scripts, I discovered he wanted me to play Dionysus. Shortly afterwards, a tall, strikingly beautiful blonde girl bounced across the room and said enthusiastically, "Are you Dionysus? I'm Ariadne!"

"Very good," I said.

That evening, something quite extraordinary happened. We congregated for a vegetarian meal, and I found myself sharing a table with a small party of Wiccans—modern witchcraft practitioners. As the meal was finishing, I went off to the loo and came back to find the witches had begun to sing. The song was called *The Burning Times*, a ballad about the witch persecutions of the sixteenth and seventeenth centuries. I later learned the lyrics had been written by the guitarist Charlie Murphy (of *Rumours of the Big Wave*) but at the time I had never heard the song before and I stood in the doorway transfixed.[27] The chorus is in the form of a chant which repeats the names of various goddesses—Isis, Astarte, Diana, Hecate, Demeter, Kali and Inanna. As the women reached it, I had a visionary experience.

I was still standing in the doorway of the dining room at Grimstone Manor. I could still see the tables and the workshop participants. But beyond them was the horizon; and beyond that, rising on the pure, sweet swelling of the women's voices, was a towering female figure. She was taller than the house itself, taller than the trees and I knew, without a second's hesitation that I was staring at the Goddess: not *a* goddess, not Isis or Astarte or Diana of the chant, but *the* Goddess, the supreme embodiment of the feminine principle. Then the song ended, the vision faded, and I sat down heavily on the nearest chair. Someone asked if I was all right.

The ritual marriage of Dionysus and Ariadne was scheduled for the

27   There's a passable version on YouTube at *http://www.youtube.com/watch?v=G-zxrpP6BD6U* as I write.

following evening and much of the afternoon was devoted to the preparations. One small group of women created a thyrsus amid much giggling: I had no idea why until I saw the thing—a thick wooden rod, veined with ivy and topped by a pine-cone. "Is it big enough for you?" asked an Australian witch-queen, Cassandra Carter-Lewis, with a mischievous grin.

Ariadne was wearing a low-cut robe and looked gorgeous. I found it so difficult to keep my eyes off her that to this day I can remember nothing of the ceremony itself. I presume the ritual went well because afterwards Ray congratulated us both on the way we'd played our parts. I wandered off with Ariadne and we chatted by the swimming pool, first about the working, then later about ourselves. I should have seen the signs, but I've always been notoriously slow about that sort of thing. We parted company sometime after midnight.

"I don't know your real name," I said as she began to walk away.

"Jacquelene Lorna St Clair Burgess," Ariadne told me.

We met again after breakfast and picked up the conversation where we left off the night before. We stared at each other during Dolores's classes over the day, sat together at lunch and went back to talking by the pool after supper that evening. Others drifted over, realised what was happening and drifted off again. We resisted invitations to join parties in the water. I discovered Jacquelene Lorna St Clair Burgess had recently given up a career as a publisher to become a crystal therapist but continued to work as a consultant to her former employers. I discovered she was not related to the spy Guy Burgess but had been followed in Moscow by the KGB because of the similarity of their names. I discovered she lived in London, having recently bought herself a flat in Cambridge Gardens. I discovered she never planned to attend the workshop: she was nervous about magic, had booked into another function altogether (which was cancelled) and only came to this one because some Swedish friends wanted a lift. I discovered I had fallen in love with her.

Most of the Grimstone accommodation was in the form of dormitories and Jacks was sharing one with several other women. But Dolores, who knew my pathological need for solitude (and comfort) had organised a private room for me with en-suite loo and shower. I took a deep breath and asked Jacks if she'd like to see it.

A little later, I found myself staring at this woman in a minor reprise of the visionary experience I'd had while the witches were singing. I knew then, beyond a shadow of a doubt, that I had just received a gift from the Goddess.

Even gifts from the Goddess can come with a price tag. Mine was that it forced me to take stock of my life. I was already in a long-term relationship—fifteen years to be precise. I was still officially married to Helen: although we had not seen one another in decades, neither of us had bothered with the formality of a divorce. I owned a thatched home in rural Ireland, Jacks owned a flat in London, reminders, if we needed any, that she was a city girl while I liked the country life. Despite Dolores's astrological insights, I still did not travel well. After several fairly disastrous relationships, Jacks had just emerged from years of therapy with the realisation that she needed no man to complete her life and was perfectly happy living on her own. This was not a set of circumstances that suggested the new lovers were likely to live happily ever after.

Over the next few weeks, we spent in excess of £1,000 apiece on international phone calls while we worried at the situation like dogs with a bone. A further complication arose—in my head at least—when I discovered that Jacks, like Helen, was a member of the White Eagle Lodge. When she told me, I felt as if I was being haunted. She went on retreat to New Lands and there sought the advice of White Eagle himself through his medium Joan Hodgson (Grace Cooke was long dead at this time: Joan was one of her daughters.)

She expected a telling-off for her involvement with a married man. Instead, White Eagle told her we were fated to be together, had spiritual work to do together, and if she left things alone, the situation would sort itself out. Jacks found the guidance more comforting than I did: I was on a guilt trip that took me beyond reassurance.

In a state of terminal confusion, I decided I needed professional guidance and presented myself at the stylish Dublin apartment of June Quinn-Berger,[28] visiting Professor of Jungian Studies at St Petersburg University, psychoanalyst and practicing therapist with a speciality in psycho-sexual and family problems. She listened to my story soberly, quizzed me gently about my early life and background, then told me two things. The first was that I had to run, not walk, from my current relationship. The second was that I must not become involved with Jacks until I reached some insights into why my previous liaisons with women had proved so ruinous. Predictably, I took the first part of her advice, but not the second. Two years later, Jacks and I were married. June, who had met her by that

28 Now June Atherton, having remarried the diplomat Sir Harley Atherton.

time and given an enthusiastic stamp of approval, was among the guests at our wedding.

White Eagle's prediction proved to be correct—Jacks and I *did* have spiritual work to do, or at least Jacks thought so. She encouraged me to develop a psycho-magical system I called Sacred Science, based partly on my esoteric training, partly on the teachings of Jean Houston, an American psychologist with an extraordinary capacity for harnessing mythic dramas to therapeutic and evolutionary effect. I was keen to keep it low-key, but Jacks pressed me to come down from the ivory tower and we began to run workshops together, first in Ireland, then in the UK, sometimes in London, sometimes in the North of England usually under the auspices of John and Elizabeth Fox, two highly experienced magicians with Martinist and Rosicrucian interests. At about this time, I agreed to join with Dolores in presenting a series of magical master classes for SoL students. Strange things began to happen.

During a Sacred Science ritual at the College of Psychic Studies in London, someone knocked over an incense burner. Red-hot charcoal scattered on the parquet floor. Jacks, who had fallen into trance—she had trained as a medium at the College in her twenties—picked it up with her bare hands and suffered neither blistering nor burns.

During an astrological ritual in the north of England, Dolores evoked entities known as Lords of the Flame. In general, it is probably true to say such evocations are as symbolic as prayers in a church—we all pay lip-service to the idea that God is listening but would be astonished if an answering voice reverberated from on high. But as Dolores fell silent, I heard the sound of wings and the chatter of a high-pitched conversation as (presumably) the Lords approached.

During a one-day workshop on reincarnation, Jacks briefly regressed a merchant seaman to the screaming memory of a cannonball that cost him his leg during the Napoleonic Wars. When he returned to normal consciousness, a chronic knee condition had resolved itself. At the same workshop, a Swedish osteopath named Matts Janander cured a young woman's ME by shining a torch through a quartz crystal to activate specific acupuncture points. I watched her being carried in on a stretcher. Three quarters of an hour later, she ran delightedly across the room to hug me.

But the most spectacular experiences were at Runnings Park, in the shadow of the Malvern Hills.

Runnings Park functioned as a hotel at that time.[29] It was an hotel with

29   The hotel is no more. The complex is now a centre for health and healing.

A gift from the goddess: Jacks and I on our wedding day.

a curious pedigree. Sometime back in the 1950s, a young man named Tony Neate found himself in contact with an entity named Helio-Arcanophus, currently described on Tony's website as 'a source of higher consciousness.' In 1957, he joined forces with the author Murry Hope to form a society called The Atlanteans, possibly because Helio-Arcanophus once functioned as a priest on that lost continent. Runnings Park was the inspiration of four families who wanted to see what they could achieve together to propagate the teachings of H-A, and to run courses on healing. A College of Healing was created and also a School of Channelling. It also became the HQ of the Wrekin Trust for a number of years when Tony Neate succeeded Sir George Trevelyan as Chair of the trust. Henley and Tricia Thomas started a very successful Therapy Centre. The hotel idea came about because of a need for financial viability.

Given the background, you might guess Runnings Park proved sympathetic to magico-spiritual functions; and so it did. Dolores held many a workshop there, usually residential five-day affairs, and Runnings Park was the venue for our joint Master Classes in magic. Our partnership was an interesting mix. Dolores tended to specialise in ritual training and practice. I introduced my obsession with magical experiment.

It was an obsession that produced some extraordinary results.

In 1972, a sub-group of the Toronto Society for Psychical Research in Canada embarked on a project aimed at manufacturing a ghost. The group was led by a former nurse, Mrs Iris Owens, and included her husband, the mathematician Dr George Owens, and Margaret Sparrow, a former MENSA chairman. No one involved claimed to be psychic.

As a first step in the process, the group created an historical romance centred on a fictional character named Philip Aylesford. Philip, they decided, was a seventeenth-century English aristocrat living at the time of Cromwell. A royalist and Catholic, he had married Dorothea, the daughter of a neighbouring noble. They lived together in Philip's family home, Diddington Manor, where Dorothea proved a dutiful wife, if somewhat cold.

One day while riding through his extensive estate, Philip came across a gypsy encampment and there saw for the first time the dark-eyed Margo with whom he fell instantly in love. His feelings were reciprocated and before long he had installed Margo in Diddington Gatehouse, close to the stables. Their affair lasted several months, but inevitably Dorothea discovered the love-nest. In a fit of pique, she denounced Margo as a witch, not to mention a husband-stealer. The girl was arraigned, convicted and burned at the stake. The dastardly Philip, fearful of his reputation, declined to speak in her defence. Or perhaps he was not so dastardly. He had, at least, the decency to experience remorse and took to pacing the Diddington battlements in an agony of despair. The day came when his despair grew unbearable, and he flung himself to his death.

One of the Toronto group members made a sketch of Philip, a cheery, square-faced man with a full beard, but despite the wealth of detail, Philip's entire story remained fiction except for a single element—there really *was* a Diddington Manor: members of the group hung photographs of it around the walls when they conducted their experiment.

The experiment itself had an elegant simplicity. The group held a series of Spiritualist-style séances at which they attempted to make contact with Philip's fictional ghost. The sittings began in September 1972 and continued for about a year. Philip was endlessly discussed, visualised, meditated upon. Some group members claimed they seemed to sense his presence, but nothing really evidential occurred.

At about this time, Iris Owens became aware of the work of a British psychologist and psychical researcher named Kenneth Batcheldor. During the early 1960s, Bacheldor became intrigued by Victorian reports of table-turning and decided to find out if he could duplicate the phenomenon. He formed a group which patiently engaged in 200 table-turning séances. One hundred and twenty of them produced no noticeable result. In the remaining eighty, the table moved. Eventually, Bacheldor was able to record total levitations using infra-red photography.

The most important thing about Bacheldor's experiments was not the phenomena, but rather the approach that produced them. Bacheldor discovered that in the absence of scientific controls, results manifested easily, but could not, of course, be verified. When controls were imposed, phenomena ceased. But then he found that if controls were applied very gradually, phenomena would initially drop off, then slowly climb back to the previous (uncontrolled) level. He concluded that table turning was not caused by spirits, but rather by the unconscious minds of group participants *and was directly related to their current belief system.* When no controls were applied, séances held in total darkness with every opportunity for fakery produced phenomena not because sitters were actually engaged in fakery, but because the possibility of fakery allowed their unconscious to generate phenomena without insult to their rational beliefs. When controls were introduced, they 'knew' it was impossible for the table to move and consequently did not (or possibly could not) make it move psychokinetically. A low level of control, which still left some possibility of fakery, allowed the minds to generate some psychokinetic (PK) effects, *which increased as the sitters became accustomed to the level of control.*

Bacheldor also discovered that 'artefacts' played a major role in creating conditions conducive to PK. By 'artefacts' he meant naturally occurring but unfamiliar phenomena which the sitters might easily mistake for PK, especially in an unusual context. Thus table movements due to involuntary muscle twitches by the sitters might be mistaken for genuine PK in the expectant atmosphere of a séance held in total darkness. *Such mistakes then stimulated genuine PK, because the sitters had experienced what they believed to be proof that PK was possible.* Another factor in the Bacheldor experiments was participant relaxation. Curiously, results were more likely to follow when participants stopped taking the experiment too seriously, told jokes and even, occasionally, burst into song.

Iris Owens decided to apply some of Bacheldor's insights to her experiment with the fictional Philip. The original sittings had been conducted in a well-lit room. Now she decided to hold them in darkness; and she encouraged her group to relax, chat and tell jokes in imitation of the

Bacheldor experiments. Soon the Owens Group's efforts were rewarded by a distinct 'spirit' rap. They established a code and quickly discovered the communicating 'entity' was Philip, who fed back the life story the group had created for him, embellished by incidental details of the period in which he had lived. The fact that everyone knew the spirit was a work of fiction made no difference. Philip proved himself capable of moving the séance-room table (which he once caused to dance a jig on one leg), dimming and raising the lights on command, producing a visible mist and causing a cool breeze to start and stop. He even managed a full table levitation before a live audience of fifty and a television crew.

I was aware of Bacheldor's work and had corresponded with him as part of the research for a book I was writing on PK. I was also aware of the Owens experiment. The magical master classes, with their willing attendances of trained minds, seemed like the perfect opportunity to expand on the Bacheldor/Owens insights. I made the suggestion to Dolores and Dolores, who was always game for anything, agreed.

Mindreach, my examination of PK and the Bacheldor experiments, was published by Aquarian Press, Wellingborough, in 1985.

Our table-turning experiment was carried out at midnight, which seemed a suitably spooky time. The meeting room we were using at Runnings Park was still illuminated by ambient light, so we papered the windows to create conditions of total darkness. Half a dozen small wooden tables were set up and the overall group of some thirty-two people split into sub-groups to control a table each. Mindful of Bacheldor's discovery, I suggested the initial experiment take place in total darkness. Each sub-group was left to devise its own approach. Most opted for the Spiritualist line of attack, solemnly asking *'Is anybody there?'* or directly requesting spirit intervention. For some fifteen minutes, nothing happened, then one group reported a slight table movement—almost certainly a Bacheldor 'artefact' caused by involuntary muscle action. Similar slight movements followed at some of the other tables.

Patience is an important prerequisite for this type of experimental work, but standing in pitch darkness with minutes ticking slowly past like hours, I was having trouble finding it. So were some of the groups, notably the one that included Jacks. She was almost as familiar with Bacheldor's work as I was and suggested to her colleagues that a light-hearted attitude might produce better results. They were bored, took to the suggestion at once and began to tell each other silly jokes. After a moment the group became rowdy, to grunts of disapproval from the remaining groups. After another moment there was a shout of excitement as their table began to move—a distinct movement, far removed from the earlier twitches.

In short order, most of the remaining groups had adopted the Monty Python approach and almost all of them were getting results. There were shouts and cross-conversations across the room as tables shuddered, shook, jerked and slid. The noise level rose dramatically. As it approached pandemonium I decided the time had come to introduce a minor control and lit a candle. The scene was extraordinary. Most of the tables, which had been set initially in a grid pattern, were displaced from their original positions. Chairs had toppled over. Several participants were standing. Some had their hands on their tables, some not. As if attracted by the light, two of the tables shuddered towards me, followed by their excited groups. In a moment I was pinned against a wall. Someone panicked and switched on the main lights. The phenomena settled down at once.

Flushed with our success at table-turning, the group set its sights on a more subtle goal: the duplication of the Owens' experiment but using magical instead of Spiritualist techniques.

The fictional character was Coventina, a Saxon priestess who lived in Britain prior to the Roman occupation. Although there was lip-service paid to creating her life story, as the Owens group had done with Philip, participants found it difficult to agree on essentials, and the result was sketchy. Emphasis switched to the creation of a 'Coventina' entity by means of numerology and sacred geometry.

Numerology is a divinatory system based on the Hebrew idea that numbers are assigned to each letter of the alphabet, allowing you to calculate an overall value for any person or thing (by counting the value of its name) and thus discover hidden links between them. If you feel tempted to play with the idea, the tables on the following page may be helpful.

The name *Coventina* produced a value of forty. Following numerological convention this was reduced to a single figure by addition the digits: 4 + 0 = 4. Once we had the basic number, it allowed us to begin to design the evocation ritual, which would be built around hidden associations with the number 4: the colour violet, the crystals quartz, tiger eye or sodalite and so on. It also enabled us to create a Coventina sigil using the principles of sacred geometry. To do this, you begin with a circle divided into nine equal segments around its circumference, then use your basic number to calculate which of the segment points should be joined and in

Roman (English/French) letter values

1	2	3	4	5	6	7	8	9
A	B	C	D	E	F	G	H	I
J	K	L	M	N	O	P	Q	R
S	T	U	V	W	X	Y	Z	

Spanish letter values

1	2	3	4	5	6	7	8	9
A	B	C	D	E	F	G	H	I
J		L	M	N / Ñ	O	P	Q	R / RR
S	T / CH	U	V		X / LL	Y	Z	

Italian letter values

1	2	3	4	5	6	7	8	9
A	B	C	D	E	F	G	H	I
		L	M	N	O	P	Q	R
S	T	U	V				Z	

For other alphabets (e.g. Russian, Greek, Hebrew etc.) transliterate into Roman.

what order. The result is a geometric figure, sometimes simple, sometimes complex, representing the number and hence the entity behind it. Finally, we created a sigil representing the group itself by calculating birth and name numbers for everyone present, reducing them to a single digit and proceeding as we did with Coventina.

The ritual environment was created using dark violet drapes and the relevant crystals. Copies of both Coventina and group sigils were hung alternately around the walls. A flashing tablet based on the Coventina sigil was placed prominently on a central altar.[30] Dolores wrote the evocation and selected one of her senior supervisors to deliver it. None of us quite knew what to expect. I imagine the smart money was on poltergeist manifestation, with raps, furniture movements or even levitations similar to the Owens experience. What actually happened was that at the climax of the evocation, Jacks fell into trance and was possessed by the 'spirit' of our fictional Coventina. The entity answered questions for

---

30   A flashing tablet is a technical device using blocks of complementary colours which gives a flicker illusion due to optical reflex. In magical practice, such tablets are used as trance inducers and are believed to give access to the energies represented in their design.

some twenty minutes before I cut the experiment short after Jacks began to show signs of distress.

The positive results of the Coventina experiment encouraged us to abandon all caution. As the next Master Class approached, I called Dolores with the tentative suggestion that we might attempt one of the most spectacular of all magical operations, an evocation to visible appearance. In this rite, the spirit takes on material, or near-material form and can thus be seen by everyone in attendance. Part of the examination that preceded initiation into the Zelator grade of the original Golden Dawn was a requirement for the candidate to evoke a spirit to visible appearance 'at least to the consistency of mist.' To the best of my knowledge, the operation had not been seriously attempted since Victorian times.[31]

"Great idea," said Dolores without a moment's hesitation. "Who were you thinking of evoking?"

"Anubis," I said.

"I'll see if he's agreeable," Dolores told me calmly.

It turned out that he was, and I got to work on the flyer.

The single problem with evoking Anubis to visible appearance was that neither of us knew how to do it. This did not worry me since Dolores looked after all the other ritual aspects of our Master Classes and I assumed she would look after this one as well. It did not worry Dolores either, as she assumed that since the evocation was my idea, I would figure out how to do it. With the evocation to visible appearance announced as the Saturday-night climax of our five-day course, our blissful ignorance ended on the Thursday when I casually asked Dolores if I might have an advance copy of the ritual. "What ritual?" she asked.

"What are we going to do?" I asked when we realised neither of us had planned anything.

"I expect something will turn up," Dolores said.

Incredibly, something did. On the Friday afternoon, I was participating in a group exercise, led by Dolores, which involved an imaginal trip to the lower world to make contact with a nature spirit. I had always viewed this type of exercise as creative rather than spiritual, but whatever its actual nature, I was stunned to find my visualised contact explaining exactly—and in detail—how the evocation rite should be undertaken.

31   During the late twentieth and early twenty-first centuries there has been a renewed interest in evocation to visible appearance among American magicians, but the techniques used tend to involve crystal gazing and auto-hypnosis which, while perfectly valid, leaves open the possibility that any 'appearance' is actually subjective.

There were forty-one participants in the master class, plus Jacks, Dolores and myself. Four of the students elected to drop out of the Saturday night ritual, believing the experiment to be dangerous. The remainder were told to be ready for 8 p.m. The basis of the evocation was a standard technique of Medieval hermeticism in which the magician stands inside a protective circle to evoke a spirit form into a triangle drawn at a cardinal point outside it. But, on instruction from within, there were several major departures from the Medieval approach. Although both circle and triangle were drawn and fortified [32] in traditional style, three ritual officers—all senior members of SoL at this time—were stationed at the points of the triangle, facing inwards. The officer at the eastern apex, closest to the wall, was David Goddard, an author specialising in angelology and a Bishop of the Liberal Catholic Church. Inside the circle was a chair for Dolores, facing the triangle, behind it a small working altar table, then myself. Behind me, outside the circle, were five further officers (who included Jacks), arranged in an arc and facing east like Dolores and myself. The remaining thirty participants were arranged in a block of five rows outside the circle to the south.

The triangle officers were instructed to visualise the traditional Egyptian jackal-headed form of Anubis inside the triangle in order to give the spirit an astral vehicle. An incense burner was placed inside the triangle as well, so that smoke could provide a physical basis for manifestation and render the spirit visible. Dolores was required to sit in the seat inside the circle and enter a trance. My job was to take an imaginal (astral) bow and shoot an imaginal (astral) arrow into a spot on her spine associated with her contact with the Opener. The arc officers were told to reinforce my actions by vividly imagining the bow and the arrow. The remaining participants were required to perform a group chant to raise sufficient energy for the operation to work. The entire ceremony was to be held in candle light. All participants were to be robed. Everyone was instructed to keep careful watch on the triangle where the manifestation—assuming the rite worked—would appear.

The ritual began with the chant, which continued for twenty minutes without pause and had the effect of raising expectations close to fever pitch. Long before this point, Dolores was slumped into trance. In the sudden silence as the chant cut off, I picked up an imaginal bow and shot the imaginal arrow. Dolores jerked slightly and gasped. There was a crash,

32   The term relates to the inclusion of various 'holy names' and symbols believed to strengthen the protective properties of the geometric figures.

followed by a terrifying gurgling sound. I looked towards the triangle and discovered David Goddard, a heavy man well in excess of six feet tall, had been lifted off his feet and was now slammed against the wall, hanging suspended about eighteen inches off the ground. As I watched, he slid down, choking and gurgling, to fall in a heap on the floor.

It got confused after that. David's fellow officers rushed to his aid. Dolores stood up, turned to me with the blank stare that suggested she was still in trance and said in the voice of the Opener, "That was not well done." S/he then walked to the altar table and created a type of communion (using what ingredients I can no longer remember—or even imagine) which s/he shared, one after one, with every participant. When the rite finished, the Opener said, "It is done" and disappeared from Dolores's consciousness. I caught her, as she seemed about to fall, and managed to get her back on the chair, but could not rouse her from her trance state. I left her to the care of others and went to check on David, who assured me he was fine, but allowed himself to be spirited away by his colleagues on the theory that he needed a stiff drink. I returned to Dolores who was still in trance, to the consternation of her pupils. I was not unduly worried, since trance, if left alone, will eventually pass into normal sleep, from which the subject typically awakes refreshed, if bewildered. I was on the point of carrying her to her room when Mats Janander, the Swedish osteopath mentioned earlier, did something painful to her feet. Dolores's eyes snapped open and she screamed.

"There," Mats grinned. "You are awake now."

Dolores proved none the worse for her ordeal. Nor, rather more unexpectedly, did David Goddard, who told me afterwards that, at the climax of the ceremony, the jackal shape of Anubis had hurled itself out of the circle and struck him in the chest, causing him to slam against the wall.

The experience, he said, was 'ecstatic.'

Jacks and I moved into an old rectory in County Carlow, magically protected on its doors and window by sigils drawn by Paddy (Patricia) Slade, a hedge witch whose family practiced the Craft in a tradition stretching back to the fourteenth century. Dolores invited me to speak at the annual SoL Conference in London. "There's somebody I'd like you to meet," she said. The 'somebody' was Anna Branche of Philadelphia, a Voodoo priestess and guru who ran America's *New Seed Sanctuary* under the name of Shakmah Winddrum.

I'd heard a lot from Dolores about Anna. They'd met while Dolores was on one of her lecture tours in the States. Anna and several of her followers had turned up to hear her speak and were particularly noticeable as the only black people in the room. Afterwards, Dolores went into the audience to find out who they were and, within minutes, discovered she and Anna were soul-sisters. It was the beginning of a friendship that lasted until Anna's death.

In the conference hall before the main event, Dolores swooped to take my hand. "Time to meet Anna," she said; and dragged me to a large, intimidating African American woman seated in the front row surrounded by an entourage of minders. She extended her hand like a lady as Dolores made the introductions. I looked at the hand, then said firmly, "Get on your feet and give me a hug."

Anna was, in a word, adorable. She gave a talk about something or other, punctuated by enthusiastic *Yeahs* and *Right ons* from her followers. I listened with envy, wishing I had an entourage. (My own lecture received a muted reception, although I was given a shamanic staff as a gift afterwards.) But where she really impressed was ritual. The *New Seed Sanctuary* website has described Anna as 'a powerful ceremonial magician, blending spiritual practices from Eastern, Western and African traditions.' When her group got going, I had frankly never seen anything like it. The rite was finely choreographed, spectacular, professionally performed. Dolores played a major role with her usual aplomb, and I was dragged in to walk around, feeling majorly outclassed, with my staff. The impact was profound and showed clearly on the faces of the conference delegates.

Afterwards, I became vaguely aware some members of Anna's entourage were looking at me strangely. Several months later, I discovered why. Anna held regular meetings of her group in Philadelphia at which she communed with spirits and, occasionally, prophesied. At one of them, some years before, she had forecast a meeting with a bearded white man 'who had an important lesson to impart to her followers and herself.' After we hugged at the SoL Conference, a few of her closest confidants wondered aloud if I was the one. In a moment of misplaced enthusiasm, Anna confirmed that I was—a decision I suspect she lived to regret. But for the moment, I became The One and was addressed with wide-eyed respect by members of the entourage. Since they were some of the sweetest, most attractive women I had ever met, it was a heady—and intensely puzzling—experience.

When the Conference ended, a select group of us repaired to Jacks's London flat. Anna sat beside me on the couch and turned on the full force of her personality. "You and Jacks have to visit me in Philadelphia," she said.

"I don't fly," I told her. "I'm afraid of flying."

"I'll fix that for you," Anna said.

Everyone I knew had their own ideas about how to cure me of my fear of flying. None of them understood that I didn't want to be cured, because that would mean I would have to fly. "I haven't time to go to Philadelphia," I said.

Anna, who was not above bullying when charisma failed, gave me a stern look and said fiercely, "If you don't come, I will put a spell on you."

I burst out laughing. "Darling," I said, "you've bewitched me already!"

We cut the crap after that and arranged for Anna and two of her closest aides, Lyrata and Avizahn, to come visit Jacks and me in Ireland. When they did, Anna introduced us to Menelyk.

Perhaps a year or so earlier, Dolores called me up in something of a panic with the news that she had acquired a second indweller. The entity was, however, a temporary contact whom the Opener required her to carry to the States, then pass on to Anna.

"I didn't know you could do that," I told her.

"Neither did I," said Dolores.

But apparently you could. Dolores shared her head with two 'secondary personalities' for a few weeks, then flew to Philadelphia where, in the course of a ritual, she passed one of them on to Anna. The entity concerned was Menelyk. Dolores clearly expected me to recognise the name, but I did not. Before Anna's visit, however, I made the effort to find out who he was.

According to the *Kebra Negast,* an early fourteenth-century Ethiopian book of Scripture, Makeda, Queen of Sheba, was not an Arabian as many

Bewitching: Voodoo priestess Anna Branche (Shakmah Winddrum.)

scholars believe, but an African. She learned of Israel's King Solomon from a merchant in her kingdom and was so intrigued by stories of his wealth and wisdom that she decided to visit him. With an entourage that would have put even Anna's to shame, she travelled to Jerusalem where she was so impressed by Solomon that she immediately vowed to abandon sun-worship in favour of the God of Israel. Solomon, it transpired, was equally dazzled by Makeda, but for rather less spiritual reasons. He tricked her into sleeping with him on the understanding there would be no funny business 'unless she stole something from him,' then claimed her favours after she drank a cup of water in the night.

The result of this little comedy was that Makeda became pregnant and gave birth to a son—Menelyk—on her journey back to Ethiopia. Twenty-two years later, Menelyk travelled to Jerusalem in the hope of obtaining his father's blessing. He identified himself to Solomon by means of a ring the king had given to his mother and received a royal welcome. Solomon wanted him to stay and, eventually, inherit the throne of Israel, but Menelyk elected to return to Ethiopia. Solomon sent with him a company formed from the first-born sons of his country's Elders. These young men, dismayed at leaving Israel, stole the Ark of the Covenant as they left and took it with them to Ethiopia. Menelyk became king of Ethiopia when his mother died and established the line of rulers that endured until the Emperor Haile Salassie was overthrown in a coup in 1974.

Anna slipped easily into trance while seated on a sofa in my Irish cottage and brought through the spirit of Menelyk. He had almost as engaging a personality as Anna's own and seemed oddly familiar. He claimed we had met before and discussed the fact that war wasn't what it used to be when men fought one on one with the potential of genuine self-sacrifice and heroic acts. I got to know him quite well in the next few years and we even conversed in Philadelphia, something I still consider a minor miracle.

It came about not by Anna's magic, but through the efforts of Dr Maeve Byrne-Crangle, an aviation psychologist who ran a *Fear of Flying* course at Dublin airport. I enrolled, paid a reasonable fee, and attended weekly sessions with a small group of the afflicted, most of whom still flew occasionally despite their terror, mainly for business reasons. One of them told me she preferred to travel Aer Lingus 'because they have priests bless their planes.' She was not even a Roman Catholic, but I understood her perfectly.

Dr Maeve proved a sympathetic, understanding woman. I have the impression she may have been an air hostess before she received her doctorate. Certainly she enjoyed flying and felt deeply for those unable to do the same. Her course was an interesting mixture of information, relaxation, suggestion and gradual acclimatisation to airports and aircraft. It culminated in a fifteen-minute flight to Cork. I was by then one of the less nervous passengers. I managed the return flight as well and shook hands with Maeve on the tarmac feeling extraordinarily pleased with myself. Jacks booked us a celebratory trip to Egypt. While there, I renewed my contact with Nectanebo II.

The business with Nectanebo is one of the more bizarre aspects of what seems to me in retrospect to be a singularly bizarre life. It began during the 1980s while I was heavily involved with fantasy role play and game books. I began to experiment with writing an FRP scenario featuring a fictional character I called Nectanebo, whom I visualised as a powerful, ruthless, sorcerer. I decided he was born in Ancient Egypt, where he studied dark arts and eventually became Pharaoh.

While researching historical background for my scenario, I discovered there really had been a Pharaoh called Nectanebo. In fact there had been two—uncle and nephew. The nephew, Nectanebo II, Egypt's last native Pharaoh, bore a startling resemblance to my fictional creation. He had such a fearsome reputation as a sorcerer that he was credited with the ability to part water as Moses did at the Red Sea. The more I researched, the more points of similarity I unearthed between my Nectanebo and the real one. I knew the most likely explanation was that I had read about the real Nectanebo at some time, then dredged forgotten memories out of my unconscious when I began work on the module. But that was not how it felt. How it felt was *spooky*. I dropped the idea of a simple role play scenario and gave Nectanebo his head in a novel. The result was a science-fiction thriller about an ancient Pharaoh resurrected by cloning.

It failed to sell, went through several rewrites, then eventually sold to David Goddard (the bishop assaulted by Anubis in our evocation experiment) who had just joined a new publishing company. Before it made its way into print, David left and the company closed down. Rights reverted and fresh rewrites started. The book became an obsession, and during our Egyptian trip I was thrilled to discover that part of the Temple of Philae was built on the orders of Nectanebo II. I commissioned an Egyptian jeweller to create a special ring inscribed with the name *Nectanebo* in hieroglyphs.

When Anna discovered I had flown to Egypt, she renewed her invitation for us to visit her in Philadelphia; and this time I agreed. Unfortunately, by the time the trip was scheduled, Maeve's magic had worn off and I climbed aboard the plane in a state of terror, modified only by the realisation that my fate was sealed, I had already died and all I could do now was wait for the actual crash. Miraculously, the plane landed in Philadelphia intact, US Customs proved warm, welcoming and polite, and while the airline lost our luggage for a day, Jacks's tears were dried instantly by a compensatory payment of $300 counted out in crisp new bills.

"See? You've only just arrived in the States and you're making money already!" Anna remarked when we told her the story.

The Philadelphia trip proved magical. The Seed Sanctuary was a large, comfortable, all-female commune centred around Shakmah/Anna and her teachings. Hospitality was generous. Anna hosted a ceremonial workshop given by Jacks and myself, plus a lecture by me on the relationship between spirituality and quantum physics. We took part in a ritual during which Anna communicated with several entities, including Menelyk, his mother Makeda and an Arabian djinn. Jacks had healing chakras in the palms of her hands opened during a frightening ceremony that involved boiling oil. Towards the end of our stay, Anna cured a recurring health problem of mine by sticking brown paper to the soles of my feet in a Voodoo rite. But the flight home was a nightmare, and when we eventually reached Dublin, I swore I would never set foot on another plane. As a result, my next meeting with Anna was in Ireland for a mystical experiment in Newgrange.

Newgrange is Ireland's premier megalithic site, situated in the Boyne valley, five miles east of Slane and seven miles southwest of Drogheda. It comprises a tumulus surrounded by a megalithic circle and is the focus of the very earliest surviving Irish epics which detail the mythic history of an ancient race called the *Tuatha Dé Danaan,* who were banished from heaven and sensibly elected to inhabit the next best place. They arrived in their airships on the mountains of Connemara, pushed out the indigenous *Fir Bolg* population and ruled Ireland for just short of 300 years before being displaced in their turn by the Milesians, ancestors of the modern Irish. But the *Tuatha* were not pushed into the sea. Instead they took refuge in the 'hollow hills' including *Brú na Bóinne* (Newgrange). Should you visit Newgrange, however, you will quickly discover its internal chambers are not big enough to house a family, let alone an entire race. The myths refer, it seems, to a mysterious otherworld to which the physical mound was only an entrance. In the palace halls of the otherworld, 'three times fifty sons of kings' lived a life of perpetual festivity, fed by three great trees which were always in fruit and a cauldron from which no company ever went away dissatisfied. It was an eternal realm in which no one ever died, accessible to the *Tuatha* only because they were fearsome magicians. I had it in mind that my own little coterie of fearsome magicians might attempt contact with whatever aspect of inner reality the Newgrange myths might represent. My only problem was the Board of Works.

Newgrange is, of course, a national monument. In the early 1990s, a small admission fee entitled members of the public to join a guided tour. Since there was no way we could engage on magical experiments with tourists walking in and out, I wondered if it might be possible to have the monument to ourselves for a few hours. It seemed, on the face of things, unlikely, but I wrote to the Board of Works anyway. To my surprise I received a reply outlining the terms under which Newgrange could be made available to private parties outside of public visiting hours. What I needed was £50 to underwrite an overtime payment to the caretaker and sponsorship letters from two recognised academic or religious bodies. Since the nature of the religion was nowhere specified, I asked Anna to provide one letter on Seed Sanctuary notepaper. The other was provided by my old friend Dom Kim Langridge, who headed the occult Order of St Gabriel in St. Albans. The Board of Works accepted both without question but dropped a bombshell with the news that I would also have to provide a £1million insurance policy indemnifying against damage to the monument. Although I had no plans to damage Newgrange, I quickly discovered that the one-off premium for such a specialist policy was well beyond my means. It seemed like crash and burn for the project, but when I wrote to the Board to say I was not in a position to provide the insurance they required, the *Tuatha* must have intervened because the Board responded by dropping their requirement. As a result, an eight-strong party—Dolores, Anna, Lyrata, Avizahn, the fantasy author Jim Serwer (who wrote as Seamus Cullen), the astrologer Ed Garry, Jacks and myself—gathered in my home the night before the experiment to engage in some preparatory work.

The preparatory work was a pathworking headed by Dolores who insisted if we planned to contact the *Tuatha* in their home, we should at least knock first. Our visionary journey took us overland to Newgrange where we were met by a representative of the *Tuatha* and Dolores ascertained we would be welcome. The next day we made the journey in reality. We were met by a representative of the Board of Works, who pocketed her £50 cheque, told us to get on with it, then disappeared into the warmth of the wooden entrance hut. The rest of us walked up the grassy slope to Newgrange.

Newgrange was built about 3100 BCE, a vast stone and turf chambered mound about 280 feet in diameter and forty-four feet high. As we approached, we could see the tumulus was bound by a kerbing of large stones, many with carved designs of spiral, lozenge, zigzag and other symbols. But what really caught the eye was the white facing wall (reinforced by a cement backing wall to prevent the mound slipping) on top of the southeast sector of the kerb. This was erected by archaeologists during excavations between 1962 and 1975, based on the position of the white quartz layers found outside the kerb. It was meant to restore the appearance of the monument as it had been in prehistoric times.

Some distance away were the remaining twelve stones of an original thirty-four in the great stone circle that once enclosed the mound. This circle was built about a thousand years later than the original structure, dating probably from the Beaker period. There was a triple spiral carved kerbstone in front of the slab which blocked the entrance. Above the entrance passage was a 'roof-box', which aligned with the rising sun at the winter solstice, so that the rays touch the ground at the very centre of the central chamber.

Entering the great mound was an unforgettable experience. Many of the upright stones along the walls of the sixty-two-foot passage, which follows the rise of the hill, have finely carved geometric decorations. The passageway is extremely narrow in parts and there were some worries whether Anna, a bulky woman, would make it through but we all reached the central chamber without mishap. The cruciform chamber had three recesses and a nineteen-foot-high corbelled ceiling. On the floor there were massive stone basins, one in each of the left-hand and rear recesses and two set on top of each other in the recess on the right. There were two bowl-shaped depressions in the surface of the topmost of these. The overall effect was of unexpected sophistication.

Our experiments were based on three premises. The first was that Newgrange was built for religious purposes. The second was that virtually all primitive religions include the element of trance. The third, more controversial, was that specific structures (including Newgrange itself) influenced the nature of the trance experience and hence the development of the religion which arose from it. It was this theory which the experiments sought to test. To do so, it was proposed to attempt to duplicate—in so far as possible—the mindset of the builders of Newgrange by means of induced trance at the site.

We planned two types of experiment. The first involved individual trance inductions of Dolores, Anna, Jacks and Lyrata—chosen because they were all good hypnotic subjects—within the central chamber. The second involved a guided meditation by Dolores involving us all, also within the central chamber of the tumulus. Anna, Jacks, Lyrata, Jim and Avizahn decided to use self-induced trance as part of this exercise.

[241]

In the individual experiments, the subjects entered the tumulus one at a time. I induced trance and recorded the results. No subject was aware of what happened to the others until the experiment was completed. Nonetheless, three of the four described their impressions of the original builders in identical terms—short, dark, very muscular and squat. The fourth envisioned them as powerfully built, but not necessarily short. There was also general agreement on the method of construction. Dolores gave the most comprehensive account, suggesting that earth ramping was used as an aid to placing the stones with the earth later dug away to create the inner chambers.[33] Three of the four 'saw' the megaliths manhandled into position. One specifically mentioned 'ropes' of some sort and a 'sling' effect using trees. Another felt each major stone was individually cut, decorated where necessary, and placed in position in strict sequence (rather than, for example, all stones being quarried first, then moved collectively onto the site). She had the impression that the builders believed the sequence made construction easier.

There was broad agreement that the tumulus was used for religious purposes. All four believed that ceremonial practice had taken place within the mound and that this practice was mainly, or exclusively, a female prerogative. Two of the four—Jacks and Lyrata—independently expressed the opinion that the stone bowl in the chamber to the right was used for birthing. (Anna, however, saw its use as a container for herbs and liquids.)

Three of the four reported that they could sense an 'energy vortex' associated with the corbelled roof. Dolores, a particularly deep trance subject, reported the sensation of being 'drawn up' into the vortex.

"What's happening?" I asked.

"It's still operational. It's pulling me in."

"Into the centre, you mean?"

"In and up. I'm being drawn up towards the roof. I think it's taking me out of the mound."

I began to worry. "Can you resist the pull?"

"I don't know. I don't think so."

"I think perhaps you should try," I said.

The entranced Dolores said, "I'm not sure I want to. It's going to take me right out of this world! This is how it was done! They used the mound to take you through! This is how you get to the *Tuatha!*"

"We're not geared for this," I told her firmly. "I'm going to bring you

---

33 Somewhat similar theories have been put forward by archaeologists to explain the building of the Egyptian pyramids.

back." And so, to her chagrin, I did.

The experience had a lasting impression on Dolores. She had not the slightest doubt the vortex was an artificial phenomenon purposely created by the builders of the mound: "It was spiral in form. But it went both upwards and downwards. They built a mirror image of the spiral going down into the earth. It's like looking at the reflection of a mountain in a lake. There were two spirals, one above, one below. They were broadly egg-shaped."

She believed the builders had a method of shutting down each of the twin spirals individually and that by doing so, they could change their function. Sometimes the power of both was allowed to go through the body of a priest, a king or a pregnant woman. When this happened, they were plunged into deep trance and their consciousness was taken into a parallel world as an observer.

"This is a doorway to two different worlds," she told me afterwards. "The downward spiral is equivalent to the region of the summer stars, an inner place in the Earth's aura. Ever since my trance experience, I have had the conviction that the *Tuatha* never left Ireland, only shifted."

It sounded fanciful, but several months later something happened to make me wonder. On my next visit to Newgrange, as an ordinary paying customer this time, I was chatting with the Board of Works guide inside the tumulus when she mentioned she had brought through a party of professional dowsers from England a few weeks before. They had surveyed the entire site using their rods.

"Did they find anything interesting?" I asked.

"They said there was a spiral of energy just over there," she told me. She was pointing at the spot where Dolores had been drawn up into her vortex.

My therapy with June Quinn-Berger lasted only a matter of months but gave me a taste for self-examination. I had long wondered what it would be like to undertake a full Jungian analysis and felt this might well be the time. I liked June, was hugely grateful for her intervention in my life and, more to the point, admired her approach. We discussed the possibility of an analysis—analysts have to be careful of their clients since the psychoanalytical procedure changes both patient and doctor—and June decided to take the risk. We embarked on a process that lasted ten years and left us firm friends.

Unlike Freudian analysis which concentrates (so I understand) on one's sexual peccadilloes, Jungian analysis makes much of one's dreams. I learned the art of remembering mine and kept an ongoing dream diary on computer. For each session, I arrived in June's consulting room equipped with print-outs of that week's dreams, which disappeared into her files. Much of the hour would then be devoted to discussion of my previous week's dreams which she would have examined and annotated in her own time.

Dreams, Freud famously remarked, are the royal road to the unconscious, and June was adept at relating the symbolism that emerged in mine to problems in my daily life. Not all the symbols were personal. It is the basis of Jungian psychology that we are burdened not only with an individual *sub*conscious, but also a collective *un*conscious common to humanity as a whole.[34] This area of the psyche is inhabited by entities who appear repeatedly in the world's mythologies. Sometimes they walk into our dreams.

One dream I presented to June related to Gibraltar, a place I had never visited in waking life. In the dream I was walking near a cliff when I was approached by the colony's famous Barbary apes. When we discussed the relevant batch of dreams the following week, I noticed she had annotated this one with the single word:

Thoth?

"Thoth?" I asked her, echoing the question mark.

"In mythology, apes are Thoth's messengers," June said. "They were believed to be forerunners of an appearance by the god."

"What do they mean in my dream?"

---

34   There are curious similarities between the collective unconscious of Jungian theory, the spirit worlds of shamanism and the Astral Plane of magic.

"I'm not sure. But archetypal symbols tend to be important."

Over the years of my analysis, I noticed a predictive element. This was neither spectacular nor mysterious. Typically, June would spot something in my dreams that suggested a particular event. Three weeks later, I would find myself involved in a similar event in waking life. Since involvements are usually the results of our own actions, I took this to indicate that I was making decisions at an unconscious level three weeks before working them out in reality. A similar process—and timing—often presaged personal changes. It never occurred to me that Thoth's messengers might fall into the predictive category of dream, but over the following three weeks a sequence of events occurred that resulted in a profound—and magical—life change. One was an unexpected phone call from Sweden. The caller was Karina Hultquist, a formed SoL student who now ran her own esoteric school. She had a query about initiation which, from memory, I could not answer.

On a trip to London several months earlier, Jacks and I paid a visit to the British Museum. While walking through the Egyptian Gallery, I was drawn to a massive stone sarcophagus, heavily inscribed with hieroglyphs. There was slight damage to one side, but otherwise the artefact was well preserved. I bent to read the display plaque. I was standing beside the sarcophagus of Pharaoh Nectanebo II. I went off to find Jacks to tell her I had just discovered Nectanebo's tomb. As I reached her, I had the feeling that someone was staring at me and turned to look into the startled face of Karina Hultquist.

My first meeting with Karina occurred under peculiar circumstances. Dolores had promised her she would receive her formal ceremonial initiation, marking an important stage in her spiritual journey, at one of our Magical Master Classes. The first I heard of this arrangement was when Karina knocked at the door of my room in Runnings Park, told me the plan and asked if I could be the one to initiate her.

It was a flattering request—she had clearly been far too impressed by one of my lectures—but it was also an embarrassment. I explained that I was unqualified to initiate anybody and, moreover, I was not a member of SoL. Karina ignored my first point and met my second by asking if I would be prepared to carry out the initiation should Dolores agree. I knew there was no chance of Dolores agreeing, so I said yes. Karina went off to find Dolores, who told her I could not perform the initiation because I was not qualified, nor was I a member of SoL and that was that. Except it wasn't.

Karina's initiation (by Dolores) was scheduled for the afternoon of the following day. Just after lunch someone whispered in my ear that Dolores needed to see me urgently in her room. When I went to find out what the problem was, her room had been laid out like a little temple, and while Dolores's body was waiting for me, Dolores herself was absent: she had been completely taken over by her indweller. There followed a bizarre conversation between the Opener and myself which began with his asking if I would be prepared to initiate Karina. I told him I was not a member of SoL. He said it didn't matter. I told him Dolores was going to initiate Karina later that afternoon. He told me Dolores was going to do nothing of the sort: for the initiation to be valid, it had to be carried out by a male. I told him I was not qualified to give initiations. He told me that 'if I was prepared to accept the gift' he would initiate me immediately into the Third Degree, which would authorise me to give initiation to anyone I chose...including Karina.

It was a weird experience. Dolores was running SoL, an organisation in which I had no official standing whatsoever. Dolores planned to initiate Karina. I wanted to ask her if she would mind my doing it instead. I wanted to ask her *how* one carried out a SoL initiation anyway—I had never seen one or read the relevant ritual. Dolores was standing in front of me, to all appearances, yet I could ask her nothing, because Dolores was no longer in charge of her own head. I decided if she didn't like it, she could always fight it out with the Opener. "All right," I said, a little gracelessly.

The Opener swung into action at once and put me through a brief, but fascinating ceremony that involved, among other things, anointing the palms of my hands—a process that left them buzzing for weeks afterwards. The whole thing took perhaps fifteen, twenty minutes. "You can go now," he told me when he had finished. "You'll need to be robed and ready for Karina at 4 o'clock."

"What about...?" I gestured vaguely towards the body he was wearing.

"She'll be fine," he said; and I took my leave.[35]

The point of this story, apart from its intrinsic interest, is that from then on, I instinctively associated Karina with initiation—hers and my own. Our meeting in the British Museum—she was in London with her family on holiday—was clearly coincidence, but I wondered even at the time whether it might be what Jung called *meaningful* coincidence: synchronicity. "Perhaps you have another initiation coming," Jacks remarked when I discussed it with her. The meeting itself was certainly spectacular

35   Some years after the event, Dolores offered me a Third Degree SoL initiation. She was stunned to discover I'd already undergone one.

The sarcophagus of Nectanebo II, which I came across unexpectedly in the British Museum.

enough: we had scarcely got past the social pleasantries when alarms went off and museum guards arrived to usher everybody out. There had been a bomb threat.

Karina's subsequent phone call left me with the oddest feeling something was about to happen, although I had no idea what. Like most of these intuitions, there was no rational justification, but something in me stubbornly insisted I was caught up in a pattern with Karina; one that involved initiation.

Some three weeks after my dream of apes and perhaps ten days following Karina's call, I awoke in the early hours of the morning to find a tall, powerful figure standing at the foot of my bed.

 The figure was not human. Although it was in human form, it was too tall and too alien to be human, but for some reason, I felt no fear. I was simultaneously aware of several things. One was that I was fully conscious: I was in bed, wide awake, with Jacks beside me and there was no question that I might be dreaming. Another was that I was not in my normal state of consciousness. The creature staring down at me was not imaginary, not hallucinatory, not ghostly, but it was not physically present either, at least not in the way I would usually define 'physical.' I was in the grip of a major visionary experience, but there was a marked difference to the parkland vision I had during the séance with Eileen Boyd. Then I was rooted in mundane reality while viewing a landscape scene as if through a window. Now it was as if I had entered the alien scene; or, more accurately, as if the alien scene—including the powerful figure— had invaded my reality, imposing itself upon it. I realise this description is unsatisfactory, but it is the closest I can come to communicating the essence of my experience.

There was communication between the figure and myself. This was not verbal: nobody spoke. I suppose you might call it telepathic, but here again it was not telepathy as I would normally imagine it. There was no voice in my head, no transfer of emotion or meaning for me to interpret. I simply knew what the figure wanted me to do and why. More to the point, I knew it all of a piece.

The bed in my room is aligned north/south. There are two windows in the eastern wall. To the northeast of my home, some fifteen miles away at Donard, is the megalithic site of Castleruddery Stone Circle, an untidy layout of forty stones about 100 metres on diameter with two enormous (fifteen-ton) quartz boulders acting at portal stones at the entrance. The circle is surrounded by a low earthwork and a great many fairy trees, as thorn bushes are called in Ireland. Beyond is a ditch, no longer visible from the ground. Official estimates date the site to about 2500 BCE.

To reach this circle in physical reality, you would turn off the N81 some five miles north-east of Baltinglass and follow the signs. From the altered reality of my bedroom, I saw the intervening countryside stretched like an open plain and the circle itself luminous in the moonlight. In many ways this *was* like my séance vision: the wall of my bedroom had vanished, as had the two (curtained) windows. But now I was no longer a passive observer. I was carried across the landscape—which distorted and shrank to accommodate the journey—to find myself standing inside the circle.

I became aware of two entrances a few yards apart set into the ground. I was aware from previous visits that no such entrances existed in my ordinary reality; nonetheless I knew where they led. Under soundless, wordless instruction from the creature in my bedroom, I entered one of them and found myself in the world of the *Sidhe*, the underworld guardians, in Irish mythology, often identified with the *Tuatha Dé Danann*. They appeared to me as tall, slender, silver-skinned humanoids with emotionless faces. Frankly, I did not like them much and sensed the feeling was mutual. Nonetheless, they did what I asked them and agreed to permit me to enter the faerie underworld. I emerged from the *Sidhe* world to find the second entrance in the ground now laid open and ran down what seemed like ancient stone steps into yet another level of reality.

In sharp contrast to the cool *Sidhe* world, this one was delightful. I found myself surrounded by little people who mobbed me like a horde of happy children. It was impossible to feel anything but delight in their presence. None of them stood higher than my waist and while their faces and bodies seemed mature, they chattered and laughed and played like youngsters. I explained what I needed, and they agreed without the slightest hesitation.

What I needed (on the silent instructions of the creature in my room) is a little complicated to explain. I had recently met, on Anna's recommendation, a married couple who believed the wife to be contacted, like Dolores, with an Egyptian indweller. Whatever entity appeared in my bedroom 'explained' that the couple required a more balanced relationship in order to achieve their full spiritual potential. To this end, my curious trip to Castleruddery was meant to arrange a specific faerie contact for the husband. If he accepted the contact, this would, it seemed, permit him more independence of action than his current situation where he largely functioned only as a support system for his wife.

With agreement for the contact now in place, I returned to my room in a state of high excitement. The entity who had sparked the whole experience was no longer there and the curious overlay of realities was receding. It was now four in the morning, but I knew I would not sleep, so I went to my study and emailed the husband of the American couple with news of what had happened. I was wary of sharing details—some part of me recalled the ridicule experienced by Whitley Strieber when he reported the appearance of flying saucer aliens in his room—so I confined myself to telling him that a contact was on offer if he was prepared to accept it. Then I went back to bed.

"Where were you?" Jacks asked as I entered the bedroom.

"I've just had the most extraordinary experience," I told her. "There was a figure at the foot of our bed."

"I know," Jacks said. "I saw it."

We speculated about the figure, of course. Jacks thought it might be Thoth because of my ape dream. I felt that unlikely, to say the least. I called Dolores to tell her the story, keeping all Thoth suspicions to myself. "It was Thoth," she said categorically. At that point, I *did* feel frightened. After a moment I said, "How do you know?"

"I can see him hovering around you," she told me.

I began to wonder about archetypes. From my analytical experience and studies, I was aware that Jungian archetypes—the Hero, the Crone, the Wise Old Man—could possess individuals and force them to lead archetypal lives. I even knew one woman who was doing so. I was also aware that for many Jungians—and Jung himself—the mythical gods and the psychological archetypes were one and the same thing. It put a new perspective on meeting with a god: contact was made not because you were special or holy, but because enough aspects of your psyche resonated with its archetypal nature. Thoth was the lunar god of scribes and magic. I had dedicated my entire life to writing and the study and practice of magic. I was as lunar as they come—sun and moon both in Cancer in my birth chart, more female friends than male, visions of the Goddess: I was even aware of cyclical mood swings that coincided with full moon. It seemed to me that if there was an archetype likely to emerge from the Collective Unconscious to make contact with my psyche, it would almost have to be Thoth.

At the same time, the contact was not a subjective experience. Some magical creature had appeared at the foot of the bed; and Jacks had seen it too. Clearly, Jung's explanation of this type of phenomenon was limited.

Steve Peek flew in from the States. I told him my story with trepidation, but he resisted any urge to take the piss. Our conversation turned to fairies. "Do you know anything about butterfly names?" he asked. I blinked and shook my head. "Humour me," said Steve. "Get yourself a book on butterfly names and tell me they wouldn't be perfect for fantasy characters in a fairy story."

The following morning I searched my local bookshop until I found the *Collins Pocket Guide to Butterflies and Moths*. Steve was right: the names were wonderful—the Purple Emperor, Brimstone, Black Hairstreak, Holly Blue. Even the Latin names were wonderful: Pyrgus Malvae, Apatura Iris, Hamearis Lucina, Cynthia Cardui…

Characters began to appear inside my head and would not go away.

A few days later I started to write a novel, my first in more than thirty years. I called it *Faerie*. I could feel Thoth pressing in on me throughout the entire process.

With Murray Pollinger now long retired, my literary output was in the hands of Sophie Hicks, then joint managing director of the literary agency, Ed Victor Ltd. She auctioned the manuscript on the day of 9/11. In 2003, the book, re-titled *Faerie Wars*, was brought out by Bloomsbury Children's Books in Britain and the US. It inspired me to write a quartet of magical novels set in the Faerie Realm, which went on to be published in more than twenty-four countries and became an international bestseller.

INDEX